Spirit
of the
Wilderness

Spirit
of the
Wilderness

BRUCE GRAHAM

GPM
FreeRein

2023

GPM Publishing
FreeRein Press

GPM
FreeRein

Copyright © 2023 by Bruce Graham

Illustrations by Kevin Ritchie with permission

First hardcover edition, 2023
ISBN: 979-8-9857865-4-5

First paperback edition, 2023
ISBN: 979-8-9857865-5-2

1 3 5 7 9 10 8 6 4 2

First Printing

*This book is dedicated to my father and to
Jean Broux, who initially inspired me with
the wonders of nature and adventures into the
wilderness, which became a lifelong passion.*

TABLE OF CONTENTS

*If history were taught in the form
of stories, it would never be forgotten.*

Rudyard Kipling, 1865–1936

INTRODUCTION

The stories that have been compiled here are taken from a lifetime of fishing and camping adventures in Canada, Alaska, and the remote mountains of Colorado. They begin with me as a young man and continue through my life until just a few years ago. The stories I've picked to tell involve not only wilderness adventure and fishing but also complex interpersonal relationships with fishing guides and people who dwell outside urban environments at the edge of "civilization" many of whom live a subsistence lifestyle. These people are as unique and varied as the world itself. Each of these individuals is presented with various life dilemmas, and each respond with their own individual abilities.

Against the backdrop of wilderness adventure topics, such as spirituality, extrasensory perception, canoe adventures, wilderness survival, the lives and stories of Native Americans, personal happiness, bear problems, the cowboy life, the Rocky Mountains, life goals, personal relationships, coming of age, and other issues involving the human condition are interwoven.

I've always been drawn to the wilderness, even as a young man. I seem to have a deep need to return to something that is ancient. To return to a place that is simpler and, in effect, truer. When I return to remote, "uncivilized" regions, I sense a renewed relationship with the earth, something that has been obscured by the hustle and bustle of modern city life. It seems that I have a stronger connection and better access to the "Great Spirit" who resides in us all. This connection is easier when I am away from the noise of the human zoo and concrete jungle of "civilization." I have found that if one is searching for direction in life or answers to life's dilemmas, being alone in the wilderness is the first place to start the journey of discovery. The Great Spirit is more discoverable in the solitude and silence of lonely places away from civilization.

There is no fooling the wilderness. If you take it for granted and don't respect it, there can be great danger and dire consequences. Nature does not suffer fools. The solitude, beauty, and potential danger tend to heighten your awareness, giving greater focus on yourself and your environment. This can elicit a feeling of being more alive and exhilarated. Being in this environment tends to enhance ancient senses that have lain dormant until you return to the ancient place where humankind began.

I have always been fascinated by individuals who live their entire lives in this ancient and wild world and their ways of thinking. I have, in a way, envied their unique freedom and their rhythm and dance with nature. Frequently, they seem to be devoid of all pretentiousness and falsity because the wilderness demands that you be yourself and nothing else. However, over the years, I have seen changes occur that were caused by the slow encroachment into even the most pristine wilderness areas. Many of the individuals depicted in this book are Native Americans. This book glimpses their culture on an individual basis and describes how steadily increasing contact with the White world has slowly changed their lives and ways of living through each succeeding generation.

These essays will hopefully elucidate the wonder of the wilderness and in effect bring us closer to our true selves. Lessons can be learned from the stories and interactions with people who live in the bush and the wisdom of an ancient way, long since lost in our affluent, "civilized" society.

Bruce D. Graham

SPIRIT ISLAND

The clearest way into the Universe is through a forest wilderness.
JOHN MUIR

I was a young man on our yearly fishing trip to northern Canada. My father, his good friend Bob, the guide, Jean Broux, and I were in an aluminum fishing boat together. The region was experiencing a record heat wave, with temperatures never seen before this far north so far as anyone could remember. The lake was nearly one hundred miles long and had very little fishing pressure since it was so remote. But the fishing was terrible; we hadn't caught one fish since our arrival four days before.

We fished hard, from before sunrise until sunset. We tried every type of lure and different ways of fishing. We cast the banks of the lake. We worked through large, shallow bays filled with lily pads. We jigged off the bottom in deep water, trolled around rocky points, and cast below small waterfalls from streams coming into the lake. Not a single bite. The lake was renowned for its large and numerous northern pike, walleye, and lake trout. We'd had great fishing success in the past, but not now. The fish seemed paralyzed, most likely from the sudden onset of the record heat wave.

Jean Broux was the most respected guide in the region. If he couldn't get you on the fish, no one could. We knew Jean well and had worked with him on two previous trips. Bob, who had planned and organized the trip, was starting to get frustrated. Bob was a big, burly man with a crew cut in his midforties. He had played football as a lineman in college. He was now a pharmacist and owned several drug stores. He was an experienced sportsman who spent most of his time in the outdoors, hunting and fishing, rather than at his drug stores. Fortunately for Bob, he had a dedicated and reliable pharmacy staff managing the stores while he was out in the boondocks. "Big Bob" was gregarious, friendly, and outgoing, but even he had his limits. He began to complain that he had pretty much had it. He put down his fishing rod and said to Jean, "We're paying you and this lodge thousands of dollars and have come thousands of miles to catch nothing, Jean. You've got to do better than this!"

My dad and I were silent, but we were frustrated as well.

Jean was calm and matter-of-fact. "Well, Bob, that's why they call it fishing and not catching." But I could tell that he was bothered. Jean took great pride in his work and could usually get his clients fish when everyone else was unsuccessful. Many of the other guides were jealous of him because he was in such high demand. Jean worked harder than any of the other guides as well. He was quite competitive, never to be out fished. He had a lighthearted personality and an easy smile and was quick to laugh. When you fished with Jean, the conversation was usually easy and ongoing.

I had a special affinity with Jean since he treated me with respect and as an adult, even though I was fifteen years old. He took time to show me how to tie knots on the fishing line and how to land and clean the fish. He had a lot of great stories about living in the Canadian bush. He was in his late twenties or early thirties, stocky and muscular, around five foot seven. He had expressive bright blue eyes with an uncanny way of looking at you during conversation, almost as if he were opening a door into your soul past any facade or pretense, affably acknowledging what made you tick so he could fully communicate with you. He studied people's personalities as he would follow the tracks of a moose until he found it silently grazing among lily pads in a shallow lake. He probably spent more time with wild animals in the bush than he did with humans in civilization.

There was something about Jean that was mysterious, though. It was hard to put a finger on it. He wasn't like any other person I had ever met, possibly less influenced or affected by people and civilization. With just a short conversation, I could sense high intelligence along with his insight into other people. He had a rugged, handsome appearance. His skin was deeply tanned from long days in the sun and wind. He was missing a few teeth; however, it wasn't too conspicuous unless he smiled widely. He had the look of an ice-hockey player or a halfback on a football team. He nearly always had a smile on his face and a cigarette in his mouth, and he went through at least two packs per day. Canadian cigarettes were much shorter and burned far more rapidly than their American counterparts, which was a constant source of annoyance to Jean. He was always trying to get his American clients to bring him a carton of Marlboros or Pall Malls.

Jean had grown up at the very edge of civilization and had been hunting and fishing his entire life. He made his living as a fishing guide in spring and summer and a hunting guide in the fall, and he trapped furs in the winter. He would shoot a moose or several caribou, which would sustain his wife and two children through the year with meat. His wife tended a large vegetable garden by their house. The lodge he worked for let him use its freezer to store fish and other meat. The remainder he smoked and salted in his own smokehouse.

One evening Jean brought his wife and two little kids over to the lodge to meet us since we had been good clients and had helped provide a good income for him for the past few years. His wife was pretty, petite, and friendly but reserved. She had a nice smile as she held one of her children while the other held her leg. I could tell Jean was proud of his wife and children. He beamed and smiled broadly as he introduced them. They lived in a cabin he had built in the woods several miles outside a tiny town in northern Manitoba.

As youths, he and his identical twin brother would disappear into the bush for months at a time, hunting and fishing and living off the land. His parents thought nothing of it because they had been brought up the same way. Jean was from a long lineage of mixed French and Native hunters, trappers, and voyagers. His life was not much different than the lives of his ancestors hundreds of years in the past.

Although Jean had a limited formal education, having attended school only to the eighth grade, he was highly intelligent and quick-witted. One evening in the lodge after the day's fishing, Jean, Bob, my dad, and I were lounging in large leather chairs and discussing schooling. I had recently taken an English literature class from an outstanding teacher, which I had greatly enjoyed. I said that the class was my best academic experience to date in high school. Jean then brought up the subject of poetry. He asked if we liked it and if we would like to see some of his. We all said sure, surprised that this rugged woodsman had this kind of interest. He went into another room and brought out several loosely bound notebooks filled with poems he had written.

We all read several of the poems. They were astonishing in their beauty and rhythm. The words glowed like embers, illuminating every page. The words seemed as if they were written especially for whoever was reading them. Many of the poems were about animals in the bush, giving them almost human characteristics. They made me think that humans and animals were not that dissimilar. Others were about the meaning of life and love. Some had a deep, almost spiritual quality that was almost haunting. We all looked at Jean with amazement, overwhelmed by the insight and true beauty that we had read. Bob's jaw nearly dropped as he looked up from the paper and gazed at Jean.

Along with the poetry, he had sketched beautiful art with an ink pen with a point nearly as fine as a needle. Others were sketched in pencil. These sketches were associated with the poetry, making the poems come even more to life. The drawings were precise and elegant, like his poetry. Jean was an accomplished artist as well as a poet. It was hard to imagine this work of art coming from the source that it did. He nonchalantly related that he had been doing this all his life and just did what came naturally to him. He was thrilled and somewhat amazed that anyone would have an interest in his writings. He had never shown his works to anyone besides his wife before. There was a lot more depth to this man than I had ever imagined. I was intrigued to learn more about the other side of Jean that we had not seen until now. Little did I know that what I was about to discover was a depth that was fathomless, a world that I had no awareness of and would find somewhat frightening.

The next day the fishing was no better despite hard and lengthy effort. Nerves were a little frayed, especially Bob's. Bob looked at Jean, exasperated, and said, "Look, Jean, there's got to be a way to find the fish. I don't care what we must do! We've spent five days out here in this boat for absolutely nothing!"

After taking a deep breath, Jean looked at Bob and said, "I understand. I don't like this either. I think this record heat wave has affected the fish. I've never seen it like this in my life."

Jean hesitated for a while, seemingly in deep thought. "I do know of one place where I think we might be able to catch some fish. But it's a long distance from here and a little difficult to get to. It's also in kind of a creepy area that the Indians like to avoid. However, I don't know much about that. There's a small river that's fed by a large natural spring. I've never been there, but I'll bet there will be cool water. It would probably take us two hours just to get there and it's getting late. Plus, I don't like those clouds in the distance."

We all turned around and saw the entire northeastern sky filled with billowing dark, almost black clouds. They had a foreboding appearance. A slight wind began to blow. Jean said, "I think the weather is about to change in a big way. What you see is a big storm coming in from Hudson Bay."

Hudson Bay is connected to the Arctic Ocean and brings cold air into the interior of Canada, like the Gulf of Mexico bringing warm air into the southern United States, both of which are frequent sources of storms.

"I don't like the looks of things at all. I suggest we go back and start over tomorrow. I have a bad feeling about this; it's better we go back."

"Look, we can run up there, spend a half hour fishing, and then come back. I think we can do it," Bob replied.

My dad agreed with Bob. However, I wanted to go back to the lodge and not tempt fate, especially in the middle of nowhere. Of course, I had no say in the matter since I was only a young lad. I'm sure Jean thought of the potential loss of a well-paying, unhappy client. Bob and my dad were well known to tip significant sums for fishing success, and Jean had a family to support. I suspected that Jean's competitive nature, as the premier fishing guide in the region, was influencing him as well.

Jean took off his hat, brushed back his hair, and then replaced his hat and said, "OK, I'm willing if you guys are. But there may be hell to pay if that storm catches us."

One thing in our favor was that the sunset was at nearly midnight in the summer that far north.

So away we went. Jean turned the forty-horsepower Johnson outboard motor to full throttle. The boat was around eighteen feet long, which was relatively cramped but functional with three large men and a young teenage boy. It was a beautiful, scenic ride up to the unknown river, past numerous rocky islands covered with tall, statuesque pine and spruce trees. We were totally alone in this unspoiled wilderness with no hint of humankind or civilization. We sped through several long, narrow, rock-walled channels between islands. The sound of the motor echoed through the canyon-like walls. I thought that this would be a great place to fish, but probably not now with the ongoing heat. I motioned with my hands to Jean to indicate my thought of a good potential site to fish in the future. He acknowledged me by smiling and nodding his head. It looked perfect for big walleye. After we came out of the channel, we took a hard, sharp turn, creating a broad wake in the water and entering a wide, large area of the lake. After about another hour on the open water, we took another hard turn through several small islands and entered a beautiful, crystal-clear small river.

The river was approximately fifty yards wide and strewn with large, smooth, car-sized granite boulders. Large drooping pines and groves of white birch trees lined the banks. The river was stunningly beautiful and looked like a scene from a postcard. It had a slow current and was easily managed by the boat. The depth of the water varied from seven to about fifteen feet. At the bottom of the crystal-clear river, we could see bright green vegetation slowly undulating with the steady, slow current. It appeared to be the ideal habitat for northern pike. I put my hand in the water, and it was dramatically colder than the main lake. I asked Jean how he knew of this place. He told me he had flown over this area in his pontoon bush plane, and it had looked like a great fishing spot from the air. The river was not marked on the standard map of the area, and its existence was unknown to the outside world. There was a giant natural spring at the source of the river several miles ahead. He didn't think anyone had ever fished in this area.

Jean throttled the motor down to a slow troll and said, "Gentlemen, let's go fishing!" He then put both feet up, lit a cigarette, and took a big drag.

We all cast in different directions and slowly retrieved our red-and-white daredevil spoon lures. The lures were just above the vegetation, slowly wobbling back to the fishing rods. Suddenly we saw multiple large northern pike dart out from their ambush sites in the vegetation below to attack the lures. All three of us had fish on. The fish hit the lures with ferocity, typical for pike. My fishing rod was nearly jolted out of my hands. The fight was on for all three of us. The fish went under and around the boat, making us all change positions back and forth.

Jean let out a big whoop. "That's it, go get 'em. We've got a triple on!"

After another big drag, he took his cigarette out of his mouth and threw it into the lake despite having just lit it up. He was grinning from ear to ear, showing his occasional missing teeth. After an epic triple battle with the big fish, we finally landed them. Jean tried at first to bring the fish into the boat with his hand, as he usually did, by grabbing and compressing the gill plates, which temporarily paralyzes the fish. However, these fish were too wide for his hand to get around, so he brought them into the boat with a net.

"These fish are real doozies," he said.

All three fish were trophy-sized, over forty inches long. All weighed over twenty pounds. The pike squirmed and flopped in the bottom of the boat, making it feel like we were in a small enclosure with several huge anacondas from the Amazon. We all unhooked our fish with Jean's help and released them back into the river. Jean lit a cigarette and took a big drag, exhaled, and gave a big smile and a laugh.

"That's it, boys, we're on to them now." His cigarette bobbed up and down in his lips as he talked.

After the release of the fish, we all resumed casting our lures into the river. We caught big pike one after the other. It was a real sight to see—one I'll never forget. Several of the hooked fish broke the water, violently twisting and shaking their long green-and-white bodies in the air. Their mouths were wide open, showing their multiple long, sharp teeth, and they then splashed back into the water to continue the fight, bending the fishing rods nearly in half. There was a circus-like atmosphere in the boat, with Jean as the ringmaster. Jean was really getting a kick out of us catching so many fish. Two of the pike measured nearly fifty inches.

Bob was boisterous in between his booming laughs. Altogether, we caught over twenty big northern pike. Jean suggested that pike from all over the lake may have migrated to this place to get out of the heat. He surmised that the biggest pike chased away or ate the smaller ones for the prime real estate of cooler water and verdant vegetation in which to hide and make an ambush site. These fish had probably never seen lures before. It came to us all that we were probably the first human beings to ever fish in this river. If we never caught any more fish on the trip, it would have been worth it just for this experience. Many well-seasoned fishermen spend their entire lives without having an experience such as we were having, with each catch a trophy.

During the fishing extravaganza, Jean said, "Gentlemen, I hate to stop the fun, but we really need to go." I saw him looking up at the sky while he spoke. The heavy gray clouds were now overhead and enveloping us in darkness. The wind blew with more force. There were sprinkles of rain coming down. We put our fishing rods down and put on our rain gear. The temperature dropped dramatically within minutes. All we had on under our rain gear were T-shirts since it had previously been so hot. We secured the equipment in the boat for the long ride back to the lodge.

Jean turned the boat toward the main lake and again gave the engine full throttle, quickly motoring out of the river. I remember looking back at that beautiful clear, spring-fed river and thinking of our memorable time there. Little did I know that a profoundly greater memorable time was just ahead.

As soon as we entered the main body of the lake, we were hit by gale-force winds and heavy rain. It was like a sudden slap in the face by a cold, hard hand. Jean's warning of the risk of being caught in the storm and having "hell to pay" was now a reality. We had gambled, and we were now potentially going to pay the dreaded consequences. I was sick with fear. I just put my head down and was silent.

We turned to face Jean at the stern of the boat, putting our backs toward the oncoming wind and rain. Unfortunately for Jean, he had to face the oncoming elements head-on while driving the boat, keeping his hand on the throttle, and steering with the rudder. He was having some difficulty seeing with the wind and rain battering his face. He really needed goggles in this situation.

The waves were starting to become a significant problem. There were whitecaps and large swells up to five feet. This made for a very rough ride. We hit the bottom of each swell with a traumatic jolt, causing discomfort and pain for all. I could tell that the pounding was causing my dad significant pain because of his chronic bad back. But he remained stoic, as usual, and didn't say anything.

We then began seeing freezing rain and occasional sleet. It was now freezing cold, and we were all shivering. The wind was becoming much stronger, and the boat was beginning to take on water. The wind and the waves began pushing us sideways along with the up-and-down action of the waves and swells. This was a particularly serious development.

The rain and sleet were coming at us almost horizontally. I could see ice forming on Jean's eyebrows and hat. The boat was taking on even more water. We frantically began to bail the water out with Styrofoam cups, which were woefully inadequate. With more water in the boat, it became heavier, sinking closer to the water level. The excess water also made the boat slower and more difficult to maneuver. The bow would occasionally dip below a large wave and soak us all with ice-cold water. With each soaking wave, everyone gave a collective low groan. We were all bounced around like rag dolls as we held on to the seats and sides of the boat, but without much success in stabilizing ourselves.

The visibility was next to nothing. I didn't know how Jean could tell what direction he was supposed to go. It seemed like an eternity fighting against nature's force. We needed land NOW! But all I could see was blackness and water. We were at great risk of going under. I began thinking of all the lives lost on the *Titanic* in the cold waters of the northern Atlantic and all the shipwrecks and lives lost on the Great Lakes due to storms. All these ships had been captained by experienced sailors with great knowledge of storms and navigation but were nevertheless lost because of nature's overwhelming sudden fury.

I held on tightly to the side of the boat and put my head down between my knees to avoid the wind and rain. I had images of how it would feel to drown after the boat capsized. The initial shock of total sudden immersion in the frigid water causing a gasp for air, all the while trying to tread water while the weight of my clothes and heavy boots pulled me down to the depths. Then struggling to breathe while attempting to keep my head above water until I slowly sank below the huge waves splashing over my head, gasping for one last breath until I couldn't stay above the surface any longer. With my last breath, I would inhale a mouthful of water into my lungs, eliciting immediate coughing and shortness of breath, only to inhale more water. My eyes would bulge out with terror and my mouth open, trying for one last breath, but I would only inhale more water. With my last bit of lucid brain function, I would realize that I was going to die within a minute, followed by a burst of outright terror, followed by unconsciousness.

I imagined my cold, lifeless body slowly drifting down to the lake bottom and eventually being eaten by bottom-dwelling creatures. My thoughts then turned to my mother and how devastated she would be at losing her husband and youngest son in the middle of nowhere, where bodies are rarely found. I silently prayed, *Please save us, Lord; please don't let us die.*

Just then Jean yelled out, "Gentlemen, we're going to have to pull in for the night." I knew we were far from the safety of the fishing lodge. We were in the middle of nowhere with no possible help available. I had never been so afraid.

Jean began to turn the boat with great difficulty toward a large, dark mass in the distance that I could barely see. I don't know how he saw this while he was fighting the waves with the boat. I took the dark mass to be an island. Turning the boat toward the island made the force of the wind and waves hit us broadside making the situation even more treacherous. This produced a real fear of capsizing. I could tell Jean was doing an amazing job of steering and handling the boat. He would turn into the wind and waves at the crest of a large swell of water, then sharply turn toward the island at the bottom of the swell. He would again turn toward the storm and waves and so on, making a kind of zigzag maneuver. By doing this, we missed the big broadside hits of the waves. I could tell it took a tremendous amount of skill to navigate the boat under these conditions, especially with a heavy load of big men and extra water on board.

We finally came close to the shore of the island. It was dark, but we could make out the rugged shoreline, strewn with large rocks and boulders. Large waves crashing against the shore made white froth between the rocks. The edges of the island rose steeply into a tangle of dark, thick, inhospitable forest. The wind was whipping the branches of the pine trees like moving arms motioning us to go away. It looked like something out of a horror movie.

We followed the shoreline in hope of finding a suitable place to land. We were around twenty feet from the sharp, irregular rocks on which the violent waves were crashing. I felt some comfort knowing that if we capsized now, land would at least be close, even though the shore was dangerous. On the other hand, we could easily be dashed on the rocks and damage our boat or ourselves, along with losing all our gear. The thought of losing our boat and being stranded on a distant deserted island with no help for possibly weeks also struck me with concern. We were walking a fine line between sinking in the raging lake and being smashed on the rocky, menacing shoreline.

After what seemed like hours, we came to a rocky point leading into a large, protected bay. We all thought, *Finally, a stroke of good luck! Thank God!* Jean turned sharply into the bay and headed for a sandy beach, a perfect place to take the boat to shore. The bay was a welcome sanctuary from the hellish lake, as the waves were dramatically reduced within it. What a huge relief! God had heard my prayer.

As the boat hit the beach, we all jumped out and proceeded to pull it as far up on the shore as possible. Our rain ponchos flapped in the hurricane-like wind like fluttering flags in a tempest. Our hats blew off, and we just had to hope we could retrieve them later. Thunder and lightning seemed close and everywhere at once. I hoped we could quickly get to shelter before we were struck by lightning. My dad, Bob, and I removed all the gear from the boat while Jean removed the engine and gas tanks. Jean then instructed us to carry the boat to a location between three boulders and turn it upside down to make a makeshift shelter. We were surrounded on three sides by large granite boulders with the boat resting on top, making a type of man-made cave. The wind and the rain were so loud that we had to yell at the tops of our voices to hear one another. Jean took out a tarp, secured it to the edge of the boat with rope, and staked it to the ground. This effectively enlarged our little shelter. It was a slight improvement to our miserable condition.

Jean gathered pine branches and thick caribou moss and laid them on the ground under our shelter. He cut patches of moss on the ground with a hunting knife and rolled up large sections of the moss like a carpet. We removed some of the larger rocks so we wouldn't be lying on them. We laid the moss over the pine branches, which made a nice rudimentary mattress. This was a definite improvement over lying on the wet, rocky ground. We all curled up in fetal positions close to one another, trying to conserve as much heat as possible. We were soaking wet and freezing. I was shivering so hard that it felt like I was having a seizure. We placed more of the thick caribou moss over us to serve as a primitive blanket. The moss was thick, with a damp sponge-like consistency. At the base was a thin layer of dirt, which quickly transferred to our bodies, but we didn't care. It was a definite improvement in our comfort. It was pitch black with no source of light, making everything much more difficult. The conditions were such that it was impossible to start a fire. Despite all our efforts, we were still miserable. There was nothing further we could do to improve our situation.

Jean said, "Gentlemen, I suggest we try to get some sleep. It's going to be a long night." Under our shelter, we seemed to revert to a primitive state, like dogs huddling together for survival. Despite our primitive mattress of moss and pine boughs, there was no getting comfortable. With every move there was a new hard spot or a branch poking up.

After several hours I heard snoring from Jean and Bob. I wondered how in the world they could sleep in such terrible conditions. I envied their ability to do so. I thought they were probably not as cold as I was because they had more body fat. I was still wet and freezing.

I tossed and turned all night, waiting for daybreak. Hundreds of thoughts passed through my mind during the sleepless night. In the pitch black and raging storm, curled in a shivering ball, I wondered, *What if the storm lasts for several days, or even a week? What will the people back at the fishing lodge think? Probably that we're all dead! What are we going to eat; will we starve? Could we all die of hypothermia?* We were woefully unprepared for weather like this. Thank goodness we had brought our rain gear. Without it, we would have been in much worse trouble. The only thing I was thankful for was being off that raging lake and avoiding drowning. I had been sure we were all going to die. Anything was better than that, no matter how miserable I was.

I realized that my greatest fears and darkest thoughts were, as the saying goes, in the dark right before the dawn. I was hoping the storm would pass and we could sort things out in the morning. Although we were in a relatively protected place in our small, makeshift, upside-down boat shelter, the wind was still howling with a ferocity I had never experienced before. Sticks, small broken branches, and other debris were flying through the air. *Could this be a tornado? Could we all be swept up and killed? Do they even have tornados in northern Canada?* I thought. *Anything is possible at some time or another.*

All the trees and bushes on the island were shaking back and forth violently. Large tree branches were waving up and down as if they were living animals trying to uproot themselves and walk away. The entire island was moving, as if it were one large evil, hostile creature that wanted us to leave. My thoughts still wandered in fearful directions. We were on an island that was possessed by a demon causing convulsions. I had previously thought I was going to die on the boat and had been rescued by land, but now I had the terribly lonely feeling of being surrounded by evil. I felt hopeless and alone. I began to fall into despair while I shivered, curling up in the cold, wet moss. I fought these thoughts because I knew they weren't helping my situation. I tried to force myself to sleep, which never works if you're not relaxed and comfortable, let alone when you're frightened and miserable.

While unsuccessfully trying to sleep, I looked across the bay from where we were camped under the overturned boat. Through the raging storm I saw a bright blue-green light slowly moving through the forest. At first I thought it was a human creating the light; however, it was much too bright and large for that. There was also no civilization for a great many miles. The light seemed to slowly pulsate with finger-like extensions moving upward to the treetops and to the sides. The finger-like projections would slowly extend and then retract in several different locations at once. There were traces of yellow and purple as well. It reminded me of the aurora borealis, or the northern lights, that I had witnessed in the past. However, this was moving through the trees instead of across the sky. The bright colors were indescribably beautiful, something I had never seen before. The light then slowly came closer to the shoreline but stayed inside the edge of the forest directly across the bay. It was as if it were trying to get a better look at our beleaguered camp.

The light seemed to pulsate in an irregular beat, as if it were a living organism. The colors changed and fluctuated, almost as if it were forming bubbles of color in different areas at different times. Watching this strange but beautiful light had an indescribably soothing effect on my worried mind. In an unusual way, the light was comforting instead of frightening amid the stormy night. I had the sensation that it was singing to me, although I couldn't hear any sound but the storm itself. It suggested a feeling I hadn't experienced for a great many years. I recalled as a child being held and rocked by my mother while she softly sang to me when I was afraid. I became enthralled and captivated by this strange entity. I could feel the presence of something within the light, but I couldn't see a face or any human-like structure.

Whatever it was, it seemed to be looking at me and trying to communicate in a strange and unusual way. I don't know how, but I could somehow sense intelligence within the colorful orb. Possibly this was just wishful thinking by someone needing to be comforted. Why this event was not frightening I cannot explain. I knew that in the middle of the night, one's imagination can come up with many unusual thoughts that the next morning one would think obviously absurd. My curiosity about the colorful moving orb only increased the more I gazed at it. I noticed that my convulsive shivering had stopped while I gazed at the light across the bay. I pulled off my damp covering of caribou moss and sat up with my knees up, continuing to peer at the lights.

I had heard stories of swamp gas producing lights. Methane is produced in swamps and bogs from decaying vegetation, which can reportedly make glowing colors. There certainly were plenty of swampy areas in the North Woods. In fact, there are vast areas of swamp and bog in northern Canada. Possibly the storm was disturbing the bottom of a swampy area, causing the release of large amounts of methane and producing beautiful but quite unusual light. However, I couldn't explain the emotional effect it was having on me. It seemed to be drawing me toward it, as if calling me. I wasn't about to investigate this in the middle of the storm, even though I felt a great need to get closer to it. The feeling I had was much greater than pure curiosity. Whatever it was, I was still cold and miserable. However, my shivering, despair, and worry were gone. My main concern was trying to keep warm and less wet despite my compulsion to move closer to investigate it further.

The light stayed for quite some time before slowly melting back into the deep forest and over the hill. I rolled back onto my rocky sleep area and replaced the large cover of dirty, damp moss back over myself. I closed my eyes and attempted to sleep, again without success, and eventually watched the sun slowly rise.

After a sleepless night, the morning was sunny and bright with no clouds in the sky. However, it was still cold and windy. We all rolled out of our little shelter, still wet, cold, and dirty. Jean made a large fire, which felt wonderful as it warmed the deep chill out of our bones. It was an improvement but was only partially effective in eliminating our cold, wet misery. We began the process of drying out our soaked clothes. I rotated my body next to the fire, first my front and then my back, in a vain attempt to dry out evenly and distribute the heat over myself.

Unfortunately, we had no substantial food available. We had cooking equipment for a possible shore lunch if we had kept any fish and only a few condiments. Jean made hot tea with pine needles placed in boiling cups of water. It was not great, but it increased our core temperature. The taste of the pine needles soothed the sensation of hunger somewhat.

"We're going to have to wait for the wind to die down before we leave. The waves should settle down by this afternoon," Jean informed us. I told Jean about the light I had witnessed the night before, and he didn't know what to make of it. Bob mentioned something about "spook lights" that were occasionally seen in the Missouri Ozarks, but even they were a source of mystery. I now wished that I had awakened everyone to see what I had seen and to feel what I had felt while staring at the mysterious light.

The bay was remarkably well protected from the wind. Its mouth faced southwest, directly opposite the wind direction from the northeast. It was surrounded by steep, heavily forested walls except for the small sliver of land where the sandy beach was in front of us. On close inspection, there was nothing unusual about the appearance of the forest where I had witnessed the light the night before. A few small waves were within the bay; however, on the main lake I could still see large waves with whitecaps. I was glad we were waiting for the wind and waves to die down. After the harrowing experience of nearly capsizing the evening before, I never again wanted to step into another boat.

I carefully looked at the surrounding forest and around the bay to glean information about the light I had witnessed. As I did, I spotted an old aluminum boat about two hundred yards away, partially covered by brush. The boat was turned upside down and pulled far from the shoreline, making it inconspicuous unless you looked hard. There appeared to be a suggestion of a trail through the forest leading away from the boat. I pointed out my findings to Jean.

He said, "Good eyes, young man. Let's go check this out." He told Bob and my dad that we were going to investigate the island and would be back later. We walked down the sandy beach to the old boat, which was well worn but clearly serviceable. There were multiple dents on the aluminum hull, and the paint on the sides was nearly worn off. As we investigated the area, sure enough, there was a trail heading through the forest upward toward the summit of the island.

Jean said, "Look at that," as he pointed to the top of the island. There was smoke emanating from the area above us where the trail was leading. "Well, now, let's see about this."

"What do you make of it, Jean?"

"It seems we're not alone on this island, young man."

As we started up the trail, it seemed as if we were entering a dark green cave with a long passageway ahead. It was a pathway into the unknown, leading to a mystery at the top of the island, which was a little unsettling. As we walked on a steady incline along the trail, I noted that the branches from the trees were cut and perfectly manicured to form an archway. All was silent and still within the green pathway. There was no wind within this tunnel, as there was outside, which was a relief. It was perfectly protected from the elements. However, my feelings changed to a slight sense of claustrophobia. It was like being in a tubular cage, or possibly like entering a large trap of some kind. The only sound we heard was the soft, muffled sound of our feet rhythmically treading the trail. The path was uniquely groomed. This was uncharacteristic for a Canadian forest path. It had the sign of willful intelligent design. The only thing it lacked was pavement. Instead, the surface of the trail was soft earth, like firmly packed peat moss, better suited to moccasins than thick leather boots. I could tell that extraneous rocks and branches had been removed for easier travel. The trail took several gentle turns around large boulders beautifully covered with deep green moss. It almost gave me the feeling of entering a Japanese Zen Garden. At this point in the trail, we took several steps up rock stairs, perfectly and painstakingly chiseled out of a wall of smooth granite boulders. My mind was filled with questions as to what lay ahead and who had made this path. The beautiful and unique manicured trail obviously had taken a lot of time and effort to make, especially the steps chiseled into the wall of granite. It was almost as if it had been created by someone who was quite dedicated to their art. Why in the middle of nowhere would someone go to all the trouble to groom an unusual but beautiful trail? I thought, *Does this unusual path have anything to do with the strange light I witnessed last night, and if so, what?* I now had a great foreboding as to what lay ahead.

I quickly glanced at Jean. He was uncharacteristically silent and totally focused on the trail ahead. He didn't even pull out a cigarette. I knew Jean had flown over this entire area in his bush plane and seen no significant human habitation for hundreds of miles. The next thing that came to mind was what Jean had mentioned before we had started—that this area was avoided by the Indians because of something "spooky."

Whether it was merely a rumor or not, it was still strange that this region had that reputation.

After a half mile of an easy walk up the hill, we abruptly came out of the green tunnel into a large, wide-open clearing bathed in bright sunlight. It was a sudden and stark contrast to the dimly lit trail from which we had just emerged. We had entered a bright new world from an imaginary birth canal. I could breathe more easily outside the beautiful but somewhat claustrophobic tunnel. We felt immediately refreshed by being in the sunlight but still anxious as to what may lay in store for us.

In front of us, multiple wooden structures lay in the large clearing. The open area with the wooden structures was surrounded by tall, stately white pine trees, much taller than the usual pine trees of the area. These majestic trees approached seventy-five to one hundred feet tall. I had the sensation that we were entering a natural arena of some kind, with no audience and in total silence. The area was protected from the wind and elements by the surrounding huge trees and massive boulders, which shielded the wooden structures from the northeast wind. I could see the tops of the trees swaying in response to the wind. However, it was perfectly calm and sunny in this clearing on top of the island, in stark contrast to the windy and cold campsite we had left by the lake.

There was a small log cabin with several wooden outbuildings and sheds surrounding it. One of the sheds contained a huge woodpile, protecting the firewood from the elements. A small wooden house-like structure with a closed door rested on four long poles at least twelve feet high. A ladder was next to it for access to the top. This is a commonly seen structure in the North Woods. Jean said that it was a cache where meat was stored in the winter so animals couldn't get it. This implied that whoever lived in the cabin had spent a long time here, including winter.

Around thirty yards from the cabin there was a commanding view of the lake, looking out over the distant blue expanse. A rudimentary wooden chair was strategically placed facing the view. Adjacent to the chair were two large, smooth granite boulders with a flat rock between them, giving the appearance of a primitive altar in some crude sacred setting. The huge pine trees close by were like the dark green spires of a cathedral, seemingly protecting the area.

The cabin was well built and solid. However, the structure was nothing fancy. The large logs making the walls were notched at the ends, so each log fit snugly in place with the next. It showed signs of having been built by someone who knew what they were doing, according to Jean. Moss was tightly stuffed between the logs for insulation. This was the traditional way to build cabins in the North Woods instead of using the more recently manufactured synthetic insulation or rubber grout. There was a large rack of moose antlers above the cabin door. We could see smoke emanating from the stone smokestack on the roof. Jean said, from his practical experience, that the chimney had taken a lot of time, effort, and expertise to make, as opposed to a metal stove chimney. The entire area was clean and tidy, with no extraneous debris, machinery, or wood scattered about, as could usually be seen in most lived-in northern camp areas. The ground around the camp area was soft, with no rocks or dead wood to step on, again implying constant care. One could even walk around this area in socks without fear of injury. We stood there silently in front of the cabin, looking at the area and trying to gain more information by further visual inspection.

I asked Jean in a low voice, "Who in the world would live here so far from all human contact?"

"I don't know, maybe someone like me," he answered as he smiled at me and chuckled softly.

"Do you think there might be a crazy man inside with a gun? I've heard that sometimes criminals running from the law hide out in the bush to avoid prosecution."

"I don't think so, but one never knows, so get ready to run if anything bad happens. At this point we are stranded on an island with no supplies. We could sure use some help. Whoever is in there clearly has food, and we don't know how long we're going to be stuck here. We're in a position where beggars can't be choosers. Plus, whoever is in there is going to find out we're on his island anyway, so we might as well meet him now," Jean said.

I looked at the cabin door with some trepidation and a little fear as to who or what might come out that door. I remembered what Jean had originally said about this area, that the Indians didn't like to come to this region of the lake because of "spooky things" like spirits inhabiting the area.

Jean cupped his hands around his mouth and gave a loud shout: "YO! THE CABIN." We waited for a while with no response. We looked at each other, anticipating what to do next. I now definitely had a creepy feeling and was ready to bolt if anything untoward transpired. I took a few steps back behind Jean. Jean then repeated the call: "YO! THE CABIN." Giving a yell first was less intrusive than knocking at the cabin door in the middle of nowhere. We waited again.

After a long while, which seemed longer than it probably was, the door of the cabin slowly opened. There stood an old Native man with a big smile. "Good morning. Come in; I've been expecting you," he said.

Jean and I looked at each other quizzically and slowly entered the cabin. We were both wondering how the old man could have been expecting us. As we walked into the cabin, we were enveloped with a gush of comforting warmth. I was still shivering despite our attempts to warm up by the fire at our campsite.

"Have a seat," said the old man. Jean and I sat down in chairs next to a table. All the furniture was quite sturdy and was clearly handmade. The furniture even had some type of glossy finish over the wood, making it smooth and attractive in a rugged way.

The cabin was warm from a fire burning in the round arched stone fireplace. It was instantly comforting to be indoors out of the cold wind. Within minutes my continual shivering stopped. An aroma of recently cooked food pervaded the cabin. Just the smell of food made my stomach churn. I looked around the cabin. It was well kept and clean and had a homey, comfortable feel. There were large burlap bags hanging from the rafters, filled with wild rice. Glass Ball jars of home-canned goods were on nearby shelves. A large black bear fur was on the wall next to a well-made bed. I caught Jean's eyes looking at a lever-action hunting rifle on the wall. I could tell he was suspicious of the old man.

"Would you like something to eat?" said the old Indian with a kindly smile.

I said, "Sure, I'm starved." Jean was silent but nodded, looking at the old man with some reluctance.

"I have some hot wild rice porridge with fresh blueberries I picked yesterday. I also have some smoked fish. I have a lot, so you can have as much as you want."

He placed two large, smooth handmade wooden bowls in front of us, filled to the brim with the hot porridge and blueberries. Large wooden spoons were placed on the table next to the bowls. The rice porridge had the consistency of oatmeal but was better in taste and texture. The blueberries were delicious. It was the first time I had ever eaten smoked fish, and it was excellent. Jean and I wolfed down the food, and the old man quickly gave us seconds. He smiled as we ravenously consumed the food.

"Good, eh? There's more where that came from."

He gave us what he called "Labrador tea," the leaves of which were from a local bush. It was a well-known local medicinal plant used to soothe an upset stomach and nausea but also used as a routine beverage by the Indians.

The old Indian introduced himself as Ben Clover, but he said most people just called him "Dark Eye." I could see where he had gotten the name because of a large, dark crescent-shaped birthmark around his right eye, extending to his cheek. He had a long, braided ponytail of mixed black and gray. I estimated he was in his late sixties. However, people living in the bush frequently look much older than they are because of long exposure to the elements. He was short, with large, thick calloused hands from years of obvious hard manual labor. His movements were unexpectedly quick and coordinated. He seemed in excellent condition despite his age. His dark brown eyes were clear and cheerful. They seemed to almost sparkle as he glanced at us. His soft smile revealed a genuine appreciation for our company. He was warm, gracious, and polite. He seemed like a grandfather who had not seen his grandchildren in a long while.

Dark Eye said, "I harvest my own wild rice from the bays and shallow areas around the lake. It takes a lot of work to dry it and remove the husks, but it's worth the effort. I like it much better than oatmeal, and it's free. I have pretty much all I need living out here. I hunt and fish for meat. I'll usually smoke or can the fish. One moose will usually last me all winter. Cattail and arrow plant are wonderful vegetables that I gather from the area as well as blueberries and rose hips, which are quite abundant this time of year. I store everything in jars so I can have them year-round, but they're better freshly picked like today."

Dark Eye didn't ask us any questions about ourselves, which I thought was unusual. It was almost as if he had known us for a long time and felt quite comfortable with us, as if we were old friends who had dropped by for a visit. Jean shifted the conversation and said, "So what brings you out here?"

Dark Eye said, "It was getting too noisy and confusing back in town. I couldn't even sleep without being awakened by people or spirits. I still have a small cottage just outside the reservation. The 'res' is about fifty miles away. I must go there every once in a while, but I don't like to stay long."

There was a small Cree town located on a reservation at the north end of the lake. It was extremely remote, and access by any means was not easy.

"It takes about a two-day boat ride to get there," said Dark Eye. "It's not that I don't like people—I do. It's all the baggage that people have that I can't take for very long. I used to be a carpenter and mechanic, among other things, when I was living on the res. I even lived a short time in Winnipeg, but that was way too much. It took me nearly a year to build this place. I've been living here at least twenty years. It's like heaven to me. It has brought me great peace."

Dark Eye seemed to enjoy talking as he moved around the kitchen area. I was impressed with his openness and the ease with which he talked.

Jean said, "Spirits, people's baggage, what do you mean?"

Dark Eye sat down at the table across from us and placed his hands together on the surface. He mainly talked to Jean, but periodically he would look at me. He maintained a disarming, gentle, and soft smile.

Dark Eye replied, "I'm able to see the other side. In all people, no matter what their race or culture, there is always an intuitive sense of the spirit world. My ability is more advanced than others'. I'm not sure if it's a gift or a curse. I have had this all my life. It was quite frightening when I was a youth."

Jean said, "The other side?"

"Yes, the spirit world. I can see people's past and future, and sometimes I can sense their thoughts. Some people are easier to read than others. When I was a young boy, I couldn't tell the difference between the living and the nonliving spirits. It was terribly confusing and sometimes frightening. My parents thought I had a vivid imagination with imaginary friends.

"I was raised in the Catholic church. When I grew older, I told my priest and teachers what I was seeing and that I was hearing voices. They thought I had a mental disorder. I was sent to a neurologist and then to a psychiatrist in Winnipeg, who gave me the diagnosis of childhood schizophrenia. I was given medication, but it made me feel sleepy and lethargic. I hated the feeling of being dull. My maternal grandmother had the same gift, but not as strong as mine. She too had a mark above her right eye. She reassured my parents that they should be honored to have a son so close to the Great Manitou, or the Great Spirit of all life. She understood what I was seeing and taught me how to manage the gift. When I'm around a lot of people, I'm able to see too much with all their history and sometimes future, along with the spirits associated with them. Many times, it's hard to carry on a normal conversation with someone with all that going on. For the most part I'm unable to help people because their fate is usually already set. I usually never tell people their future unless there is a good chance that I may help them. Occasionally I'm able to help people make life decisions and give comfort to them. The Indian people know where I live and will sometimes make the long trip to visit me. However, with the changing times visits now are few and far between."

Jean looked at him skeptically and said, "You said you see spirits?"

"Yes, all the time. They are always present to some degree. For in-

stance, your twin brother, Dean, is right next to you now. I know that
you occasionally see him."

The old man leaned closer, earnestly looking at Jean. "You also have
the gift to a degree, but you try to ignore it. The gift can be developed
with practice. Most people have some level of sight into the other world
but don't realize it. It may be a dream or the feeling that there is a presence with you at times. Sometimes people will hear a voice. Dean was
with you in the boat last night helping you steer. I know it must have
been quite difficult. Dean told me it was about as bad as the time you
both were in a storm on North Cranberry Lake. Some people call them
guardian angels or helpful spirits. They're sent back from paradise, an
area I cannot see into, to guide the living."

Jean looked at Dark Eye with astonishment. He nearly had his mouth
open. I could hardly believe what I was hearing. However, the way Dark
Eye explained everything was convincing. He was so matter-of-fact. It
took a while for Jean to utter any words.

Mildly raising his voice, Jean said, "How do you know my brother's
name? How do you know we were in a bad storm on North Cranberry
Lake years ago?"

"I told you, I 'm able to see and communicate with spirits and see
the other side of this reality. I don't mean to offend you. I'm here to
give answers to the questions you've been asking yourself for years. It's
possible that you were sent here by the Great Spirit for some reason."

Jean said, "Yes, the storm on North Cranberry was nearly as bad
as last night." Jean continued, "Dean was my identical twin brother.
We were very close. We lived in the bush together for months at a time
when we were kids. We always had an intuition about what the other
one was thinking."

"About five years ago I woke up in the middle of the night. I sat up,
and there was Dean standing at the foot of my bed. I asked him, 'Hey!

What are you doing here?' He raised his hand, waved, and walked out of the room. He didn't say a word. I got out of bed and followed, but I couldn't find him anywhere. I went through the house and then outside. I didn't see his car or any trace of him. I thought, *That was weird!* I then went back to bed, expecting to talk with him tomorrow. The next day I got a phone call and was told that Dean was killed in a car accident the night before about the time I saw him in my house.

"Dean usually comes to me the night before some big event in my life. The night prior to my wedding, before each of my children was born, and before each of my parents died. He appears so real and is smiling. He never says anything, but he gives me a calm, reassuring feeling."

Jean continued, "I was confident that nothing bad was going to happen to us in the boat last night because Dean didn't appear to me the night before."

Dark Eye said, "Dean is a very strong spirit, and he is always with you. Why he was taken away at such a young age, only the Great Spirit knows, but there is an infinite plan for all human beings. Life passes very quickly; it is but a second compared to your spirit in eternity. I am convinced that one day you will be with your brother again. Until then, listen to him. Search your soul in a quiet place, away from noise and people. It may take time. Some people fast while they are looking for guidance and a connection to the spirit world. The Great Manitou wishes only good for you." Dark Eye gently smiled and looked at both Jean and me with expressive eyes.

"You have a good wife. Her name is Susan, is that correct?"

"Yes, her name is Susan!"

"I see her spirit living in you. That is good. When one is truly in love, they give a part of their spirit or soul to you. It then resides with you forever. That is something that you can never give back, no matter what happens to the relationship. She also carries your spirit within her. You are very lucky to have this. This is what was meant to be. It was given to mankind by the Great Spirit. However, your wife is different, and she will never see Dean or have any connection to the other side while she is on this earth. There is nothing wrong with this. It is what is meant to be by the Great Spirit."

"Susan, Dean, and I used to be great friends. He had a girlfriend, and we would go out and have so much fun together. I miss those days."

"Although your wife will never see Dean, your son will. I sense that a part of Dean's spirit, or you may call it his love, is within him. Like I said, eventually your son will see Dean, so don't be alarmed when this happens. It is all for the good."

"He's only four years old!"

"Yes, I know," Dark Eye said with a soft smile.

After several minutes of silence, I looked over at Jean. I could tell that talking about his brother and his family had significantly affected him.

Jean took a deep breath and slowly exhaled. He took his hat off and brushed his hair back, then replaced his hat. He said quizzically, "Why did you come to this island when there are so many other places?"

Dark Eye replied, "This island has been known by the Cree people for centuries as a place of great spiritual power. Many of my people have called this a floating island. It has been said that the island changes location at times. Some people will see the island in the distance one day, only to find it gone the next day. Some people have great difficulty finding this place. I heard that a man in a canoe once attempted to paddle to the island, but the island remained on the horizon no matter how long he paddled. He eventually gave up and went home. I think people who cannot find the island were not meant to come here or were coming for the wrong reasons. I have never seen the island move, but one thing I do know is that this place has great power, and I would not be surprised at anything. This place seems to be a place where our reality and the spirit world overlap. This island is inhabited by powerful but good spirits, primarily the She-Manitou. She appears to me as a beautiful Indian woman. When I'm able to see her, she hovers in the air just off the ground. There is a mist or a light fog around her. Her smile is gentle and beautiful, as if she understands, but she never moves her lips. I never hear her voice, but she speaks to my mind. I can feel great love and comfort from her. I'm not exactly sure who she is except a wonderful spirit that takes away suffering. Maybe she is Mary, the mother of Jesus? Maybe she is Jesus in a female form? Possibly she is my guardian angel sent by the Great Spirit. I'm not sure exactly who she is. She will sometimes show herself if I call for her. Occasionally she shows up unexpectedly, usually at dawn or late evening just before sunset. She gives me great comfort, and I'm always happy to see her. Just to talk about her makes my heart soar."

Dark Eye turned his head, looked at me, smiling, and said, "I think you may have encountered the She-Manitou last night young man. Sometimes she may appear as indistinct colors, other times a voice, and other times in human form. I think she was checking on you boys and saw you were in distress." Dark Eye continued, "In the old days Indian people would come to this island to seek direction and guidance in life, much like a pilgrimage. Young men especially would come here when reaching a difficult crossroads in their lives. Some people still come here, but not so often anymore. I am here to help people interpret their visions, just like with you, Jean."

Dark Eye went on, "There is now a great evil pervading the Indian peoples. They have lost direction, and they don't listen to the spirits. Drugs and alcohol numb the spiritual mind, and evil spirits will take advantage of a human in that condition. They then forget how to live properly. Suicide, murder, and violence of all kinds are now common.

In the past these problems were rare with my people. It is so hard to hear the good spirits with television, noise, and large numbers of people around. Nowadays many people, especially the younger ones, think I'm crazy and fear me because they don't understand.

"I sometimes find myself walking a thin line between the natural and the supernatural, unable to distinguish or explain the difference between the two. Just the same, the supernatural has been our companion since the beginning of time as we know it. It is separated only by a thin invisible veil. There is a reality that exists beyond this physical world that we engage with much more than we think."

Jean and I sat there, pondering the fate of modern society and its lack of spiritual guidance. We both realized that it wasn't just the Indian peoples who needed help, but everyone.

We all sat there in silence while Dark Eye smiled and finally asked, "Would you like some more tea?"

Jean looked at me and said, "No, thank you, we really need to be getting back. I think the wind has died down and we should be on our way." I could tell Jean was getting a little anxious from talking about things that were too close to home that he had never discussed with anyone before.

Jean and I shook hands with Dark Eye. Looking at Jean, Dark Eye said, "Please come back anytime, Jean; you're always welcome."

He then turned and looked at me as if seeing into my soul while shaking my hand and said, "You have a long and interesting road ahead of you, young man."

I wasn't quite sure what to make of what he said. I just thanked him for his hospitality, and we walked out the cabin door.

As we walked through the camp area, Dark Eye yelled, "Oh, Jean, Dean told me to tell you that there's no red river porridge where he is."

Jean smiled and waved, and we went on our way through the camp and down the winding trail to the beach. What had been barely an hour with the old man seemed like a day.

As Jean and I walked down the trail, I asked him, "What's red river porridge?"

"It's a thick porridge made from cracked wheat, rye, and flaxseed. Cranberries are frequently crushed and placed in the porridge, giving it a red appearance. It's a traditional breakfast food of the Canadian north, mainly Manitoba. My mother would make Dean and me eat the stuff every morning, and we both hated it. It had the texture of thick glue with no taste. No matter what she did to try to improve the flavor, it was always terrible."

Jean remained somber as we wound our way down the path to the beach. He didn't even pull out a cigarette. While we silently walked down the trail, my mind was racing. Was Dark Eye a crazy old man, a lunatic trying to maintain his sanity by living alone? However, he seemed so normal in every way, and so gracious. His thought patterns and mannerisms were quite orderly. He was so calm and polite. Was he taking psychedelic drugs and was delusional? But how did he know all those things about Jean that no one else knew? Had we just imagined our conversation with the old man—were we delusional?" I didn't have a clear explanation for our encounter with the mysterious old man.

Then it came to me. It was all about Jean!

I don't think Dark Eye would have been forthcoming about spiritual things and about the She-Manitou if it had been just me, my dad, or Bob. I'm sure he would have been gracious and given us food and supplies. However, Dark Eye really wanted to see Jean. Maybe Dark Eye had been waiting for weeks to see Jean, maybe months— who knows, maybe years. I think he had a message to give Jean from the beyond. That was why he had said he was expecting us. It made sense when I looked at it that way. Dark Eye had been so clear and explicit in his descriptions of his life and the spirit world. I don't think he would have gone into all that except for a purpose. During our conversation, Dark Eye had been looking at Jean the whole time, with only occasional glances at me. I don't think he was necessarily expecting me or anyone else besides Jean. It seemed that Dark Eye was drawn to Jean like a magnet to steel. It reminded me of a master talking with a new apprentice who didn't quite understand everything yet. I think Dark Eye had planted a seed in Jean from which he expected something to grow. What that would be, I had no idea. I had a feeling that this would not be the last time Jean and Dark Eye would be in contact.

When Jean and I returned to where we had beached the boat for shelter, Bob and my dad had cooked up an amazing shore lunch. They had gone to the rocky point of the island to fish. The luck with fishing had changed with the weather. They had caught a whole stringer of walleyes, filleted them, covered them in a cornbread batter, and fried them in a large skillet. They had found some coffee, and it was ready to serve. Everything smelled wonderful. We were right on time for a shoreline feast. We all sat on the sandy beach, plates in hand, savoring the freshly caught walleye and coffee. Jean and I had no problem taking in a second meal. We were all in good spirits, as if nothing had happened, except for Jean, who was uncharacteristically quiet. He wasn't even smoking his typical cigarette.

The wind was now just a slight breeze, and the sun was shining. More importantly, the waves on the lake were minimal. The huge swells and whitecaps we had experienced the night before were gone. After lying on the beach for a while, savoring the warmth of the sun and our full bellies, Jean got up and said, "Gentlemen, I say we break camp and go home."

We carried the boat down to the beach and flipped it over into the water. Jean got the motor and gas tanks and placed them in the boat.

We cleaned up the dishes and placed the cooking equipment back in the large wooden shore-lunch box. We then all climbed into the boat and pushed off. Jean pulled the starter cord of the engine, put the throttle on full, and sped out of the bay into the main lake.

As we rounded the rocky point at the bay's entrance, I noticed an ancient Indian painting on a stark cliff extending into the lake. I waved my hands to get Jean's attention and then pointed to the petroglyph. He slowly turned the boat around for a closer look. The figure painted on the cliff above the waterline was stained red and slightly faded by time. It was a primitive picture of a single stick-like man in a canoe with both arms raised toward a circular spiral above him. This spiral I took to indicate a spirit. I thought that for some ancient Indian to take the effort to make this art, there must have been some great spiritual connection to this place. Jean was silent and for the most part looked away during the viewing. We lingered in front of the petroglyph for several minutes, giving our ideas on its meaning. Then we turned toward the main lake and motored off, again at full throttle. I wanted to go back and talk with Dark Eye again. It seemed that we had just scratched the surface of his knowledge, and I wanted to know more.

The lake was smooth as glass, with no wind or waves. The temperature was mild. It was a pleasant ride back to the lodge. The lake was beautiful again, a far cry from the night before. The boat glided over the surface of the water as if on a tapestry of silk.

We finally saw the large log fishing lodge with its dock in the distance. It was a great relief to know that we would soon be back in safety and comfort. We pulled into the boat dock, where the manager of the lodge was waiting.

He said, "What happened to you boys?" I asked him if he had been worried about us. The manager said, "No, we knew you were with Jean, and we knew he would take good care of you. We did figure you probably had a rough night, though."

The manager said to Jean, "How are you doing my friend?"

"I'm fine," Jean said quietly without expression or making eye contact.

The manager could see that Jean was not his usual outgoing self. "What's the matter, Jean? It looks like you've seen a ghost."

Jean didn't say anything as he unloaded the boat.

I thought, *Maybe he did see a ghost.*

THE CHURCHILL
RIVER

Look deep into nature, and then you will understand everything better.

ALBERT EINSTEIN

J ean Broux and I were busy packing his pontoon bush plane with
material to finish building a fishing camp on the Churchill River in
northern Manitoba. We had been planning this trip since our last
trip to the region one year before. I was thrilled that our adventure
was about to begin. It was 1967, and there were no fishing camps
where we were headed. We'd be the first people to fish in this large
river. The thought of fishing such a major river system where the fish
had never seen lures before filled my thoughts with anticipation of
great adventure, like setting out on an expedition into the unknown.
All year I had studied maps of the area and read about the region's
history, including explorations of it and its Indigenous people. Who
knew what monstrous fish lay in the depths of one of Canada's largest
rivers? We were hoping to catch trophy northern pike and walleye.
However, our main goal was pike, which could grow to more than

four feet in length. Pike are known for their aggressiveness and fighting ability.

One reason for the pike's rapid and large growth is its aggressive feeding style. The pike is a killing machine whose nickname is "water wolf." One thirty-inch pike, for example, was found with a twenty-inch fish in its stomach. Not only are pike cannibalistic, but they will eat just about any fish, as well as rodents or ducks and almost anything else unlucky enough to float by. Most of the day pike lie in ambush among vegetation or lie at the bottom of deep pools, looking like logs, waiting for a dawdling fish to wander by. If the water is clear, they will charge with incredible ferocity from the bottom to snatch a fish close to the surface. A pike will sometimes stalk its prey, following its meal to the surface or around a barrier before lunging at it with a rapid aggressive thrust. One person described a pike as having a German shepherd's face and a snake's body with fins!

Jean was energetic and upbeat, as usual, as we packed the gear into the plane. He seemed as excited as I was for the upcoming trip. It had been a year since I had last seen him. I had gotten to know Jean well over the past three years from our yearly summer fishing trips. This year Jean seemed just a little different. He was still his outgoing self, but now he seemed just a little more serious and formal. The difference was not obvious unless you knew him well. The change was subtle, and no one but me seemed to notice it. I wondered if the experience we'd had with the Native shaman, Dark Eye, the year before had influenced him. I was eager to know if he'd had any further contact with Dark Eye. However, I was hesitant to ask since Dark Eye had told him a lot of personal things about himself and his family that Jean was clearly quite sensitive about. I would have to bide my time and wait for the right moment.

I had never told anyone, including my parents, about the unusual light on the island and Jean's and my encounter with Dark Eye. To begin with, I didn't think anyone would believe me; they would probably brush it off as a young man's fantasy. It would be like people who report seeing UFOs, Bigfoot, ghosts, or other strange and unexplained rare phenomena. I worried that people might think I or Jean was a little odd. Also, there was a lot of personal information about Jean that I didn't feel comfortable spreading around without his permission. I knew what Dark Eye had said greatly affected him. Little did I know what revelations Jean had in store for me in the upcoming week.

Jean had scouted the area for the lodge and was optimistic about great success. He had flown up to the river just after ice-out and fished for several days with phenomenal results. He had filled us with stories of giant northern pike and massive schools of walleye, the likes of which he had never seen before.

He had begun building the camp on a rocky peninsula jutting into the river about a mile down from a large cascading waterfall. Jean had already made wooden platforms for the tents and set up a propane stove for the cooking tent. He had made several tables and chairs and brought in cooking equipment. He had built a small dock on the downriver side of the rocky point in a small bay where planes and boats could dock. He had done all this alone in an amazingly short period, accomplishing the job with more efficiency than three people could have shown in the same amount of time. The lodge paid him a significantly higher salary than customary because they had no need to hire others when they had Jean. Jean was an excellent carpenter as well as a superb fishing and hunting guide. He could do just about anything the lodge needed. That included being a bush pilot and transporting clients to remote fishing locations. He was also an accomplished mechanic who was able to break down, diagnose and fix airplane as well as boat motors. Now he just needed to add the finishing touches to complete the camp with me as his assistant.

Jean and I were going to fly in first, followed by a larger pontoon plane carrying my dad and the rest of the fishermen along with more supplies. I had begged my father to let me go first with Jean, and he'd given me permission. I was thrilled. Over the years Jean had become a mentor and almost a hero to me. He represented a completely different way of life, one of freedom, independence, and adventure. This was a life a sixteen-year-old boy would obviously be attracted to, something like Huck Finn and Jim running away and floating down the Mississippi River.

My dad thought highly of Jean and approved of the friendship. Jean had taught me how to land and clean fish, tie knots, and improve my fishing skills. Although I was sixteen years old, he treated me as an adult, with respect, probably because by the time he was sixteen, he and his brother, Dean, had dropped out of school and were living on their own as fishing and hunting guides. He had grown up in the bush at the edge of civilization. He'd done what his parents had done as well as other family members for generations before and grown up living off the land with very little need for the things you'd find in a town.

After packing the plane with our equipment, I released the rope tethering the plane to the dock. I pushed the plane farther into the lake with significant effort. At the same time, I vaulted from the dock onto one of the hollow aluminum pontoons. I grabbed the ladder and scampered up through the open door into the cockpit. I jumped into the seat and looked over at Jean, who was already in the pilot's seat of the single-engine propeller plane, strapped in and ready to go. After I strapped on my safety belt, Jean gave me a big smile and a thumbs-up. He threw his nearly omnipresent cigarette out the window into the lake below and said, "Are you ready?," maintaining his big smile with one missing tooth.

"Absolutely. Let's go!"

We put our headphones on to dampen the loud noise of the large De Havilland engine so we could hear each other talk through the microphone system. Jean turned on the engine, which gave a loud, chugging roar as the propeller began to turn slowly. Smoke momentarily came out of the engine. Seeing some concern on my face, Jean reassured me that the smoke was normal. He made a final check of the instruments and taxied onto the main lake. He then increased the throttle of the engine while taxiing over the water before giving it full power. The roar of the engine increased dramatically, and we began skimming across the surface of the lake at great speed, bumping along the waves. Jean pulled on the flight stick, and we slowly became airborne from the water. There was a sudden transition from rapidly skimming along the rough surface of the lake to immediate smoothness as we lifted into the air. The momentum of the lift pushed my back deeper into my seat. It was an exhilarating feeling to be airborne above the lake and viewing the lodge below. We quickly gained altitude and then banked over the dock from where we had come. We could see my dad and several of the other fishermen like small insects waving at us. Jean slowly tipped his wings up and down in response. We turned and headed north.

As we gained altitude, looking northward, we were greeted by a vista of forest, lakes, and rivers, with some areas of exposed rock as far as the eye could see. There were so many lakes that it seemed as if nearly half of what we saw was water. This topography carried on beyond the horizon. The view was majestic in its vastness, with no human habitation. I felt the country's expanse, its huge space, and its unexplored distance. I had the sensation of excitement as I felt my heart rate increase. We had just left the edge of human civilization with total wilderness extending thousands of miles north to the Arctic Ocean. It felt good to be back in the northern wilderness again. It almost felt like coming home in a strange and deep way.

What we were seeing is called the Canadian Shield, which is the geologic remnant of glaciers gone eons ago but leaving their effect on the land by gouging deep crevices out of granite rock, forming lakes and leaving behind large amounts of water. The Canadian Shield extends from the Great Lakes at the U.S. border north to the Arctic Ocean, an enormous area. I realized how alone we were now and going still farther from any civilization—farther and more remote than I had ever been before. This was exhilarating. I looked at Jean, smiled, and gave him a thumbs-up. He seemed to know what I was thinking, and he gave me a big smile and nodded. I think he felt the same way I did, even though he saw this every day. I thought, *This is why he loves what he does; he never gets used to it.* It was the feeling of freedom and independence away from the noise and hassles of urban living.

It was a mild, sunny day with only scattered puffy white clouds. The ride was smooth, and I was enjoying looking at the wilderness below. Jean motioned to me to look down out the window on my side. I saw a large cow moose with a calf wading and eating vegetation in a shallow bog. A few minutes later he pointed out a black bear walking across an exposed area of rock separating two large areas of forest.

There were many beautiful lakes that looked like excellent areas to fish, especially since none had ever been fished before. As we continued our flight for around forty minutes, I noted one sizable lake that had the perfect structure for an excellent fishing area. It was a beautiful gem of a lake, like you might see on a postcard. There was a small, slow-moving river flowing into the lake and a large bay with weeds and lily pads close by. This led out to a rocky point with a steep drop-off in depth. From the air we could determine the relative depth of the lake by looking down at the crystal-clear water. The lake was surrounded by large pine and spruce trees. I pointed this out to Jean, and he nodded in agreement.

He said, "It looks good. Do you want to check it out?"

"Now? You mean fly down there and land on the lake to go fishing?"

"Sure, I do this all the time. It won't take long to quickly check the lake out. You're right, it's a beautiful lake that looks like an excellent place to fish."

I knew that Jean frequently flew around in his pontoon bush plane looking for new areas to fish so he could give his clients an excellent and unique wilderness fishing experience. He would also tell the lodge manager of any new lake that he thought was productive enough to put an outpost camp on.

I said, "Sure, let's go fishing!"

"OK, here we go."

Jean precipitously banked the plane to the side and slowly lowered the altitude. With the nose of the plane pointing in the direction of the lake, I felt as if we were going on a strafing mission. I thought it was very cool to spontaneously fly down to explore an unknown lake and fish on a mere whim. The landing was smooth. We skimmed across the lake surface and then taxied into the bay next to the river. It was even more beautiful on the water. Jean kept the motor running with the propeller slowly moving as the plane glided slowly across the smooth surface of the water, like a slowly trolling boat. Jean told me to grab my fishing gear and cast toward the bank close to the weeds and then into the entrance of the river.

I opened the cockpit door and slowly descended the ladder onto the pontoon, fishing rod in hand. I began casting with a yellow-and-red five of diamonds spoon lure with a steel leader. The use of a steel leader at the tip of a fishing line is a must in the north country because northern pike, and to a lesser extent walleye, have many sharp teeth that would cut any fishing line easily without it.

I began to slowly retrieve the lure when I felt a sudden violent hit that nearly jolted the rod out of my hands.

"Fish on!"

The fish jumped out of the water, bending its long green-and-white snake-like body as it tried to throw the hook. It was a big pike! I had to walk up down and around the pontoon to land the fish. Just when I thought the fish's energy was spent, it would speed off, stripping more of my fishing line with an audible whine. Eventually, after a significant fight, I landed the fish and held it up to show Jean.

"Excellent, that's a good one!"

I unhooked the fish and placed it back in the water. I caught several more big pike, hooking one with nearly every cast.

"Let's see if this place has any walleye." Jean turned the plane out of the bay and motored toward the rocky point.

When we got to the point, he told me to let the lure fall to the bottom and then retrieve it with a slow jerking motion. I did what he instructed, and halfway through my retrieve, I felt a heavy thud and then a continuous pull. I knew it wasn't a snag because it was moving. I could feel the fish trying to dive deeper into the lake. It wasn't like the violent, aggressive jerking and twisting struggle characteristic of a pike. This was something different. I slowly brought in a large, beautiful brown-and-gold walleye. It was at least twenty-six inches long, a definite trophy. Wow, was I having fun! Who would ever think of fishing off a pontoon plane instead of a boat, trolling around the lake with an airplane propeller instead of a boat motor? What an incredible experience. I couldn't wait to tell my friends back home about this. Little did I know that the unique adventures were just beginning.

Jean said, "I think we now know this is a great place to fish. We'll need to come back here someday. Let's mount up and get to the Churchill."

I climbed back into the plane, happy to have had the experience of fishing from a plane instead of a boat. I had never heard of anyone fishing in this manner before. We taxied onto the main lake, gave it the throttle, and became airborne toward our destination, the Churchill River.

After approximately an hour, Jean said, "That's it down there. That's the Churchill." I looked out the window and saw a large, winding river that widened into many areas of large bays and associated lakes. There was a large waterfall just ahead. It was larger than I had expected. Massive volumes of water cascaded down several levels and around huge house-sized boulders to one large fall at the end. Large clouds of mist billowed up from the base of the falls, creating an impressive appearance of great power. I could see the rocky point where the camp was. Jean banked the plane and slowly brought it down to the main area of the river.

The Churchill River is one of the major rivers of northern Canada, flowing east toward the tundra and emptying into Hudson Bay, which is an extension of the Arctic Ocean. The river drains a vast area of forest and thousands of lakes. During the fur trade from the seventeenth to the early twentieth century, it was used as a trading highway into the interior of Canada. Native Americans, the French, and later Scottish and English voyagers brought furs downriver in large canoes to trading posts on Hudson Bay and the town of Churchill.

We taxied slowly over to the recently made dock. There was no current in this protected small bay adjacent to the camp. Boats and motors previously transported by plane were there. I could tell that making this camp had required considerable time and effort, mainly by Jean. I opened the cockpit door and jumped onto the pontoon. Jean had maneuvered the plane perfectly, bringing it to within two feet of the dock.

We removed the canvas tents and the rest of the gear and set up all the tents on their frames over the wood-plank floors. We placed an aluminum chimney flue through a hole in the top of the kitchen tent and attached it to the propane stove. We placed two fold-up cots per tent for sleeping.

It was late afternoon, and we hadn't eaten all day and had done a considerable amount of work. We were both starving, since the larger plane with my dad in it had all the food supplies. This plane wouldn't be arriving for several more hours. While fixing up the kitchen tent, Jean spied an old half-opened, partially rusted can of Spam on a back table that he had probably left there weeks before. He grabbed the old can and started removing and eating the contents. While he was busy munching away, I looked closely at the processed meat he held in his hand. There appeared to be a kind of movement to it, something barely detectable but out of the ordinary from my vantage point. I walked closer to Jean. Yes, there was a subtle, squirming component. I came even closer, focusing on the meat, and saw many tiny, thread-like white worms burrowing into the canned meat and writhing on the surface.

"Do you want some of this? I'll split it with you."

"Jean! Those are maggots crawling over that Spam!" They weren't the largest maggots I'd ever seen; in fact, they were likely newly hatched, but nonetheless, maggots! Just small ones.

Jean looked quizzically at the writhing, half-decayed piece of Spam and said, "So there are. Well, I've eaten worse." He began brushing the maggots off the processed meat and then resumed eating it.

"Are you sure you don't want some?" he asked as he nonchalantly chewed and swallowed.

"No, no, I'm sure. I'll be just fine." I'm not very squeamish, but I had to look away while he downed the remaining decaying and infested meat.

Jean definitely had spent a long time in the bush. If that wasn't the worst thing he had ever eaten, I'd have liked to see what was, but I wasn't going to ask. I kept waiting for Jean to get sick, but he never did. He was healthy as a horse the whole trip.

The campsite was in a perfect location. There was a constant slight breeze coming down the river canyon. It was also away from the dense forest in an exposed position, which reduced the problem of mosquitoes and biting flies. The small bay on the opposite side of the current created perfect protection for boats. There was a gentle slope from the sheer granite camp area to the bay shore, which made it easy to pack the gear to and from the boats. The camp area itself was high enough above the water's edge to be safe from flooding. Jean told me that this area had been used as a campsite for centuries by Indians and voyagers alike for just those reasons.

Later that evening we heard the distant steady drone of the larger pontoon plane coming our way. This far north the sun didn't set until after eleven o'clock, and even then, it was more like dusk. The sound of the two-engine propeller plane grew slowly louder until we finally saw the plane overhead. The landing was smooth, and the plane taxied up to the dock, where Jean and I secured it with ropes. My dad and the rest of the group left the plane and went up to the camp area. Fortunately, they had brought plenty of food as well as a cook and camp manager. They immediately went to work fixing a big dinner of steaks, green beans, salad, and potatoes with butter and sour cream. It was a true feast. While I was enjoying my steak, I thought, *This sure beats decayed spam with maggots!*

That evening everyone got their fishing gear ready, and we all made plans for the next day's fishing. I couldn't wait to get out on the boat and begin the great adventure. I slept like a rock that night.

The next morning I was awakened at dawn by the smell of bacon, eggs, and brewing coffee. I quickly got dressed, put my boots on, and walked over to the kitchen tent. It was around five times larger than the individual sleeping tents so there would be room to feed all the fishermen and to serve as a small lounge area. After we had a hearty breakfast, we went to the boats with our fishing equipment to start the day's fishing adventure. Jean was already in the boat with his feet up in a relaxed position, smoking a cigarette.

"Good morning, gentlemen. What do you say we go fishing?"

My dad and I replied, "Sounds good. We're ready; let's go!"

As Jean pulled out of the small bay and onto the main river, he went over the game plan for the day. Jean was always good at keeping his clients informed and telling them what he was thinking.

"We'll spend the morning fishing in a big bay for giant northern pike. The pike are in the shallows now, trying to warm up since the end of the spawn and the ice-out. They should be big and hungry. At some point we'll fish below the falls. I'm not sure what we'll catch there, but it should be interesting. Most likely walleye. That area would be a good spot to have a shore lunch."

After motoring in the boat for about fifteen minutes, we saw the entrance of a large, shallow bay half a mile wide with no real distinguishing features. Jean cut the motor down to a very slow troll before entering the bay. I could see the mud and sandy bottom. The water was five to seven feet deep and as clear as the rest of the river. I could see many large, dark objects I took for logs. Jean stopped the motor and slowly and carefully dropped anchor.

I asked Jean, "What's with all the logs on the bottom?"

Jean replied, "Those aren't logs, my friend; those are the things we're after—they're big pike. I mean big!"

I couldn't believe it. They were the biggest pike I had ever seen, and so many of them in clear sight! Usually if you see fish in the water, they look smaller than they really are, but these things were enormous just to look at.

Jean said in a muffled voice so as not to startle the fish, "OK, gentlemen, let's go fishing!"

My dad and I both cast out and slowly and steadily began to retrieve our lures. I saw one of the "logs" turn its head and begin to follow my slowly wobbling lure. When the lure was nearly at the boat, the enormous pike darted upward from the depths, opened its gaping mouth filled with teeth, and inhaled the lure. Its mouth was large enough to put two fists into, and I could see down its deep white throat. Its red gills flared to open its mouth to maximum size. The lure then disappeared. The fish quickly turned its long body away from the boat, slapping the water with its broad tail as it fled to the depths. The fishing line whined out from my reel. The fight was on! The pike took out yards of line on a long, powerful run. It reminded me of the old accounts of whalers in the 1800s, like the novel *Moby Dick*, being dragged by the rope in their rowboat after harpooning a whale.

As I was fighting the fish, I glanced over at my dad and saw that he was in the process of setting the hook on a strike to his lure. He forcefully jerked his rod into the air, bending it nearly in half with the heavy weight of the fish. We now had two fish on!

Jean yelled, "Hey, hey, a double! Both of you take your time, and I'll get the net."

These fish were not tiring out; they had real power. They were both making runs back and forth and under the boat. This caused my dad and me to switch places in the boat several times. Both of our heavy rods were seriously bent by the strength and weight of the fish. All the while Jean was coaching and giving us encouragement.

"Easy now, let him run, don't force him in. Keep playing him until he wears out, then slowly reel him in." These fish were so strong that unless they were played well, they could easily break our line.

Jean kept saying in a low, reassuring voice, "Be patient, be patient. Let him run, then slowly bring him in when he stops." He was giving us instructions as a coach would talk to an athlete during a competition.

After nearly twenty minutes my fish began to tire, and I was able to bring it closer. It looked like a torpedo next to the boat. With a rapid two-handed deep scoop of the net, Jean pulled it into the boat. While in midair, the fish suddenly flipped out of the net onto the bottom of the boat because the net was too small for such an enormously long fish. It hit the bottom of the aluminum boat with a noisy thud that reverberated through the boat. It must have weighed at least thirty pounds. As soon as the fish hit the bottom of the boat, it began thrashing about violently.

I tried to control the fish and remove the lure, but I was having difficulty. It's no simple task to remove a lure with sharp hooks from a large, powerful, struggling fish with razor-sharp teeth. Jean was busy trying to net my dad's fish. With another lightning-fast scoop of the net, the second pike was now in the boat, flipping out of the undersized net. Both fish were flopping and flipping around, banging against the aluminum sides of the boat and creating a racket. Both had their mouths wide open, showing their needle-like teeth. Their red gills were opening and closing in a living rhythm. Both my dad's and my fishing lines were becoming entangled, encircling both fish as well as both fishing rods. It was becoming a real mess. The two fish had the appearance of a giant anaconda writhing around in the bottom of the boat. Each fish measured forty to fifty inches long.

Northern pike have a slimy protective coating over their scaly skin. The slime was all over the bottom of the boat as well as us as we attempted to untangle the fish and remove the lures from their toothed mouths. We both knew that a cut from a pike's teeth in conjunction with its slimy coating spelled instant infection. There was total chaos in the boat with the two slimy giant pike writhing around at our feet and becoming more and more entangled. Both powerful fish were frantic to free themselves, squirming back and forth and rolling like trapped alligators.

All the while Jean was laughing and having a great time. You could tell he really loved this. Between the three of us, we eventually got control of the fish. We used a metal mouth spreader and then removed the hooks from the fishes' mouths with long-nosed pliers, carefully avoiding their sharp teeth. We then gently picked each giant fish up, took some photos, and released them back into the water. The pike slowly swam off in good condition. My dad and I both gave a big sigh of relief.

We sat down and looked at one another, and we all started laughing. My arms and wrists were sore from the fight with the pike! It felt as though we had been through a war already, and this was our first catch of the day! To catch two fish like that would have satisfied most experienced fishermen for the rest of the day, and we were just starting.

After a few minutes' rest, Jean said, "Well, gentlemen, shall we try for some more?" He lit another cigarette, inhaled a big drag, and then blew out two columns of smoke from his nostrils like a medieval dragon.

My dad and I looked at each other and said, "Sure, let's do it!"

We continued to catch and release numerous huge pike. It was quite an experience to fish by sight, seeing the fish move and attack the lure. I decided to switch to a top-water bait that mimicked a mouse swimming on the surface of the water. I slowly jerked the lure across the surface, making a small disturbance. The pike attacked the furry lure like crocodiles to a piece of meat. It was a thrill to see them come out of the water, open their fearsome mouths, and devour the fake mouse. They slapped their tails on the surface as they dove into the depths with the mouse in their mouths.

After I landed several pike, my mouse lure was destroyed and lay in shreds minus its tail. We noticed that a large amount of paint on our other metal lures had been torn away by the sharp teeth of the pike. I had the momentary thought that I would not wish to go swimming in these waters.

After several hours Jean said, "How about checking out the falls, gentlemen?"

"We're good with that. It'll give us some time to rest our arms."

Jean pulled up the anchor, pulled the starter cord on the motor, and sped out of the bay. We motored into the main channel of the river. After about fifteen minutes we came around a bend in the river and were greeted with the loud, continuous thundering noise of an enormous waterfall. There was a cascade of smaller falls before the largest one. The falls created a cloud of mist and spray around the entire area. Large whirlpools moved downstream from the falls along with white foam circling in the turbulent water. The Churchill River is just a bit smaller than the Missouri River and garners a tremendous amount of power as it descends the falls.

Jean motored the boat to the shore, where we beached it on the side of the falls. We got out and started fishing around the area. Jean even brought out his rod and reel and began fishing, which he rarely did. We all began to catch good-sized walleye. Jean told us to keep the walleye so we could have a fish dinner and a shore lunch. In a short while, we all had full stringers of walleye. These fish were here in abundance. There must have been literally hundreds of them schooling just beneath the churning swirling water. Walleyes are well known as one of the best eating fish in the world, and I certainly agree with that, especially when freshly caught.

Jean and I stopped fishing and began fixing a shore lunch. We made a fire and brought out the shore-lunch box, which was filled with cooking equipment. In short order we cleaned, battered, and fried the fish. Along with the fish, we had sliced fried potatoes with onions, beans, and coffee. The meal was delicious. After we ate, we all just sat on the sandy riverbank and viewed the magnificent scenery by the majestic falls. The air seemed alive with the active thunder of the water.

With his hands behind his head and lying on his back, my dad said, "This is really nice."

Jean replied, "There's nothing like a good shore lunch after a great morning of fishing. I think this may be what heaven is like."

While my dad and Jean were taking in the picturesque surroundings and slowly cleaning up, I started to go farther up the falls to explore new areas to fish. As I started to climb the rocky incline next to the falls, Jean quickly turned around and, with an urgent and firm demeanor, told me not to go up there. His face was stern, which I had never seen in him before. Jean was usually easygoing and not risk averse. He then turned his head and gazed solemnly at the lake. I came back to the sandy beach and sat down next to Jean and my dad.

"There's a deep crevasse halfway up there that's hard to see. There was an Indian long ago who was portaging around the falls with his canoe. His foot fell into the crevasse, and he broke his leg. He fell all the way down here. He had a terrible fracture and couldn't move. He was alone and helpless. He lay there all day and through the night in terrible pain. However, his problems were just beginning. Later that night, a big bear came along and got him. He had lost his bow and arrows in the fall, and his knife wasn't effective in fighting off the bear. It was a slow and painful death. The bear fed on him for several weeks until nothing was left. After a month or so members of his tribe searched for him and found some of his bones. They retrieved what was left of him and buried the remains in their sacred burial place. This has always been an area that bears frequent. Sometimes fish coming over the falls hit rocks and injure themselves, making an easy meal for any predator that comes along, usually bears. It's always risky traveling alone in the bush, and the Indian knew that. He took the risk and lost, paying the ultimate price. There's a good chance he wouldn't have made it anyway because of the severity of his fractured leg, even if the bear didn't show up."

My dad and I stared at him with amazement while he was talking. "This all happened right here?"

"Yep, many, many years ago. There have been a lot of mishaps portaging around these falls, but that was the worst. It's always risky carrying heavy loads around rocky areas, especially on a descent with a canoe over your head. Sometimes the rocks can be slippery too. That crevasse is bad, though; you can't see it well. That spot has been a real problem for people over the centuries."

"Is this area still frequented by bears?"

"Oh, yeah. You just have to be aware of your surroundings and don't do anything risky."

"You mean like having a shore lunch here today?" I said.

"No, we're fine. In life there's some risk to anything one does. It's just a matter of degree," Jean replied.

"Have you been up there on top of the falls?"

"Nope."

"Then how do you know about the crevasse and the Indian?"

"I just do."

My dad and I looked at him quizzically and didn't say anything more. I remembered the unusual gift of Dark Eye and that Jean may have had some of this gift as well. I wondered whether he had a premonition and was protecting me from some mishap. I let it go and began packing up our gear and putting it back in the boat.

That night I had trouble sleeping. I sat up in my cot and saw firelight from the outside. I put my clothes and boots on and went outside the tent. There was Jean, sitting motionless by a campfire he had made close to the lake. This was odd behavior for Jean, who usually went to bed before the sun set and slept soundly no matter what commotion was going on. I remembered last year he had slept soundly, curled up on the ground under an overturned boat in the middle of a terrible storm. I walked up to the fire.

"Hi, Jean."

"Well, hello, young man. Have a seat."

I sat down on a large log adjacent to the fire.

"What are you up to?" I asked. "You usually hit the hay early."

"I was interested by the events and by all the people who have been here before us."

"What do you mean? I thought we were the first people to fish this area."

"No, I mean long ago. It's quite interesting and kind of funny to see what went on."

"What do you mean 'see'?"

He didn't answer the question and just stared into the fire.

"This has been a favorite campsite for Native people and European trappers for hundreds of years. This river was like a highway from the rich fur-trapping interior of Manitoba and Saskatchewan to the trading post on Hudson Bay. They would usually camp here after portaging all their equipment and canoes around the falls. Portaging around the falls was no easy thing and usually took all day."

"It must have been tough in those old days."

After a long silence, Jean began laughing while staring into the fire.

"What's so funny?"

"There was an old trapper from Quebec named Barboneau who had accumulated many furs over a two-year period. This required several canoes to carry the furs to sell at the trading post at the town of Churchill on Hudson Bay. He hired a group of Indians to help him transport the furs. Midway through the journey, they camped here. The trip was far more strenuous than the Indians bargained for, plus they were short on food and had to go on minimal rations because of poor planning by Barboneau. They had what you might call a mutiny right here at this campsite."

Jean pointed to the shoreline right in front of us as if we were currently spectators to the dramatic event. He chuckled.

"The Indians told Barboneau that they were going back home unless he doubled their pay. This made Barboneau furious. He cussed and yelled at them. He even jumped up and down and threw things, but there was nothing he could do. He couldn't threaten them because he was outnumbered. Barboneau then tried to negotiate a lesser increase. The Indians were serious and wouldn't budge from their demands.

They were alone in the middle of nowhere. So he agreed to double their pay.

"They never liked him in the first place, though. He had a reputation for cheating people with bad business deals. He tended to push people around when he knew he could get away with it. He was not a respectful person; you might call him quite self-centered. The Indians had a derogatory nickname for him, 'Dog Face.' He was an ugly guy. He had a large nose that seemed to point out straight like a woodpecker's beak and a large jaw with a pronounced underbite. His lower teeth stuck out, making him look like a strange dog. However, I can't blame Barboneau too much because the Indians did agree to the deal, even though he was not a nice guy."

"How do you know about this?"

"I'm able to see things. It's so much clearer now."

"What do you mean 'see things'? You mean like Dark Eye?"

Jean stood up and began to put out the fire. "Let's hit the hay. We've got a big day tomorrow."

As he put the fire out, I asked, "What do you think is going to happen to this river in the future?"

Jean stopped putting out the fire and stared at the river. He stood like a silent statue in the partial light of the unextinguished flames. He had a pensive look in his eyes for a long moment. I stared out into the darkness, noticing the thick night mist rising from the nearby river. It appeared in sheets of cool water vapor slowly reaching upward, as if from a huge witch's cauldron.

"It's going to be smaller. The river will be much smaller somehow." Jean shook his head as if coming out of a momentary trance-like state and said, "Let's get to bed. We've got a lot of fishing to do tomorrow."

The next several days were filled with catching large numbers of northern pike and walleye. Every day was like a fisherman's dream come true. It reminded me of films of a tuna boat, catching large numbers of fish one after another.

Once after a long day of fishing, my dad asked Jean if there was some way we could bring back some of the walleye fillets without any access to ice to preserve them. "Sure, Smoked fish! The Indians used to smoke their fish to eat later while traveling. I do it all the time for my family. We could rig up a smoker here if you want, but we would have to take off a day of fishing to do it."

The next day we took a break from fishing to prepare a smoker for the fish. The smoker was made of large sheets of plywood with several wire racks on the inside. It was a five-foot-square wooden box with an opening at the base to put in firewood. We prepared numerous fish fillets, soaked them in saltwater, and then rubbed pepper and more salt along with other spices into the meat. We then placed the fillets on the wire racks within the smoker. We built a birchwood fire and maintained the coals at a slow burn. We smoked the fish for over twenty-four hours. The results were excellent—very tasty smoked dried walleye that could be transported easily and eaten whenever one was hungry.

There was an area along the water's edge where beverages were placed to keep them cold in the river. A semicircle of rocks extending above the water had been made next to the rocky shoreline to enclose the beer and soda pop. I had seen the adults take beer from the enclosed improvised beer cooler. It looked so refreshing, and the fishermen all seemed to enjoy it. Neither my dad nor Jean drank any alcohol. I was curious but underage at sixteen years old.

While Jean and my dad were occupied making and preparing the smoker, I strolled over to the enclosed natural beer cooler at the river's edge and looked down. It was packed with beer and soda pop. I had always wondered what beer tasted like. I had seen the fishermen drink lots of it. They seemed to treat themselves to a beer after a long day of fishing, and it looked so good. I had seen a lot of beer commercials on TV. What stuck in my mind was the jingle for Hamm's beer: "From the land of sky-blue waters comes the beer refreshing!" The beat of an Indian tom-tom followed the little jingle. I thought, *I don't see any Hamm's beer.* I began to chuckle. I then thought, *Should I risk it?* I looked around to make sure no one was looking and quickly grabbed a bottle of beer. It wasn't Hamm's, but it did look refreshing and enticing to my curious young mind.

With one instantaneous confluent move, I stuffed it under my shirt. My heart was pounding as if I were committing a felony robbery. I strolled nonchalantly away into the bush. I found a small clearing in the forest and sat down on a log. I was looking forward to drinking my first beer, anticipating how it would taste. I'd seen Western movies where the cowboys came into the saloon after a long trail drive and ordered beer for everyone. Then the entire saloon would erupt in cheers. This was something grown men drank and enjoyed. My heart rate went down now that I was secure in my forest hideout. I pulled the bottle out from under my shirt. To my shock, I found out that I needed a bottle opener. OH NO!

I set the bottle down on a log, walked out of the bush, and went to the kitchen tent, where I stealthily lifted the needed instrument. I strolled back into the woods, acting as innocent as possible with my heart still racing. I came to the clearing and sat down on the log, making myself comfortable. I took a deep breath. My heart rate and anxiety settled down again. I was sure no one had seen me. I picked the bottle up. It was Canadian Black Label beer. It wasn't Hamm's, but it would do. The black label was outlined with red, and the glass bottle was dark brown. I popped the cap open; some foam came out, which I disregarded. I first took a small taste.

Hmm, not too bad, very different, I thought. There was something special about this beer. It was exciting. I was taking forbidden fruit that no one knew about. I was a teenager, and like most teenage boys, I wanted to be a grownup as quickly as possible. This was going to be my first of many rites of passage. I began swigging the cold liquid. I thought, *Not sweet like pop, not too bitter, definitely carbonated, not too bad.* In around six big swigs I finished the bottle. I thought, *Wow, my first beer!* I stared at the empty bottle. *Not bad at all.* I put the bottle under the log. I didn't dare take the extra risk of carrying it back to camp. I had gotten away with it!

I walked slowly back to the kitchen tent and replaced the borrowed bottle opener, feeling smug that I had gotten away with a crime. As I walked out of the tent, I unexpectedly came face-to-face with Jean. I was startled and said, somewhat nervously, "Hi, Jean, what's up?" with a big smile.

"How was the beer?"

"What—what do you mean?" I was mortified that I had been discovered taking a beer while underage. Jean just smiled. I stuttered a bit and said, "How did you know?"

"There aren't many things you use a bottle opener for in the bush." He chuckled.

"Please don't tell my dad!"

"Don't worry, I didn't see a thing. Actually, I think it's kind of funny. The Black Label wasn't too bad, eh?"

"Well—Jean, I never see you drink any kind of alcohol. How come?"

"First of all, it's unprofessional to drink on the job. You would never see your father having a beer before surgery or at lunch before seeing patients in his office. Second, I never drink in the bush. When bad things happen away from civilization, they come on suddenly. It's on you before you know what's happening. One must always be ready because potential danger is around every corner out here. I need my wits about me every second. The time you stop being vigilant is the time you get burned, and it may be life threatening. I'm responsible for all your safety."

Jean continued, "I have an occasional beer when I'm in town and if it is offered to me. I don't mind the taste. It's OK. Most of the time it's kind of a social thing."

Jean went on, "Do you remember that old Indian man, Dark Eye, we met when we were stranded on that island last year?"

"How could I forget?"

"Well, he was right. When your mind is altered even a little bit, you lose connection with the Great Spirit, and that's something I never want to do. He is our protector. If you let your guard down, danger and evil are always just around the corner. Not just on a physical level but on a spiritual level as well. I have seen so many people destroy their lives with alcohol. It's a real problem up here. We have long, dark winters, and people who aren't active and don't have a purpose every day tend to use drugs and alcohol too much. Then, before you know it, they're addicted. Dark Eye told you how it was with his people on the reservation." Jean patted me on the back and said, "Let's get back to smoking those fish."

The remainder of the trip was filled with incredible fishing, enjoying the wilderness, being away from urban life, and being around good and enjoyable people.

When the day came to finally end our great adventure, I helped pack Jean's pontoon plane with our equipment. We hopped into the cockpit, started the engine, taxied into the main river, gave it the throttle, and were off. I looked back at the large bay where we had caught giant northern pike, and then I could see Churchill Falls with its billowing clouds of mist. We banked over the falls and then headed south. I thought, *I hope I'm able to come back here someday.*

We again viewed the endless forests and lakes ahead of us. After a while I saw a lake that seemed familiar. Jean looked at me and pointed downward.

"That's the lake where we went fishing by airplane."

On second look, the lake appeared even more impressive than when I had first seen it. It was much larger with many bays, beautiful islands, and several rivers flowing in and out of it. It was particularly beautiful and picturesque. In later years I found out that an outpost camp had been placed there on Jean's recommendation. Later a major and renowned fishing lodge was built there with topflight accommodations, a gourmet chef, and a regular fly-in plane service with a runway. I'm always amused when I see advertisements for this fishing lodge on outdoor television shows and in fishing magazines. I find it humorous that Jean Broux and I discovered this lake, and I was the first sport fisherman to fish it, albeit from a pontoon airplane.

As we were flying, I brought up the subject of Jean's identical twin brother, Dean, who had been killed in an auto accident years earlier.

"Have you had any contact with your brother?"

"I haven't directly, but my five-year-old son has a lot. My son will sometimes say in the morning, 'Thanks, Daddy, for coming into my room and holding me last night when I was crying and scared.' I smile and don't say anything except 'I love you, son.' However, I never once went into my son's room or heard him crying. Of course, Dean was my identical twin and looked just like me. I'm certain it's him caring for and comforting my son. Although Dean and I were identical twins, there were definite differences between us. My son reminds me a lot of Dean by the way he talks and his mannerisms. Although I haven't seen Dean in physical form lately, I do feel his presence frequently. Dark Eye did say that my son would see Dean, and I think that prediction has come true."

"Does your wife know about this?"

"No, I don't know how she would take knowing there are spirits around, even if they're good and protective spirits. I figure if the Great Spirit wished her to know, she would. So I leave well enough alone. She's a good wife and mother."

Since we were speaking of the hereafter and the supernatural, and we had had an unusual experience with the Indian shaman Dark Eye one year before, I felt compelled to ask more questions about the afterlife that I had no idea about. I had only recently been confronted with this world by exposure to Dark Eye and Jean.

"Jean, do you believe in guardian angels?"

"Absolutely. Dean is my guardian angel and probably my son's as well. Just as old Dark Eye said, these spirits are sent from God to guide and protect us from harm and evil. You just have to listen to them. You can't hear the spirit if your mind is clouded by alcohol, drugs, or anger. The problem with city life and with most people today is that there's too much noise and activity. The spirits are usually subtle, and only rarely are they made obvious to you. That's why it's good to be alone occasionally, and the bush is a good place to do it, especially if you're seeking answers to questions in life. We are all given free will to make good or bad choices in life. It's always a good idea to seek wise council, and the wisest of all is the Great Spirit, who always has your best interest in mind."

"Do you think that being in the wilderness like you are brings you closer to God?"

"Many of the prophets in the Bible, including Moses and Jesus, went out alone in the wilderness to come closer to God and find direction. There are a great many lessons to be learned by being alone in the wilderness. We often think of being alone as a negative, a state to avoid at all costs. However, there are certain times when being alone is a blessing. This is because when we are so full of ourselves or preoccupied with our relationships with others, we naturally become 'God-empty.' We then find it difficult to maximize our potential and often lose our way in life. There is a certain kind of unique strength that comes from knowing that you only have God to rely on and no one else. If there are no distractions and you're alone, it's just you and the Great Spirit. He will show you direction if you ask for it. You just need to be patient and listen. I've had a while to think since we met Dark Eye. What he said I have known all along in my heart. He just reaffirmed what I always knew was true."

In the distance, we could now see the lodge that we had come from a week before. It was a beautiful two-story structure of large logs with a wide picture window looking out over the lake. Multiple smaller guest cabins surrounded the main lodge on a hill above the lake. A long flight of steps connected the main lodge to the docks below. Several boats and another pontoon plane were moored to the dock.

"There it is, my friend, our home base."

I told Jean, "A hot shower is really going to feel good after a week without. One of the good things about camping in the bush is that it makes you appreciate the small things that everyone takes for granted."

"That's for sure. I think about that a lot. You have to appreciate the simple pleasures of life. It's not money, power, or a great job that will bring happiness," replied Jean. "After being in the bush, it seems to cleanse my mind and recharge my batteries, so to speak."

"You live in the bush most of the time, though."

"That's why I like my life so much. Maybe I'm closer to the Great Spirit that way, therefore making me a more confident and content person."

"Do you ever go to church, Jean?"

"Nope. There aren't any churches around where I live. There are no people. My nearest neighbor is many miles away. The bush is my church. Remember what Dark Eye said. Plus, I don't like the singing and all the ritual; that to me has no meaning. Sure, it's great for most people, but not for me. It's all about the personal relationship with the Great Spirit and listening to him for direction. I do read the Bible and teach my kids the lessons to be learned in the book. Even if you're not religious, there is so much wisdom in the book that it should never be ignored and should always be studied. Outside of my poetry, it's the only book I read."

"Now that you mention it, have you ever gone back to visit Dark Eye?"

"Yes, once. I stayed with him for about a week. It was an interesting experience," Jean said with some hesitation.

"What did he say to you?"

"Oh, not much. He was happy to see me, though. We enjoyed each other's company."

"Did you see the She-Manitou spirit, like Dark Eye?"

Jean chuckled. I could tell he didn't want to discuss his experience with Dark Eye, so I let any further questions go.

We began our approach to the lake in front of the lodge. We landed on the water and taxied up to the dock. The owner of the lodge was on the dock and tied the plane securely. I opened the cockpit door and climbed out.

"How was it, young man?"

"We had a great time. It was fantastic!"

Then Jean climbed out of the plane and told the manager that he was pleased with the way things had gone. The manager replied, "That's what we like to hear." Later that evening, after cleaning up and having a good meal, my dad and the rest of the fishermen were loung-ing around in the great room of the lodge, looking out the large picture window overlooking the lake and reminiscing about our experiences on the Churchill. It was our last night in Canada. I was hoping I might see Jean once more before we left, but I wasn't expecting it, especially since he had a family to reunite with.

Just then, in walked Jean with his wife. He looked dramatically different than I had ever seen him. He was all washed, clean-shaven, and as flashy as he thought he could be. They were going to a party in the tiny town of Cranberry Portage. Jean and his wife didn't go out much, maybe once a year, since they lived in such a remote area. It took them thirty minutes on a dirt road to get to the lodge and another thirty minutes to get to town.

"Just thought I'd stop by and say goodbye to you gentlemen."

My dad and I stood up and said, "We're so glad you came. We were hoping to see you before we left."

Jean was without his usual fishing hat. His hair was slicked back with some type of oil, like Elvis. There was a clear demarcation line on his forehead between the pale white skin where his hat usually was and the deeply tanned and windburned remainder of his face. He wore a powder-blue, tight-fitting pullover nylon shirt with a wide collar. The top buttons were open, exposing his upper chest. He wore tight-fitting powder-blue slacks that matched his shirt and pointy black boots. There was a strong scent of English Leather cologne. He really thought he looked hot! Well, maybe for Cranberry Portage, northern Canada, in the '60s.

"Thought I'd treat Susan to a night on the town since it's been a while. Her mom has the kids."

Susan, his wife, was pretty, around five foot two and slender with short brown hair halfway to the shoulders. She was reserved but not shy. I had met her the year before on our previous trip. After shaking hands, she commented about how much I had grown since our last meeting. She seemed to be a very nice person.

After a bit of small talk, Jean turned away from the others, looked at me intently, and said, "You have learned much; you have a good heart. You will do well, my good friend; you will do well. Look into the forest and the lakes like you looked at the colors across the bay on Dark Eye's Island. Keep your mind open. Search, and you will see a map for your life."

His demeanor toward me was different than ever before over the years I had known him. He spoke in a serious but kind way, as though he knew we would never meet again. It seemed as if he knew something I didn't. As he looked at me, I had an odd but vaguely familiar sensation. It dawned on me that this was the same sensation I had felt when Dark Eye had looked at me and said goodbye a year before.

Later, I recalled the meeting with Dark Eye when he had told Jean that he had the gift to some degree but was trying to ignore it, and that the gift could be developed. Jean seemed a lot more serious than usual when he was talking with me. Possibly he was wiser and seeing something I couldn't.

After he spoke, he quickly looked away. His demeanor rapidly changed, and he broke out into his characteristic big smile and laugh. He said goodbye and waved at everyone. The couple turned and walked out the door. Jean and his wife were off to the big hullabaloo in Cranberry Portage.

I never saw Jean again, nor did I ever return to the Churchill River. I was entering a new stage of life, my later teenage years, which were filled with activities other than Canadian fishing trips. I later learned that much of the water from the Churchill River was diverted hundreds of miles south to the Nelson River for a huge hydroelectric project. This project reduced the Churchill River to 15 percent of its natural flow. Jean's premonition in front of the campfire, of the river becoming much smaller, came true.

As time went on, my thoughts slowly floated away from the mysteries of the spirit world and Dark Eye. These thoughts of the spirit world returned as I grew older with the realization that there is something beyond this reality that only a few gifted people are allowed to peer into. I have frequently thought of Jean over the years and have wondered what he did with his improved abilities to see into the beyond.

Although fishing is a great sport and adventure for me, it seems to serve as a catalyst for a far greater meaning to life. I think that is in part what Jean meant by "Look into the forest and lakes, and you will see a map for your life."

Jean was like no other person I have ever known. I was fortunate to have met him in my formative years. He gave me a love and respect for the wilderness, with the insight and deeper meaning of life that only its solitude and mystery can bring.

ON OUR OWN

In every walk with nature, one receives far more than one seeks.

JOHN MUIR

Preparation

I was attending the monthly meeting at Mr. Myers's house in preparation for our upcoming Canadian canoe trip as Explorer Scouts. Mr. Myers was an older man who was an adviser to the group. His two sons would be leading the expedition. I had been to the Boundary Waters Canoe Area Wilderness in Minnesota and the adjacent Quetico Provincial Park in Ontario three times before. This trip would be far more extensive and rigorous. Our objective was to canoe and portage between lakes with all our survival gear, traveling approximately one hundred miles in a large circle. We were to stay approximately two weeks in the northern wilderness. The meetings were to discuss what was expected of us, camping techniques, what to bring, and when and where to fish as well as to review our planned route. At one meeting an emergency-room physician was invited to discuss advanced wilderness first aid and safety measures.

Like most sixteen-year-old boys, we were anxious to prove our strength and endurance against Mother Nature. We were at the pinnacle of the scouting organization and were eager to test the outdoor skills we had accumulated over five years. All of us had just received our driving licenses and wanted to be treated as mature men. We knew that for most of us, this would be our last organized wilderness experience since we were all going off to other teenage activities and then on to college. You might say we had something to prove. Little did we know that all our outdoor skills, strength, and endurance would be tested to the limit, and all would be profoundly changed for the better. However, with profound change is usually profound pain.

Mr. Myers warned us that the first four days would be tough, but after that it should be smooth. He spread out a large map of the region we were to travel to. There were so many lakes that half of the map appeared to be water. Mr. Myers pointed out the proposed route with a marker. The old man's eyes came alive, as if he had been instantly transformed into a young man again. I could tell there were innumerable memories behind those eyes. He described each lake and each portage like people he knew with different personalities. He marked out proposed campsites and good fishing areas. He began to tell stories of each place on the map. Everyone was transfixed by the old man's stories, hoping we could make some stories for ourselves that we could tell others for the rest of our lives.

Mr. Myers was a large, bald, elderly man who carried a continuous kindly smile on his face. He seemed like a wise old grandfather to everyone. He had a huge repertoire of wilderness tales that were always enthralling. Many of the stories had a moral. Some were of the history of the region, and others included Native American mythology. Everyone looked forward to one of Mr. Myers's stories, usually told at night around a campfire. He was a great source of humor and wisdom that were assets to the Boy Scout troop and Explorers. He was greatly loved and respected by all. Before he retired, he had been a high school principal and coach. Everyone wished they had gone to his school.

As we looked at the topographical map of the area that we were to travel to, Mr. Myers pointed to one spot on the map indicating an exceptionally long portage where we would have to carry equipment and canoes overland between two lakes. He remarked that it would be rough as he smiled at us. When I examined the map, I noted that this portage was nearly four times longer than the second-longest portage on the map. However, the main feature on the map that alarmed me was that the contour lines at the beginning of the portage were extremely close together. This indicated a precipitously steep incline—almost a sheer cliff! Then the portage was exceedingly long and winding, like a snake going through dense forest. After I looked at the map, I commented, "Will we need mountain-climbing gear?" Everyone laughed. Mr. Myers said, "You'll be fine." I knew how to read topographical maps, and I was shocked that this could even be a portage. I had been on many portages before, but I had never seen anything like this. I just let it go because Mr. Myers knew what he was doing, and I wasn't leading this expedition. We came to find out that my initial concerns were well founded.

The leaders in charge of the expedition were Mr. Myers's sons, Matt and Mark. They had been guides in the area for over eight years. They had been hired by various outfitters to take people on wilderness expeditions based out of Ely, Minnesota, in the past. Both young men had been trained and were experts in wilderness survival. They had been in our Boy Scout and Explorer troop many years before us, and we thought of them as heroes. Their stories of wilderness adventures were legendary. We all felt lucky to go into the wilderness with these two. They were like gods from Greek mythology to us.

They were now high school teachers who left their summers open for their true love: guiding in the northern wilderness. Their parents had introduced them to the canoe country as young children. Mr. Myers, their father, had grown up in this area of Minnesota and had been a guide himself in his younger days. There was a one-year difference in age between Matt and Mark, but it was difficult to tell them apart. Both were tall, around six foot four inches, all raw bone and sinewy muscle. They were both in excellent physical condition. In high school they had both been star athletes in multiple sports. The two brothers had won an event held in this wilderness area in which the contestants had had to canoe and portage for nearly two hundred miles. They had completed the race in approximately thirty-five hours. The contestants were in pairs and came from all over the world to compete.

Both brothers had brown hair and short, well-kept beards. They had similar personalities, mild mannered, calm, and, as some people would say, "laid back." They were congenial and easy to get along with. They were in their mid- to late twenties. When it came to wilderness survival, these guys knew what they were doing.

One of their more memorable times as guides was when they worked for an organization called Outward Bound. This group deals with troubled inner-city youth who have difficulty dealing with authority. Mark and Matt took a group of boys into the wilderness for three weeks, pushing their bodies nearly to the breaking point. The youths would learn to listen and take instructions from the two brothers, or they would starve, be terribly uncomfortable, or be left behind in the vast wilderness. The brothers laughed and said, "That bunch of kids were completely changed after the experience." They said, "It was tough going at first, but after a while they were all taking orders well and pulling together as a team. I think we gave them a better outlook on life—less rebellious, less selfish, and more responsible."

As advanced Explorer Scouts and experienced campers, we were given a lot of leeway regarding the expedition. The Myers brothers were mainly there as advisers and teachers, if need be, but we were expected to make our own decisions.

For months prior to the trip, we had improved our physical condition with exercise, lifting weights and preparing for the strenuous time ahead. Twice a week we would take a five-mile hike with a sixty-pound pack through wooded trails in nearby parks. Mr. Myers had a canoe at his house, the same type we would be using on our trip. During our monthly meetings at the Myers house, we took turns carrying the one-hundred-pound aluminum canoe on our shoulders around the block. At sixteen years old, this was the first time I had been strong enough to lift and carry the canoe on my shoulders. I was proud of this accomplishment. It must have been quite a sight for the neighbors to see young men carrying a canoe along the sidewalk with no water nearby. The most difficult part in carrying the canoe is lifting it onto your shoulders and then afterward placing it gently into the water after completing a portage. To do this, you must use explosive momentum and skill, as opposed to brute strength. There is a definite technique that takes time to master.

The ten of us, including the two brothers, drove up to Ely, Minnesota. Ely is a quaint, clean little town with only one main street. It seemed to have dropped from the sky amid a vast forested area surrounded by thousands of lakes. The town revolves around sport fishing and canoe trips into the extensive nearby wilderness.

There we stayed overnight at the Voyagers Hotel. It was an old four-story brick building built in the early 1900s. It was no-frills, but it did have an excellent restaurant adjacent to the lobby. Supposedly it was the best place in town out of a limited selection. We had an excellent steak dinner there.

Mark Myers said, "Enjoy the steak, boys, because you're not going to have anything like this for some time."

As I looked around the restaurant, I could tell most of the customers were young men newly returned from canoe adventures into the wilderness. All had tans from sun and wind. Many had new beards and windblown hair. It seemed that all were in good spirits, talking about their recent trips into the bush. Looking at these guys gave us a thrill for getting started.

We woke up the next morning and walked out of the hotel by five a.m. The sun hadn't risen. The pine-scented northern air was cool and crisp. It was good jacket weather. We all walked down Main Street to the outfitters. The streetlights were still on, and there was a thick fog. The town was totally silent except for our banter about the upcoming trek. As we walked together down the deserted street, it felt like we were some kind of youth gang, confident and looking for action. The main outfitting store was, as expected, closed at this early hour. We went around back, where there was a gravel parking lot with canoes lined up side by side. The parking lot opened into a wide, brightly neon-lit basement area with a cement floor. It was like a large six-car garage with the sliding doors raised. All our packs and provisions were laid out in a line. Two young outfitters had set everything up for us. We thought this was a real convenience.

All the packs were the typical north-country dark green thick canvas Duluth packs with wide leather straps. There were packs designated for cooking gear and other packs for food. Each food pack was labeled for a specific day. Every person had a personal pack for their own gear and fishing equipment. We became acquainted with the equipment and made sure everything we needed was there. We threw the packs into a truck and then were taken by van to Moose Lake, where we would put in.

As we drove on a gravel road through thick pine and birch forests, the sun slowly rose, creating small beams of light that twinkled through the foliage. As we crested the hill, we could see the lake with the canoes by the dock. This gave me a thrill of anticipation. I looked at my buddy Wayne, sitting next to me. I smiled and shook my head, silently exuberant. He replied to my nonverbal communication with "Yeah, all right!" and a thumbs-up. We were thinking the same thing—we couldn't wait to get started.

The Trek

We loaded the packs into the canoes and set off. Paddling into the crystal-clear lake. I could feel my heart rate increase with excitement. We quickly got into the rhythm of paddling in unison, skimming along the surface of the water, silently piercing the heavy mist. There is a magic in venturing into the unknown, especially when one is young. We were now on the adventure for which we had been preparing for nearly a year. It felt good to finally be on the lake, gliding through the smooth, silent waters of the north country. The cool early-morning mist rising off the lake gave the impression that we were entering another and quite different world, adding to our sense of adventure. The lake was beautiful, surrounded by large white pine and groves of white-trunked birch trees. On viewing the birch trees, I recalled that the Indians in this area had made their canoes out of birch bark and sealed the sides with hot pine and birch resin. I thought how lucky we were to have durable and relatively light aluminum for our canoes and no fear of damage.

I noticed that the Myers brothers were maintaining a rapid pace with very little effort. They were in the lead canoe. We suddenly realized what would be expected of us. Thanks to our training and preparation, we were keeping up well. Around an hour later we came to our first portage. Mark Myers put on a fifty-to sixty-pound pack, then flipped the one-hundred-pound canoe onto his shoulders as if he were putting on a light jacket. He bounded off into the woods as if taking a jog in the park. Matt Myers put one pack on the front of his body and another on his back. In his hands he carried loose equipment. He jumped between the rocks and then onto the trail close behind his brother in a near jog. The rest of us slowly caught up to the brothers at the end of the portage on the next lake. They were sitting in their canoe, packed up and ready, waiting for us. It took the brothers one trip while the rest of us took two trips to transport the gear from one lake to the other. The brothers were polite and just smiled at us as we toiled away.

The next lake was Basswood. Fortunately, the mist and fog of the morning had burned off with the rising sun. It was a large body of water, and since the water was smooth with minimal wind, we crossed the middle of the lake. We would save time this way, as it was more of a straight line to the next portage. I could barely see land on the horizon. Being in the middle of such a large body of water gave me a slightly uneasy feeling. I felt vulnerable, as if I were in an unseaworthy craft in the middle of the ocean, far from shore. I quickly put my concern out of my mind and continued paddling hard to keep up with the brothers.

The next portage we came to was short, but it required us to check in at a ranger cabin. It was the national border between the United States and Canada. It was a well-kept, beautiful cabin by a picturesque waterfall. The cabin was made from large logs and had a dark-green roof and awnings. The grounds around it were well kept and manicured. The bright red-and-white maple-leaf flag of Canada flying outside the cabin set off the colors even more. Since it was close to noon, we took out some cheese, crackers, and summer sausage for a quick lunch beside the cascading waterfall. We all enjoyed this small respite in such a beautiful setting. We could imagine this scene on a postcard, and we were in it.

As we all looked at the waterfall while eating our small but tasty lunch, we were filled with optimism for the continuation of the adventure. Passing the Canadian border was like crossing the Rubicon or casting the die for Caesar. All things would be significantly different from here on, and there would be no turning back. The water in these lakes was clear and drinkable, making our lives much easier, as we didn't have to transport or purify our drinking water. After finishing our lunch, we grabbed our cups that we stored in the canoes and dipped some clear water from the falls. We sat there waiting our turn while the brothers were in the ranger cabin filling out paperwork for crossing an international border. Each of us was called into the ranger cabin individually to sign papers. We then went on our way again. We made camp for the evening after passing through several small lakes and shorter portages. We knew the "rough" portage was waiting for us the next day. We were tired from our first strenuous day, and I slept like a rock.

The next day, after breakfast, we were off again. As the day progressed, we continued to paddle and portage from lake to lake. As I paddled, my arms were beginning to burn with pain and my hands felt numb, with prickling sensations, due to keeping up with the Myers's' blistering pace. Some of the guys in the other canoes looked at me and made faces like they were suffering in misery. My buddy Wayne looked back at me from the front of the canoe and rolled his eyes. Everyone was feeling the same strain in their arms, but nobody was saying anything. Everyone was doing everything they could to keep up the pace set by the two supermen at the front of the string of canoes. The Myers brothers propelled their canoe through each lake like some type of robotic water machine with no effort at all.

We knew the next portage would be a long one. This was the rough one with the steep incline that we had noted on the map at Mr. Myers's house.

It is usually much faster, easier, and less physically demanding to spend as much time as possible in the canoe traveling by water than to portage over land. Portaging can be quite demanding and strenuous, depending on the length of the portage and the topography of the land. However, I was now looking forward to the portage so I could rest my arms and stretch my legs. It seemed that all our physical training and preparation for the trip had been trivial compared to the real thing. This was hard, all-day work. All of us were hot and sweaty before we even hit the upcoming portage.

The Portage from Hell

When we approached the end of the lake where the portage was, our hearts sank. At first sight from a distance, the supposed portage looked like the white cliffs of Dover adjacent to the English Channel. We could hardly believe our eyes. Wayne said, "Is there really a portage there?" I was silent as we drew closer and obtained a better view.

We saw a steep, narrow, rock-and-boulder-strewn trail that seemed to be chiseled out of a sheer cliff of white granite. It wound up through a narrow canyon with high walls on both sides. The trail extended at least seventy-five nearly vertical yards. It was reminiscent of the Grand Canyon, which would be traversed by donkeys. However, we would be the pack animals this time. To make matters worse, we didn't know what was beyond the cliff. I just remembered the long, snake-like trail on the map at Mr. Myers's house.

We hit the beach in front of the portage with an aggressive attack attitude because we knew what was in store for us. When I jumped out of the canoe and helped drag it to shore, I could barely see the trail as it wound upward into the canyon area of the cliff. What lay before us was a nearly sheer wall of granite. The brothers hopped out of their canoe like rabbits and scampered up the trail, carrying their canoe and packs as if they weighed nothing. They hopped from one boulder to the next with total ease. In no time they had summited the cliff and were out of our view. I was amazed at their tremendous strength and agility. I picked up the canoe, set it on my shoulders, and began the ascent. Wayne was behind me with a large sixty-pound pack. The canoe was cumbersome and heavy on my shoulders as I climbed. It was like going up a long staircase, only stepping up on boulders instead of solid, stable, flat stairs. My breathing became heavy as I felt the strain on my entire body. This was not like a regular portage of walking over a flat, forested trail. The footing was precarious at best and potentially dangerous at worst.

Halfway to the top, my legs began burning with pain as I slowly made the ascent up the boulder-strewn staircase. I noticed that it was easier on my burning quadriceps and hamstring muscles if I walked in a rhythm, as opposed to taking stutter steps. I had to keep going and stay in rhythm to make it to the top. Even if I wanted to stop, there was no place to rest the canoe, and it would be nearly impossible to remount the canoe on my shoulders in the middle of the steep trail. It would also put a halt to everyone behind me who was in the same position. I just had to suck it up and keep going. There was no other option. I not only had to watch where my feet were placed so they wouldn't slip between the rocks, but I had to ascend a large step up to another level, all the while moving through the narrow rock walls on either side. Periodically the aluminum canoe would bang against the granite walls of the trail, making a reverberating low boom. I kept reminding myself that I had to push on.

Nearly out of breath and my body burning in pain from lactic acid overload, I finally reached the top of the cliff and rested my screaming legs for a minute by placing the canoe at an upright angle against a tree. The moment I placed my heavy load against the tree, taking the weight off my shoulders, I let out a reflexive soft groan like those one usually hears in a weight-training room. I was sweating profusely. I wiped the sweat off my face and took a deep breath. I took a few steps to loosen my burning legs and stretch my aching back. I walked around and looked down the trail up which I had just come. I couldn't believe what I had just done. It was much steeper and more treacherous than I had thought. I saw the rest of the crew struggling up the trail, each in their own silent struggle. The ascent up the face of the cliff was the hardest portage I had ever done. However, I realized that the cliff was just the beginning of the portage. I was exhausted already after the long day of portaging, paddling, and now, to top it off, climbing this cliff carrying a one-hundred-pound canoe. I was pretty much at the end of my energy for the day. I put my hands on my hips and looked down the trail. I had no idea what lay ahead. All I knew was that it was long.

The trail ahead looked like a green tunnel through a dark forest. It was overgrown with dense vegetation, a clear sign that this portage was not often used. I now understood why. I put all negative thoughts out of my mind and rallied my spirit for the second stage of the portage. I heard the low, reverberating sound of an aluminum canoe banging against the cliff walls in the distance as one of the other crew members climbed up the narrow, steep trail. At least I was done with the cliff-climbing part of the portage.

I picked up the canoe and resumed the portage. The low-hanging branches of trees scraped the sides of the canoe as if they purposefully wanted to impede my progress, like nature telling me, *Go home, get out of here, you're not wanted!*

Carrying the canoe on my shoulders, I had a limited visibility of just a few yards ahead and on either side. I tipped the canoe up a bit more to get a better glimpse of what lay ahead. I looked down the trail and saw that it lead into a swamp, a large area of watery black goo. It gave off a putrid, foul smell like rotten eggs from decaying organic matter. As I approached the muck-filled area, I noted one water-soaked slippery log with no bark laid over the muck. The swamp was surrounded on both sides by a dense, tangled forest that was impenetrable, especially carrying an unwieldy canoe with limited visibility. Going around the swamp was out of the question. Traversing the swamp by walking on the slippery log while balancing a heavy load on my shoulders was the only option. I didn't know how deep the swamp was. I took my first few steps on the log while still balancing the canoe on my now aching shoulders. It was like walking a tightrope covered with grease. Inevitably, my foot slipped off the log, and one leg went knee-deep into the muck while the other maintained a tenuous foothold on the slippery log. I kept the canoe on my shoulders in a feat of balance and upper- and lower-body strength that I hadn't known I had.

The last thing I wanted was for my entire body to fall into the thick, smelly goo and for the canoe to drop on top of me. I quickly realized if I dropped the canoe, there would be hell to pay when I tried to mount it back on my shoulders while half my body was submerged and stuck in the swamp. With all my strength shifted to the partially bent leg still perched on the slippery log, I lifted my fallen leg out of the thick, gluey muck and continued my balancing act on the log tightrope. I had a fleeting sense of pride at having accomplished a physical feat that I hadn't realized I had the capacity to do. I had made it this far through this obstacle course relatively unscathed except for one dirty, foul-smelling leg. However, I had expended a tremendous amount of energy that I knew would be sorely needed before the portage ended.

The portage continued past the swamp, winding through dense forest and up and down numerous hills. I occasionally had to straddle a tree that had blown down across the trail or walk over the tops of slippery, moss-covered boulders.

My breathing was becoming heavy because of the tremendous physical strain. I could feel my body weakening and my mind becoming numb. Salty sweat was pouring down my face and dripping into my eyes, causing them to burn. I couldn't wipe the burning sweat away because I had to hold on to the canoe. I began to wonder when this trail would end. It seemed to go on forever, moving around one obstacle after another. With each boulder or log I had to traverse, I felt what was left of my strength slowly ebbing away. I was running on empty. The low-hanging pine branches scraping the sides of the canoe created more drag on my progress.

I suddenly came to a point where my body said, "That's it. I can't go any further!" However, my mind refused to be dictated to by my body. I told my body, "You have no choice; you will do as you are told!"

My body then switched into a type of autopilot. I was so fatigued and weak that my mind began to turn off because thought created too much effort. The only thought I could have was to keep putting one foot in front of the other. I resigned myself to keep going on an endless narrow trail, mile after mile. My entire body ached, but I didn't dare put the canoe down to rest for fear of not being able to pick it up again. I was trapped in a situation where I had to keep going despite the pain and near exhaustion.

Just when I felt that I couldn't go any farther, I saw a glimpse of shimmering water through the tree branches. It was the lake, the end of this portage! THANK GOD! It must have been three miles through terrible terrain, plus ascending the treacherous, energy-draining cliff at the beginning. I walked to the water's edge and placed the canoe in the water. My legs felt like spaghetti as I weakly wobbled to a place where I could finally rest. I sat down on a large, smooth granite boulder and took a deep breath.

There they were, the brothers, just smiling at me, sitting in their canoe by the shore all packed up and ready to go. As if they'd had a mere minor walk in the park!

"Tough one, eh?"

I didn't say a word. I just looked at them with my mouth open, pouring sweat, and shook my head. I stared blankly into space, not focusing on anything. I was numb. My cerebral function had not yet recovered, let alone my body. Now I was going to have to go back and do it all over again to pick up more packs. I dreaded the thought of going through that hell again. I didn't see how I could. At least I wouldn't have to carry a canoe again.

In the back of my mind, I wondered whether the brothers had planned this, like a cruel initiation ritual. For now, I wasn't going to think about ulterior motives. It was what it was, and I had a job to do that was not yet done. While I sat there catching my breath, trying to regain some strength and mental acuity, I heard heavy breathing and rustling in the bush. I turned my head and saw one of our guys coming out of the woods covered in muddy black goo. He had obviously taken a bad spill into the muck of the swamp. I couldn't imagine what he'd had to go through to get himself out of that hellish, putrid soup. He was brownish black from head to toe. His face was barely recognizable under the black sticky goo plastered on him. I was too tired to laugh. I couldn't imagine how he could avoid vomiting from the foul stench enveloping his entire body. Maybe he already had, and there was nothing left to come up. He didn't say a word as he walked past me. He appeared to be in a trance from exhaustion. He was among the living dead, just like me. I knew exactly how he felt. He took his large pack off, laid it on the ground, and proceeded to walk unsteadily directly into the lake. It was bizarre to see his whole body slowly go beneath the surface of the water and then see his hat floating away. Fortunately, his head popped up and he started walking back toward the shore. I slowly got to my feet and cleaned off the dirty backpack, rinsing it with lake water.

I finally regained some strength and walked back to the beginning of the portage to pick up the remaining gear along with my now cleaner but soaked companion. We were so tired that we couldn't talk much except to utter a few unintelligible grunts and groans, acknowledging our mental and physical state at a lower-brain-stem level. We were reduced to a state of lowly pack animals near exhaustion.

As we walked back over the trail, we passed the remainder of our crew. scattered along the way. They had the appearance of zombies, a long line of the living dead, traveling through a cave of dark green hell. All the once strong, healthy young men now had hollow, blank stares and were barely able to speak. Occasionally one of the guys would say, "How far?" The crew slowly trickled into the end of the portage by the lake.

After the return trip and the completion of the portage, everyone removed their packs or their canoes and immediately fell in a heap in near total exhaustion. Many of were covered in the thick, stinking swamp goo, but no one cared. I raised my head and gazed over the scene. It looked like there had been a massacre with dead bodies lying all over the lakeshore and the brothers sitting in their canoe, observing the carnage. Some of the crew began drifting off into a half-dazed exhausted sleep.

Still in this half-conscious state, we heard one of the brothers say, "OK, let's mount up." No one could believe what they had just heard. It couldn't be! There was no movement from the zombie rank and file. There were a few groans, but no one got to their feet. The higher cerebral function of everyone's brain had turned to mush. I slowly opened my eyes and blankly stared into the blue sky with scattered, puffy clouds while lying on my back. My mind became lost in the vast infinity. I barely comprehended what I had just heard one of the brothers say. My mind slowly came crawling back to reality, and I forced my cerebral cortex to reawaken. I wondered whether we could just camp here and call it a day. The portage had taken nearly five hours, but it seemed like twenty-four. The next call from one of the brothers came much more loudly: "OK, girls, let's go!" With that insult to our masculinity, our minds cleared. We all rolled over, first getting to all fours and then slowly rising erect on two feet. Just to stand seemed like an ordeal. I slowly and painfully arose to gain a second wind. We packed the canoes and headed off.

That terrible portage was a true testing ground for the character of all the crew members. We had been pushed to the brink of exhaustion and still rallied to continue. At the time it wasn't acknowledged by the brothers, but in retrospect it was a great accomplishment. I think the ordeal served as a bonding experience among the entire crew. There is nothing like shared pain and struggle to bring a group together. We found a new respect for one another because of this. No one had given up or refused to pull their own weight. There was not even a complaint. Everyone had fought their own demons on that portage through hell and won. In our previous camping wilderness experiences, we had seen individuals with less experience break psychologically and start crying, demand to go home, or become belligerent and start arguing. The wilderness exposes a person's true mettle. In essence, it exposes the bare truth of who you are.

As we all sat in our canoes, the brothers looked at us and said, "You did well today, boys. Let's start looking for a campsite." That was music to everyone's ears. The brothers had pushed us hard, and we had kept up, albeit with great difficulty.

Jewel Lake

As we moved onto the lake, we were all suddenly awestruck with the place we were in. This lake was different than the others. It was so impressive that everyone stopped paddling without being told to do so. Even the brothers stopped. We stared in silence at the magnificence in front of us. We immediately realized that we were in a special place. This lake was beyond picturesque. Statuesque white pines and spruce nearly one hundred feet tall surrounded the boulder-strewn lakeshore. The temperature seemed much cooler, possibly because of the envelopment and shading of the enormous trees. Several small emerald-green islands seemed to float on the blue water in the distance. They were uniquely bordered by large, bright white granite rocks along their shorelines. The islands looked as though they had been trimmed with gigantic shears. The water was smooth as glass and glittered like multicolored jewels from reflections of the setting sun. There was total silence. It seemed as if we had entered a natural cathedral. As if we were in church, everyone kept silent or spoke in whispers. The ancient white pine trees around us were like church spires pointing to heaven. This area had never been logged, and thus the trees were majestic, likely one hundred years old or more. We were in a three-dimensional natural work of art, a place of palpable majesty. It seemed that we had gone through hell only to enter heaven.

While we sat silently in our canoes, taking in the beauty, we heard the haunting cry of a loon in the distance. This truly characterized the northern woods. There was no human being around for a great many miles. Any trace of civilization was absent. This lake had been this way for thousands of years, since the end of the ice age, untouched by humans. We all felt as though we had entered someplace special, almost sacred yet somehow alive.

I remembered what Jean Broux, a fishing guide and trapper in northern Manitoba, had said to me just three months before: "Look into the forest and lakes while keeping your mind open, and you will see a map for your life." This seemed like one of those special places where there was the "positive energy" that Dark Eye, the old Cree Indian shaman, had talked about. I could tell that the entire crew was affected by this place. It was somehow soothing to the soul.

Eventually the silence was broken by the soft voice of Mark Myers:

"Isn't this lake wonderful? This is one of our favorite places. No one comes here because it's so hard to get to."

I thought, *I'll testify to that!* Who in their right mind would undertake a portage like the one we had just done? The name of the lake was Jewel Lake. I could see how it had gotten its name.

We slowly paddled along the boulder-covered lakeshore in almost reverent silence. The water was crystal clear. I could see at least twenty feet down. We found a beautiful place to camp, a rocky point jutting out into the lake like an overlook that reminded me of a giant's index finger pointing into the water as he lay on the ground covered with trees and vegetation.

We all had our assigned duties, which were rotated among us. Our initial objectives were fire, shelter, and food. Wood was gathered and a fire quickly started. All the tents were put up. The cooking detail got busy rehydrating the dehydrated food and preparing dinner. It all went like clockwork. Things moved smoothly despite our tremendous fatigue. The members of the crew were all experienced campers, so we all knew what to do and performed our assigned duties with robotic efficiency.

We were starving from the energy expenditure during the day. Our last meal had been some cheese, bread, and summer sausage, which seemed like eons ago. Beef stroganoff, corn, beans, and rice pudding, all rehydrated, sounded terrible but was delicious. Maybe it was our state of mind or pure hunger that made the dehydrated food so good. There were second and third helpings for all. I had a suspicion that the brothers had scheduled extra food for the first several days because of the anticipated energy that we would expend. After dinner, the cleanup crew took over. There wasn't much talk after dinner in our exhausted state.

As everyone went into their tents, I walked out onto the precipitous rocky point next to the lake at dusk and sat down on a large, smooth boulder. The sun had just slipped below the horizon but was still sending colorful rays of light into the sky. Just above the horizon, the sky was bright purple and orange. At the base of the billowing white clouds was a nearly fluorescent unworldly bright gold color. This array of colors contrasted with the dark blue sky. It was a sunset like no other. Although the beautiful sunset was stunning, there was something more about this place, or maybe it was a confluence of the right time and place in my life. While looking over the lake, I recalled a similar sensation over a year before on Dark Eye's Island. I was hoping to see something unusual as I had then. The brilliant colors of the sunset slowly faded and were replaced by the darkness of the night. It seemed as if the sun had temporarily run out of energy and was going away to sleep. I was watching a celestial changing of the guard. The piercing stars were just beginning to puncture the summer night. The full moon then arose, taking the sun's place as if it were its turn to guard the earth. The reflection of the moon off the lake and white granite boulders made the area shine like a flashlight beaming off polished chrome. The whole region lit up in a soft, unearthly but comforting glow. I watched as the moon crawled across the sky like a benign living organism. I then felt a subtle breeze coming from one end of the lake like a soothing hand gently stroking my tired body. I had the feeling that something was saying to me, "You did well today; now you may rest." The slight breeze then changed direction to the opposite side, as if the whole region were alive and softly breathing. This place seemed to be beckoning me to stay. However, it was not to be since we would be on our way in the morning. Again, I heard the distant call of a loon while looking out at the serenity of the lake before me. I realized I had glimpsed something special— something sublime that had touched my soul in an ancient way.

Ancient truths stand out more vividly than all others since they have stood the test of time and cannot be eroded by trivial things. I felt a true freedom of my spirit. Although my body was physically exhausted, my mind was completely clear. Something was in front of me that could not be seen. Something big, something unworldly that could only be sensed. Maybe what Dark Eye had said was right, that certain places emit positive energy and others negative. Many times, there are lessons to be learned from lonely places. Sometimes pleasure, fun, and entertainment have a way of distracting us from what we really need or what really matters in life. Maybe this was just a fleeting glimpse of the map of my life that Jean Broux had talked about that needed to be explored further. I realized that I had found a home in this ancient place, where there was no pretense, only truth in its raw and exposed form. I knew then that something deep within me was drawn to the wilderness and that I would have to return in the future.

I began to feel every muscle in my body. I was sore from head to toe. I was exhausted and after a while decided to turn in for the night, despite the compelling force of the lake. Large, dark gray clouds had begun to envelop the brilliant full moon, seemingly playing peekaboo with its reflection on the lake. The wind gently increased, making the branches of the large spires of trees move as if beckoning me to stay. Everyone else had turned in immediately after dinner. As I entered my tent, I stretched out on my sleeping bag, staring at the top of the tent in a totally relaxed state. A soft rain began to fall. It seemed as if we were being baptized from above for a difficult job well done and were being resurrected in some sacred place. As the rain gently pattered on the tent, I fell into a deep and well-deserved sleep.

The brothers let us sleep an hour later than usual the next morning. We were all up after dawn, fixing our rehydrated eggs and oatmeal. The food wasn't too bad. We were mainly concerned about filling up with calories to endure another day of tremendous energy expenditure.

After quickly cleaning up and packing our gear, we were off again. The brothers gave us a little compliment on how we had been able to break camp and pack up so quickly. To our amazement, everyone had recovered well from the grueling previous day. As we paddled out on the lake, we were again all taken back by the sublime beauty of this place.

False Passage and Insect Attack

After several hours of paddling, we came to a marshy area at the end of Jewel Lake. Because the lake was so infrequently traveled, we were having difficulty finding the portage trail to the next lake. It appeared to be overgrown from lack of use. There were two slow-moving streams coming into the lake, but the map showed only one. It was not clear which would lead to the correct portage trail. We consulted the brothers, and they weren't sure, but they suggested that we go with the larger of the two streams, which seemed logical. We all paddled for a half mile up the shallow, marshy slough to where it ended at a beaver dam with a suggestion of a trail beside it. We hauled the canoes over the beaver dam with considerable effort, removed our gear, and started following the trail, which was exceptionally rugged. The crew became bunched up in an overgrown area, as we were having great difficulty walking through this rudimentary "portage." We became enveloped by bushes and branches. It soon became obvious that the narrow path was not a portage but a game trail. It ended in a massive hundred-acre lowland swamp that went nowhere.

The brothers said, "Well, boys, what we have here is a dead end." There was a loud communal groan from the crew. It was a huge letdown to toil so hard for nothing. It felt like a defeat to turn around and go back to the area we had just come from. The Myers brothers said,

"We had a 50 percent chance, and we guessed the wrong one." In the deep wilderness, getting your bearings can be difficult. Even the brothers, who were highly experienced, could be fallible in this world.

We turned around, aware that our wasted expenditure of energy would be needed in the upcoming few hours. We headed back to the lake and started paddling up the other small, shallow stream. After a quarter mile, the stream began to get smaller. This was a contradiction of the map and our compasses. We gathered to discuss what to do. The brothers decided to explore the area ahead to avoid another false-passage situation. So we sat in our canoes and watched them rapidly fade into the distance along the small, marshy stream.

As we waited for the return of the brothers, we began to hear a continuous low humming sound, like being close to some enormous electrical machinery. It was becoming increasingly loud. We looked around and saw large gray clouds of insects coming towards us like a

storm covering the entire sky. The massive accumulation of insects turned the bright sunlight into dimly lit dusk. We watched, waiting for the onslaught we knew was to come, helplessly trapped in our canoes while waiting for the Myers brothers' return. We suddenly felt the soft collision of thousands of soft insect bodies all over us, like a blanket of writhing creatures had abruptly been thrown over us. We immedi-

ately felt the biting and itching. It would have been somewhat tolerable to be bitten in one place at a time. This was the usual case at home when attacked by mosquitoes. However, this was an entirely different world that we had never experienced. We were being bitten in multiple areas at once, leaving us nearly defenseless. We broke out our insect repellent, but it was minimally effective at best. Large gray undulating clouds of mosquitoes appeared to envelop each of the crew members so that we looked like large moving gray bubbles. Everyone was swatting with their hands and waving their arms to protect themselves from the hungry hordes of flying insects. Everyone was yelling as if that would somehow deter the hordes of determined attackers. They crawled into my ears and nostrils. I had to close my eyelids so they wouldn't crawl onto my eyes and impair my vision. If I talked, they entered my mouth, causing coughing and choking. We had heard of large mosquitoes in the North Woods; however, this was an insect attack on a gigantic and horrific scale. The mosquitoes were far more numerous, but the biting flies were more painful. The biting flies seemed to have a predilection for the neck, possibly because the skin is less thick there or possibly because of easier access to blood. Each painful bite left a raised mark along with swelling. The initial pain was equivalent to a bee sting, but the discomfort didn't last as long. I was even getting bitten through my T-shirt and pants. I tried putting my shirt over my head for protection, but the insects were still able to find ways to get me. I could feel them crawling over my body. I considered jumping in the water, but it was shallow and swampy with a thick, mucky bottom from which I might find it difficult to extract myself. The close shoreline was not solid ground, as it seemed. It was what is called "muskeg," a floating mat of vegetation that is unable to hold a person's weight. It looks like solid ground, but if you step on it, you fall through into the water and become mired in muck.

We just had to sit in the canoes and take it until the brothers returned. I took off my baseball hat and began swatting the air indiscriminately. This left my scalp open for attack, even though I had a thick head of hair. There was no relief!

Just as we were going to turn and retreat into the main lake, the brothers finally returned after what seemed like hours but was only twenty minutes. They gave us good and bad news. The good news was that we were going in the right direction. The bad news was that beavers had built a dam obstructing a previously navigable small river, making two smaller streams and then a small lake above them that had submerged the portage trail. The beaver dam had completely altered the topography of the map. No wonder we had gotten lost.

We paddled upstream to the beaver dam with clouds of insects in tow. The dam was a sizable structure, at least four feet high. Wayne and I got on each side of the canoe and struggled to pull it over the dam in several successive attempts. The canoe along with the packs weighed over two hundred pounds. This required us all to jump in the water up to our hips to pull the canoes over the dam. The beaver pond beyond the dam was filled with flooded trees and bushes, making it impossible to paddle through.

We continued to be harassed by the clouds of mosquitoes as we slowly walked the canoes through the shallow, muck-filled beaver pond. Each step required extra effort to slowly pull my leg out of the thick, calf-deep muck and then extend my leg for the next step down into the squishy muck. It was slow going for everyone. We finally came to water that was waist deep, crawled back into the canoes, and paddled through into the main lake. As we did, we felt a gentle breeze blowing our tormentors away and delivering us from insect hell. Everyone cheered our deliverance. What a relief! We were saved from our terrible affliction!

Going through several smaller lakes and portages, we again struggled to keep pace with the brothers. We figured they were trying to make up for the time lost in the false-portage debacle.

That evening at our new campsite, we all went swimming to clean up after the swamp adventure. It was then that we noticed something on our bodies. Along with numerous insect bites causing red welts on our skin, we noted small black things attached to our lower legs. They didn't rub off. I grabbed one, and it started moving. LEECHES! Insects were not the only blood-sucking creatures that we had attracted in the swampy beaver pond.

The brothers had a big laugh. They said, "You can use those things for good fish bait, or if you're really hungry, they're a good source of protein." Everyone let out a spontaneous communal groan and removed the parasites one at a time.

After several days, the going was becoming less strenuous, and we were becoming used to the pace. Everyone's muscles seemed to be adapting. It seemed that we were getting into a rhythm. We could tell the brothers were pleased, but they said nothing. That evening there was a heavy rain, but we were comfortable and dry in our tents. It was somehow soothing to hear the rain beating on the tent while I was dry, snug, and warm.

The Bear

The next morning the brothers had an announcement before we continued with our journey. They told us we were about to enter bear country, and we needed to take extra precautions. Absolutely no food in the tents. We'd have to clean up well after dinner and leave no food scraps in the area. We would also need to store the food packs high above the ground, hanging them from a large pole between two trees. The brothers reassured us that most black bears are like big dogs and are easily scared away by humans. They told us to stay far away from a mother and cubs and to avoid getting between a hungry bear and its food source. Given a chance, they will leave you alone. However, despite this reassurance regarding the usually benign disposition of black bears, we were all aware of occasional unprovoked attacks by predatory bears that had severely mauled or killed people.

That evening at camp, Wayne and I were assigned to hang the food packs. We cut down a small tree, removed its branches, and made a long, strong pole. We put the pole through the leather straps of the food packs and placed it between the branches of two trees, elevating the packs approximately eight feet off the ground. Then we turned in for the night.

I was suddenly awakened from a deep sleep by a commotion in the camp. I rubbed my eyes, clearing my blurred vision. When I unzipped the tent, I was shocked to see an exceptionally large black bear rummaging around the camp. The bear was lean and large-boned. It had longer legs than most bears. It was the largest black bear I had ever seen—not fat, just big, and with good muscular tone, almost athletic in a strange, animal-like way.

I yelled, "Get out of here, bear!" I could hear some of the others yelling. The bear paid absolutely no attention. It didn't care about us at all. I thought about throwing a rock at it but decided not to, fearing it might provoke an aggressive response. It was frustrating because we were helpless against this bear. All we could do was watch as it tore things up. Sleep was out of the question.

After about an hour of walking around the camp sniffing what seemed like every inch of ground, the bear went over to the elevated food packs. It stood up on its hind legs and was able to barely touch the base of the packs, but it couldn't get a good grasp. It swatted at the packs, but it wasn't getting what it wanted. It then attempted to climb the trees holding the packs, but they were still just out of reach. This bear was determined. It knew there was food to be had in the packs. After a prolonged time, it slowly scooted backwards down the tree, inch by inch. I was hoping that by then the bear would finally be frustrated and leave. Instead, it walked about twenty feet away from the packs, rose up a little on its back legs as if starting a race, and then bolted toward the packs like a galloping missile. I was shocked at the sudden sprinting speed of the bear. At just the right moment the bear leaped into the air and grabbed the end pack with its front legs as if they were the arms of a football player making a tackle. It held on to the pack, with its lower legs dangling off the ground. Because of the weight of the bear and its momentum from its jump, one end of the pole holding the packs up slid out of the tree branches. The packs then all slid one by one to the ground like a line of falling dominoes.

The bear then went to work aggressively tearing the packs apart and getting at the food. The vicious intensity of the attack on the food packs was frightening. With repeated rapid movements, the bear bit the canvas packs with its teeth while tearing them apart with its claws. It grunted and snorted as it wreaked destruction. We were defenseless, trapped in our tents, which were made of material many times weaker than the thick canvas Duluth packs that the bear was tearing up with ease. I thought about how much weaker our skin and flesh were than the thick canvas of the packs. We hoped the bear wouldn't turn its attention to us next!

One pack, then another and another. The claws of the bear made deep tears in the unusually thick canvas packs. We heard the loud sounds of tearing and ripping. Our hearts sank as we watched the bear feed on our food supplies. I said to my tent mate, Wayne, "This bear must be starving!" It wouldn't stop eating! It continued to eat for at least an hour. It was unnerving and frightening to have this ravenous bear just a few yards away. I momentarily thought we were going to owe the outfitters a lot of money for the destroyed packs when we got back. The bear seemed to be enjoying itself. It periodically raised its head and looked around while chewing away. It almost seemed to smile at times, as if proud of itself.

After going through all the food packs, the bear eventually went down to the gently sloping rock edge of the lake. It put its head down to the water and drank for a long time. Then it raised its head, seemingly taking a breather, before putting its head back down to the water and resumed drinking.

This bear is drinking a lot of water, I thought.

Then it came to me: it had eaten nearly ten days' worth of dehydrated food for ten people. Rehydrated food quadruples in size, if not more, after water is added. I thought, *It is going to be interesting to see what happens to this bear when all the dehydrated food in his belly starts to swell. No wonder he is so thirsty and is spending so much time drinking.*

After nearly twenty minutes of drinking water intermittently from the lake, the bear raised its head and let out a deep, prolonged moan. It sat down on its backside. I could see its abdomen begin to slowly increase in size. The bear put its front paws on its steadily growing belly and started to moan again. The abdomen grew to tremendous proportions. It looked as if the bear were pregnant. Its belly was now larger than a basketball. When we first saw the bear, it had been lean. Now it appeared bizarrely deformed with a massive abdomen. The bear started moving its head from side to side, emitting a continuous loud groan, panting, and drooling copiously. This bear was obviously miserable.

I thought, *It serves you right, bear. Now you're going to have a real stomachache for a good long time, and possibly a bowel obstruction. It's not going to be pretty. I hope this teaches you to leave human campers alone.*

After an extended time, the bear finally got to all four legs with obvious difficulty and began waddling away with its head down, still groaning as he slowly vanished into the dark woods. I could hear him moaning in the distance for quite some time as he meandered further into the bush. The bear seemed to be crying. I was once told by an old Indian fishing guide that he had once seen a bear cry. I was skeptical at the time, but now I realized it was true that bears could cry.

We all stayed in our tents until dawn. We were not about to take any chances with the bear, even in his debilitated state. The next morning we assessed the damage. Several of the packs were torn into shreds. Seeing the heavy canvas of a Duluth pack ripped open impressed upon us the power of a bear and what it could potentially do to a human.

We took inventory of the food stores. To our horror, we found that the bear had eaten all of our future dinners and half of the breakfasts for the rest of the trip. The thought of impending starvation crept into our minds. Frustration and anger welled up among some of our crew. They began to blame Wayne and me for improperly hanging up the food packs, allowing the bear to get the food. We began hearing comments like "Way to go, you two. Now we're going to starve. You two ruined the whole trip for everyone!" Fortunately, the Myers brothers came to our defense.

"Hey, guys, settle down!"

"We looked at the placement of the packs, and we thought they were placed well. That bear was extraordinary. We've never seen a bear that could jump like it did. That was some athletic and determined bear. It would have won a gold medal for the high jump in the animal Olympics. It's no one's fault what happened to the packs. One thing all of you must learn: when you're in the wilderness, there can be no anger or arguing. You must never allow this to happen! We're all in this together. Everyone is trying to do their best. Even if there was a mistake made, get over it! Bad things sometimes happen. We must make the best of it, be positive, and move on. We are alone on a small ship in a sea of inhospitable, potentially dangerous wilderness. Any hostility or lack of cohesion among us brings danger to the entire group. This attitude cannot be tolerated! Let this be a lesson to all of you!"

It was the first time we had heard the brothers forcefully raise their voices so firmly and commandingly. They were no longer the mellow, laid-back guides we were familiar with. I was grateful to them for defending us. They poured cold water on a fire and immediately suppressed a bad situation that, if not addressed, could have led to anger boiling out of control and continuing indefinitely. The entire crew understood and had an immediate change of heart. Some guys slapped me on the shoulder and said, "Don't worry about it; sorry I yelled at you." Wayne and I felt bad but vindicated.

"OK, boys, let's go over our options." We sat down next to the lake with the brothers standing in front of us. "We clearly don't have enough food to go farther. We have just enough food to make it back using only the remaining breakfasts for all our meals. So, returning now is option one. The second option is to press on and forage off the land and take our chances. This would include a lot of fishing and gathering the rest of our food from nature. We could show you all how to do it. If some of you decide to go back and others to go forward, we wouldn't hold it against you. Mark will take the people back who wish to return, and I will take the remaining group on if that is what you want to do."

There was complete silence for a while. I said, "We can press on for a while, and if things don't look good, we could always turn around and skip a few days of food." There was silence again. Finally, Wayne said, "I say we forge ahead. I'm not looking forward to going back over those same horrible portages we went through a second time." The entire crew looked around at each other. There were a few questions about how we could forage and what it would entail.

We then took a vote. Matt Myers said, "OK, how many want to return?" I looked around, and no one raised his hand. There was a prolonged silence as the others also looked around.

"Well, then! It's settled—we press on." Matt gave us some encouragement and a little pep talk. "We will all do well. No one is going to starve to death. Mark and I have done things like this before. Once we went out for over a week and didn't take any food and did fine. It just takes a little time and extra effort."

Matt added, "We first need to get out of bear country and then set up a base camp so we can forage. We will have to alter our return trip a little because it will take time to gather food. Mark and I know of a beautiful place for a base camp just two lakes up."

We all packed up with some anticipation and a little anxiety for the future. I thought that this may have been how Columbus felt sailing for the new world in 1492. Would he find a western passage to India, fall off the end of the world, or discover something new and different?

Foraging

We went through two lakes and two minor portages before seeing a good area to camp adjacent to a small river that emptied into the lake. We pulled to shore and immediately set up tents and a cooking tarp and gathered enough firewood. Then the crew went fishing while the brothers went off to forage for starch and vegetables. Wayne and I had been sport fishing since we were little kids; in fact, we used to make our own lures. I have taken numerous fishing trips with my dad in the past. The most recent had been just three months prior, fishing in the

Churchill River in northern Canada. Fishing now felt much different. It had ceased to be sport and was now survival! We set out in our canoes with a single-minded determination to catch as many fish as we could.

It was a beautiful bright, sunny day, still early in the morning. We paddled the canoe several yards offshore of a rocky island that seemed to have a deep drop-off. I said, "This is a perfect spot for walleye." We used black jigs, bouncing them erratically off the bottom. I imagined the fish could mistake these jigs for leeches, something we knew all about and that the brothers said were "good fish bait." Sure enough, I felt a tug and steady downward pull on my fishing pole. I played the fish very safely and conservatively so that it wouldn't throw the hook. I thought we could ill afford to lose a fish because of trying to land it too quickly. I slowly brought the fish close to the boat, raising the fishing rod with one hand and grabbing the fish gently but very firmly with my other hand. It was a nice-sized walleye, the best eating fish you could catch. As I was putting the fish on the stringer, Wayne landed another walleye. We were pleased with our success. We were off to a good start.

The fishing continued until early afternoon when the action slowed down. By that time, we had a whole stringer of walleye. We started to paddle back to base camp. We paddled around the opposite end of the island by a point that jutted out into the lake.

Just for one last shot at some more fish, I threw my lure out behind the canoe and placed the fishing pole between my legs, trolling my lure behind the canoe as I paddled. Not long afterward, my fishing pole violently bent in half. I held the pole tightly between my legs, put the paddle down, and grabbed the pole. The fish shook and swam beneath the boat. It had power and strength, and I could feel real weight at the end of the line. The fish stripped out yards of line. I slowly began reeling it in, followed by several other runs. I was determined not to lose this fish. I knew by the feel and aggressive action that this was not a walleye. Eventually I landed a large northern pike. It was around thirteen pounds—a genuinely nice catch! I grasped it around its gill plates, compressing them together to temporarily paralyze the fish, and raised it into the air.

"Outstanding," Wayne said.

I put it on the stringer of walleyes, and we began to paddle back to camp. This stringer of fish should feed everyone for quite some time. I was extremely proud of myself and Wayne for finding the location of so many fish and then catching them without the help of an adult guide like Jean Broux. We had proved ourselves to be good fishermen and good providers for our crew.

As we paddled close to camp, the rest of the crew, who had stopped fishing several hours earlier because of no luck, anxiously came to the shoreline and yelled, "Did you catch anything?" Wayne and I could see deep concern etched on their faces. They were fearing imminent starvation. We hesitated and feigned gloom. I could see the others' hearts sink momentarily. With a sudden movement of both hands, Wayne raised the huge stringer of fish. There was an instantaneous cheer. Everyone's mood rose immediately when they saw the stringer of fish, knowing we would not starve that evening. We made a semicircle enclosure of rocks at the edge of the shore to serve as a live well for the fish so we could take them when we wanted.

After some coffee and a snack of the remaining summer sausage, we all went out fishing again. Wayne and I went back to the same place but had no luck. We moved and tried several other areas and caught some walleye, but not the numbers we had caught in the morning. We decided to call it a day and paddled back to camp again.

The Great Fish Robbery

When we were about two hundred yards from camp, we saw a large bald eagle fly off from the edge of our campsite. Its wingspan was enormous. It was an impressive sight rising off the ground with its powerful flapping wings. When the eagle gained a little altitude, we saw to our horror that the large pike I had caught was in the grasp of its claws, helplessly bent between the eagle's piercing talons. The eagle slowly flew up and into the distance, taking with it enough food to feed three

to four people. There was nothing we could do except yell at the big bird. We thought, *Well, it's only one fish, and we still have the walleye.*

As we drew closer to the camp, we saw multiple small, dark heads bobbing up and down in the water close to the shore. At first we thought they were some of the crew taking a swim. However, they were much too quick and moved too fast to be human. "What in the heck are those things?" Wayne asked. We started paddling as fast as we could and began yelling again but didn't see anyone in the camp. As we got within thirty yards of the little bobbing heads, it became obvious that they were an entire family of otters. We thought it was cool to see these animals, as it's not every day that you see this kind of wildlife. We beached the canoe and headed for the live well where the fish were kept.

Wayne let out a loud yell: "OH NO!" I went up to the rock-walled fish enclosure and saw that all the fish were gone, thanks to the otter family. There were traces of a fish massacre: pieces of tail, fins, bone, and a few heads with no bodies. The otters had made short work out of our hard-earned catch. Those otters ate more than our whole group could have eaten in several sittings.

We put the recently caught fish in the enclosure, although it was nothing like the amount we'd had before. The rest of the crew came trickling in, and we all had some fish, so at least we didn't have to go without food that evening. We had a delicious walleye dinner with some arrow plant that the brothers had gathered. We all had our fill and were satisfied. After dinner the Myers brothers informed us that it would be best to move our camp elsewhere since the otters and eagles were not going to go away, and we were an easy target for further predation.

The next morning, we all ate some leftover walleye with coffee and were off to our next camp. We traveled farther north through two lakes and had two easy portages. We set up our new base camp on a beautiful elevated rocky point. This lake was much larger than the previous lake, with many islands and numerous small, shallow bays. It looked perfect for fishing.

The Blueberries

When we entered the new lake, we noted that on one side of it and on several small islands there had been a forest fire that had burned down the trees. In their place was a thick covering of shrubs and bushes. It was prime blueberry season. Several of the islands were colored entirely blue from the exuberant growth of blueberries, and nearly all the waist-high shrubs were blueberry bushes. Wayne and I volunteered to harvest the berries while the others fished. We filled the canoe with large pots and paddled toward one of the several blue islands, where we landed and rapidly filled pot after pot as we worked our way over the crest of the island. I occasionally stuffed my mouth with a handful.

They were delicious, much sweeter and larger than the blueberries one could buy commercially at a supermarket. Each berry was nearly the size of the end of a thumb. I looked over at Wayne and saw him filling his mouth with the delicacy as well.

As I was busy picking the berries with my head down, I began to hear rustling in the bushes ahead of me. At first I thought it was Wayne, but I realized that he was far behind me and to the side. I stopped picking and looked ahead. I saw something large and dark moving around in the bushes twenty yards away. I instantaneously froze in position and silently stared at the slowly moving object. I noticed that there was a slight wind blowing away from me in the direction of the dark area in the bushes, so whatever it was would soon pick up my scent. Suddenly all movement ahead of me stopped. I realized that whatever it was, it knew I was there. I still didn't know what it was, but I had a terrible suspicion. I froze. I wasn't about to move. I tried to breathe as quietly as possible. My gaze was transfixed on the dark patch in the bushes ahead of me. My heart was pounding so hard that I thought whatever it was could certainly hear the sound. I broke out into a cold sweat. I had no weapon, but a big metal pot filled with blueberries. I had a fleeting regretful thought: *Why didn't I at least bring my knife with me?* I didn't dare move, awaiting the first move from whatever was in front of me. I didn't even swallow for fear that I might make a sound, although I needn't have worried—I doubted I could work up enough saliva to bother swallowing.

Suddenly, up and out of the bushes, a large black bear stood up on its hind legs, staring at me. It was approximately seven feet tall, most likely a big male. It had a small white spot on its chest that is occasionally seen in some black bears. I didn't move. I avoided direct eye contact and just looked at his chest to avoid anything he might consider aggressive behavior. I instantly recalled the way the previous bear had ripped the thick canvas Duluth packs apart within seconds. I realized that my skin was not nearly as thick as the canvas. I wasn't going to turn and run because it might trigger an attack, and I knew it could outrun me. I recalled the previous bear's explosive sprinting ability as it ran at the elevated food packs. There were no trees to climb, and the lake was too far to jump into. There was nothing but a few bushes between the bear

and me. If the bear came at me, I wasn't sure whether I should run or put my arms out and yell to make myself look bigger and more dangerous than I was. I was in a quandary and didn't know what to do. What to do when facing a bear only a few yards away was something we hadn't discussed at Mr. Myers's house when he was preparing us for the wilderness trek. For the moment I decided to do nothing and stay still.

The bear finally went back to all four legs and continued eating the bumper crop of blueberries. The berries were just too great a treat for him to resist for even a minute. Bears love blueberries as much as they love honey. Plus, there were no bees to contend with. The bear could tell I posed no threat. I was lucky he was not an inherently aggressive animal and that it wasn't a mother bear with cubs. I was also not between him and his food source since the delicious berries were all around.

I slowly backed away as quietly as possible, trying not to crack any shrub branches or step on any sticks that might snap. I was still terrified that the bear could turn at any time and charge me. Sweat was pouring off my forehead. It crossed my mind to wonder whether a bear could sense fear. I tried to calm myself as I took a deep breath and exhaled while I continued to back down the side of the island. I was halfway to the canoe when I began waving to Wayne to return to the boat. I got in the boat as Wayne started to make his way to shore. I didn't see any trace of the bear. I kept urgently motioning Wayne to hurry. When Wayne finally got to the boat, I told him about the bear. He was as glad as I was to get off that island. We paddled away as quickly as we could.

I felt lucky to have run into a benign, apparently nonaggressive bear instead of a dangerous one. If that bear had wanted to get me, there was no way I could have escaped or, for that matter, defended myself. Despite being scared half to death by my bear encounter, we had accomplished our goal of filling several large pots with blueberries, and we brought them back to camp to everyone's delight. We had handfuls of blueberries with every meal. One real treat was blueberries with rehydrated powdered milk and sugar. It was a true delicacy. The blueberries seemed to fulfill some natural need that was lacking in our diet, such as vitamin C and other nutrients necessary for quick energy and good health. Everyone seemed to have a big boost in energy after feasting on the treat for several days.

Camp Life

Fortunately, the lake was a productive fishery. Our new rock-lined fish enclosure was constantly filled with fish. The bears fortunately left the lunch packs alone. We had a light breakfast, a good lunch, and a feast of fried fish in the evening with a dessert of blueberries, sugar, and instant powdered milk. No one was going hungry, and we were all in good spirits.

The time at our base camp was filled with fun and adventure. Every morning we would all go fishing, usually with good success. After lunch we were free to do whatever we wished, since fishing was so good. We didn't need to worry about starvation. The weather was warm and beautiful. Everyone usually went for a swim once or twice per day and lounged in the sun on the smooth granite ledge sloping into the lake next to the camp. Big card games by the lakeshore were a premier daily event. Sticks of varying size and pebbles representing money or chips were in play. Everyone was relaxed. It was as if we were at a resort, only deep within the wilderness.

To pass the time with a little competition, we had what we called "guide fights." One person alone in an empty canoe attempted to ram another person in another canoe and tip him into the water. Since there was only one person in the back of the canoe, the front end was raised out of the water, making the boat unstable and easier to tip when rammed. Variations on the theme expanded until there were multiple one-manned canoes in a free-for-all against everyone else. It was a canoe demolition derby. Fortunately, the aluminum canoes wouldn't sink because air-enclosing rivets were built in along their sides. When a canoe was tipped over, entering it from beneath seemed like entering an underwater cavern. It was great fun.

Most of us had the time to improve our campcraft skills. We made several tables and chairs without nails by lashing wood together with rope. We made a rack between two trees that held all the cooking and kitchen utensils. A food preparation table was next to the utensil rack. We expanded our shelter area over the tables with a wooden roof and stabilizing poles to hold it up. After a while the campsite began to appear like a small village.

At night there was a campfire along with great stories and recollections of past portages, fishing, and previous events. We all had a sense of close comradery, a type of brotherhood. The stars were extraordinarily bright and seemed large enough to touch. The Milky Way was easily visible, painting a large swath of sparkling tiny lights across the night sky. The brothers were quite knowledgeable about astronomy and individual stars and planets. We all wondered how the ancient Greeks had come up with patterns of stars representing different animals, gods, and heroes. They must have had active imaginations. The sky was alive with the Northern Lights. Fingers and curtains of lime green and purple undulated silently through the heavens, making the sky seem like an enormous moving, living thing extending from one horizon to the other.

We were all having the time of our lives, and everyone was loving the situation. Having a base camp on a beautiful lake where the fishing was excellent was far better than traveling every day, working our tails off. We all came to realize that the bear attack on our food packs had been the best thing that could have happened. We'd had to change our plans and adapt, but it had all turned out for the best.

We hadn't seen another human being since we had crossed the Canadian border several weeks before. We had the feeling that this entire wilderness belonged to us.

The Return

It finally came time to pack up and make the return trip. It seemed almost strange to leave the little village we had built. We had become so accustomed to it that it had begun to feel like home. Once we got into the canoes with all the packs, reality quickly returned. We were going to return a different way than we had come. Before we got into the canoes, we studied the map of the area with the brothers and determined the route so that everyone knew what to expect. The only potential difficulty was a long, narrow lake named Agnes. This lake was so long that we would avoid multiple portages. It appeared that the return would be dramatically less demanding than our initial trek up, thank goodness!

The brothers again set out at a rapid pace, but we were now able to keep up with them with less effort. All of us noted a significant improvement in our strength and endurance. We went through several lakes and portages with single-minded efficiency. We began to feel like a well-oiled machine.

After paddling through several lakes, we came to Lake Agnes. It was deep, narrow, and twenty-one miles long in a north-south direction. The ancient glaciers long ago had made a huge claw mark through the hard granite landscape. Agnes was well known for wind whipping down the lake through the granite cliffs on each side. The lake was commonly referred to as the "wind tunnel." It could be very difficult if the wind was against you. When this happened, people would call Lake Agnes "the wicked witch of the north." However, we were lucky this time because the wind was strong and gusty but from the north, which was behind us. Despite the tailwind, it was going to be a long paddle.

Upon noticing the windy conditions, we came up with the idea of taking advantage of the wind to avoid the extra work of paddling. We lashed two boats together with pine saplings, like a catamaran. We then made a cross-pole mast between the two boats and used a canvas tarp as a sail, lashing it to the mast with rope. We were skeptical that it would work, but it was worth a try. The brothers got a real kick out of it. They thought it was a "hairbrained, crackpot" idea, but they were so amused that they went along with it. We got all the boats tied together in twos, and the brothers were going to just paddle their canoe.

We paddled to the middle of the lake, where the wind was strongest, and then set sail. The sails worked! The canvas tarps billowed out and suddenly began to propel us, sending us flying down the lake with no effort. The wind was so strong that we had to hold on to the masts with rope. The two guys in the fronts of the paired canoes held the mast in place while the two in the backs steered and paddled a little if needed. Everyone began to cheer. We felt like pirates on the open ocean flying down this long wind tunnel of a lake. It came to us that if we had been paddling the canoes in the opposite direction against the wind, it would have taken us days of ongoing toil to reach the end of the lake.

We looked back at the brothers, who were expending significant effort to keep up with the rest of us. It looked like they were in serious canoe-race mode. This created a lot of laughter and jeering at the two supermen. Every time they began to close the gap between us, there would be a strong gust of wind that would propel us farther away from them. The brothers would then respond with even harder paddling.

Although the brothers were real gentlemen and mild mannered, we unveiled their deep competitive spirit. They paddled as hard as they could for twenty-one miles while we smoothly sailed with minimal effort. We eventually came to the south end of the lake without having to work very hard. The brothers jumped out of their canoe sweating heavily, shirts open, and breathing as if they had just completed a marathon. Gone were the spring in their step and smiles on their faces. They didn't say a word. So much for the "crackpot" idea. We chuckled to ourselves when we hit the portage at the end of the lake. We were all smiling but didn't say anything, although we wanted to. We felt a degree of pride in our ingenuity and having beaten Agnes the witch. But most of all seeing the brothers work like dogs!

As we crossed the U.S.-Canadian border, we again checked in at the ranger cabin by the beautiful waterfall. We saw other people starting out on their own canoe adventures. They looked at us with deference and a little awe. Our clothes were worn and slightly tattered, as if we had been through some rough country, which we had. We must have been quite a sight, weathered, rawboned, and confident. Seeing other people seemed out of place, something we weren't used to.

We went through several lakes and small portages, finally ending at Moose Lake, where we began the journey. As we got out of the canoes and stepped onto the dock at Moose Lake, the Myers brothers turned to us and said, "Men, you did a fine job. We're proud of you." We noticed that this was the first time the Myers brothers had addressed us as men.

It seemed as if months had passed since our start. We all felt different from when we had begun, stronger and more mature. One might say we had done a lot of growing up within a few weeks. We had a great sense of accomplishment, as if we had done something many people couldn't have done. We had been tested and succeeded. All *on our own.*

SAVIOR COWBOYS

Although we say mountains belong to the country,
they actually belong to those who love them.

DOGEN

My dad, my dad's fishing buddy Bob, and I were on our way to the high mountain lakes and streams of northern Colorado to fish for trout. My dad and I had been on several trips with Bob before. He was a big man with a crew cut in his early fifties. He had played collegiate football when he was younger. He was always smiling and had an outgoing, gregarious personality. The three of us had been taking fishing trips on an almost yearly basis since I was ten years old.

It was the early summer of 1978. I had just completed my third year of medical school, and my life was changing rapidly. From here on I knew I would be extremely busy with my career, and this might be the last fishing trip we would take together for a long time, if ever.

We had heard from one of Bob's friends that there were three lakes off the beaten path in the western Colorado mountains near the Wyoming border that were filled with many kinds of trout. These lakes were remote and difficult to access. It could be done only with four-wheel-drive vehicles, and even then with some difficulty. Bob was driving his Jeep. When we arrived in Denver, we picked up one of Bob's friends, an experienced outdoorsman who had told Bob about the lakes. The friend was named W.O. He never mentioned his full name to me. He was a mild-mannered, polite, clean-cut, soft-spoken man around my dad's age, in his mid- to late sixties. He had a four-wheel-drive Jeep as well. The four of us took the two Jeeps to the high country to go fishing for trout.

The drive to the high country of Colorado was beautiful and scenic. We went over several mountain ranges with incredible views. After several hours on the state highways, we turned off onto a dirt road and traveled several hours through open range and government forest land. There were red and yellow mesas and large, gnarled rock formations that looked like a giant child had left multicolored Play-Doh on the ground after mashing it into odd shapes. The rolling hills between the rock formations were covered with gray-blue sage with bright yellow flowers. It was a stunning contrast with the blue-green mountains in the background, some with white snowcaps.

We came over the top of a hill, and in the valley below was a small cabin in disrepair, literally in the middle of nowhere. We drove past what appeared to be an abandoned post office and several collapsed wood cabins. An old, weather-worn sign on a wooden post in faded black letters read, "BURNS." We took this for the name of the abandoned town. Why or how these structures were there was a mystery, as there was no hint of any civilization for over seventy miles. We didn't even see any ranches or cattle.

As we continued into the mountains, we began gaining elevation. The scenery changed from mainly sage and brush to high alpine spruce and pine trees. The temperature became almost chilly. We eventually reached a trailhead at the end of the dirt road. A National Forest Service sign read, "To Emerald Lake, Sapphire Lake, and Lake of the Clouds." There was a small stream adjacent to the rock-strewn trail. We imagined that the stream likely originated from the lakes noted on the sign.

W.O. had told us that these lakes were some of the most beautiful he had ever seen. He also guaranteed that the fishing would be outstanding. Each lake was filled with different kinds of trout. Emerald Lake was filled with cutthroat and brook trout, while Sapphire was filled with rainbow and lake trout. Lake of the Clouds was mysterious; W.O. had never been there. Legend had it that it had a hybrid species of lake trout and salmon. Some people called these fish "splake." This lake was difficult to get to and accessible only on foot. The stories he had heard were secondhand, making the lake sound even more mysterious, almost as if one would expect to see the Loch Ness monster there or Bigfoot walking around. These high mountain lakes were stocked by the Colorado fish and game department by dropping fish fry or juvenile fish by airplanes into these inaccessible lakes.

With great anticipation, we drove the Jeeps off the dirt road and onto the narrow, rocky trail in low four-wheel-drive. We literally crawled over boulder after boulder. Driving over such a rough road was extremely slow but exciting. I was amazed at the capability of the Jeeps. The drivers, Bob and W.O., were doing a masterful job of twisting and turning the Jeeps over the boulders and rock-strewn trail. The trail was wide enough for only a single Jeep. I hoped we wouldn't meet someone coming down from above. I couldn't imagine backing down this trail, or for that matter backing up it. Either way, it would be a real mess.

We eventually came to a turn in the continuously upward-climbing trail and found ourselves facing a near rock cliff of boulders. I had no idea how we were going to get around this obstacle. We nevertheless began creeping over the large, round boulders one inch at a time. One tire, then the next. I was grateful that the Jeeps had roll bars. My dad and I got out, leaving only the drivers of the Jeeps strapped in while climbing over the boulders. It finally came to a point where it appeared that the Jeeps might tip over. Then, we used a winch with a metal cable attached to the front of the Jeeps. The metal cable was placed around a large tree adjacent to the trail above the large boulder pile. The mechanical winch was then employed to pull both Jeeps over the last few feet of the boulders. The Jeeps looked like insects slowly crawling over a rock. It appeared quite unnatural and even bizarre. I'm sure we couldn't have made it without the winches. When it was this difficult to get to a fishing spot, it was unlikely that the lakes had been fished frequently. This thought ignited my imagination about giant, multicolored trout of many different species, a one-in-a-million fishing experience. I couldn't wait to get to our destination and throw my line in the water.

After the large boulders, the trail flattened out to a large degree. We crossed several small streams and drove over some small logs. Driving through a dense pine forest, we were continually slapped by low-hanging pine branches all along the small trail. It seemed as if we were running a gauntlet of unfriendly trees.

As we drove up over a small hill just past a stream, we glimpsed glimmering water through the trees. The reflected sunlight from the partially hidden lake was like diamonds flickering through the open areas in the green trees. Emerald Lake was just ahead. We drove a bit farther out of the forest and into a clearing, giving us a full view of the magnificent sight. The lake was crystal clear, surrounded by large pine and spruce and encased by towering mountains. On one side huge granite walls, thousands of feet high, dove straight into the water. The reflection of the dark green trees surrounding the lake gave the water a deep green appearance, thus the name Emerald Lake. The sky was an almost unnaturally brilliant blue with scattered white puffs of clouds. The blue of the sky was noticeably vibrant, much different than at lower altitudes. The air was clean and crisp with a subtle scent of pine. We all stood there for a while, taking in the majesty of this place.

W.O. said, "I never get used to this. Even though I have come up to the mountains frequently for the past twenty years. When I get to the high country, it excites me just as much as if it were the first time. I'm lucky I live so close to the mountains."

It had taken us over three hours by Jeep over an extremely rough and rugged trail to get to the lake. It was late afternoon, and we were tired and hungry from the arduous journey. We began the process of setting up camp. We erected two tents and placed a large canvas tarp over a cooking area. Bob and W.O. had thought of everything. A propane stove, a small folding table, chairs, cooking equipment, Coleman lanterns, and plenty of food. Dinner was soon being prepared: big steaks, baked potatoes, apple pie, and coffee. The dinner was made exceptional by eating it next to a beautiful lake surrounded by high, picturesque mountains. Bob had even brought an electric generator for light and a plug-in CD player. The CD that he played was cool jazz. Although I liked the music, it seemed out of place and not quite right in this beautiful natural setting away from civilization. However, I didn't complain.

After the wonderful dinner and the arduous Jeep ride, we sat in lawn chairs admiring the incredible natural beauty. Something felt special about this place. It was awe inspiring. Throughout history, humans have sought out mountains and high places for inspiration. Moses climbed Mount Sinai and heard the voice of God, returning with the ten commandments. Jesus climbed to the top of Mount Hebron with two disciples, where he was raised into the air, hearing the voice of God along with meeting Moses and Elijah. Jesus taught his disciples on the Mount of Olives. Sitting Bull, the great Lakota chief, climbed a high mountain in the Black Hills to receive a vision from the Great Spirit. Why do people climb to the top of the world's highest mountains, risking their lives to get to the top? Maybe there is something special about being in the mountains that makes them feel closer to the Almighty. It seems that high places are special places for humankind. However, no one can live for very long on top of high mountains. The conditions are too harsh at the top. It seems that they are for inspiration and not for living.

The next day the fishing began at dawn. It had been a long time since I'd used my fly rod, and I was anxious to use it again, hoping my technique had not gotten too rusty. I got my waterproof waders on and headed for the lake with great anticipation.

After a few casts my casting methods came back to me. Fly casting is more than a technique; it is an art. There is a beauty in seeing your artificial fly flip through the air, driven by just the right amount of force and delicacy from your arm as you let out the right amount of line with each false cast and whip it out past your head, placing the fly in just the right spot. You then wait for a big trout to strike. It seems that nothing else in the world matters while you watch your line and wait for it to be taken under by a hungry trout lurking below the surface of the water. Even if no fish are caught, working on the art of casting is always a fun challenge.

I waded further into the cold water to just above my knees. It was still early in the morning, and I was enveloped by the clear, crisp mountain air. I was surrounded by precipitous granite mountains and forests. As I cast my fly out onto the smooth lake surface, I noted mist rising like a thin, unearthly cloud, sticking its fingers slowly skyward from the crystal-clear cold lake. Across the lake I spied a large bull elk with a huge set of antlers emerge from the shroud-like mist and then slowly amble away. I stopped retrieving my fly to fully take in this awesome scene. I thought, *Is this heaven?* In the stillness I could almost feel the presence of something unseen trying to silently communicate with me.

Suddenly I felt an abrupt, violent tug on my line, bending my rod nearly in half and instantly changing my focus to the reality of catching a trout. FISH ON! My focus was now 100 percent on the battle. The trout sped into the depths of the lake, pulling out line with an audible whine, then paused. I began reeling in the struggling fish. Not yet willing to surrender, the trout turned and headed for the surface, flying into the air and then returning to its watery realm with a loud splash. After a prolonged battle, I slowly brought the trout next to me as I grabbed the net stationed snugly in my belt. I raised my fly rod and at the same time, with my other hand, placed the net below the fish. I slowly brought the valiant fish out of the water. It was a large silver cutthroat trout, almost a shiny reflective chrome with bright red below its gills. It was a beautiful fish. After catching my breath and viewing my catch, I gently released it, none the worse for wear. I felt the surging pride of victory over a worthy opponent. I took a deep breath and again looked at the silent, misty lake.

Nearly every fourth cast resulted in a fish, the great majority of which were brook trout. Brook trout are beautifully colored. They have bright red bellies bordered by nearly luminescent white on the edges of their fins. Their bodies are golden brown with red dots. They are magnificent in appearance. They fight hard and can be acrobatic, leaving the water and twisting in the air. They were great fun to catch. We caught literally hundreds of fish and then let them go except for the ones scheduled for dinner. That evening we had a delicious brook trout dinner.

Bob and I fished again at Emerald Lake the next day, while my dad and W.O. went to Sapphire Lake, approximately one hundred yards above Emerald Lake. W.O. had brought an inflatable raft that he launched on the lake. They caught numerous large rainbow and lake trout, which were double or triple the size of the brook trout. Bob and I finished up the day fishing on Sapphire Lake and caught a few rainbow trout too, although not nearly the size or number my dad and W.O. had caught. However, we were fishing from the bank and not the boat. Most of the larger fish were to be found in deeper water. Sapphire Lake was aptly named. Its waters were deep blue, reflecting the sky and the surrounding gray mountains. I could see why these two lakes were named after beautiful gemstones.

On the following morning, Bob wanted to hike over the mountain in front of us to fish Lake of the Clouds just beyond it, the lake that was rumored to have large hybrid salmon and trout. Getting to it would require a one-thousand-foot climb to the top of the mountain, followed by a descent into a small alpine basin where the lake was supposed to be. I was up for it, but my dad and W.O. wanted to stay in camp. The hike over the mountain would be arduous, especially with the mountain's elevation over twelve thousand feet. The air could get a little thin in the face of physical exertion.

The day was warm and sunny, almost hot. Bob and I took off in the early morning and started climbing with our fishing gear. The climb took us first through a forest and then through small scrub trees; then, as we went higher, we progressed to climbing over large rocks. We were now at such a high elevation that we were above the tree line. We were within a hundred yards of the summit, and I still felt great. I'm not sure why, but I burst into a run and sprinted the rest of the way to the summit. I guess I was anxious to get to the top and see this mysterious lake from atop the mountain that we had taken so long to climb.

When I reached the summit, I took a deep breath and scanned the horizon. The view was amazing in all directions. Bob finally made it to the top and said, "How did you have the wind to do that?" I said, "I don't know; it just felt like the thing to do." In retrospect, at the time I was in my mid-twenties and still in excellent physical condition.

Bob and I stood on the summit, taking in the view. There were huge mountain ranges in all directions as far as I could see. The sight was breathtaking. I felt a sense of accomplishment at climbing to the top of the mountain, although I knew our journey to the lake had just begun.

"This is really a sight to see," Bob said.

"It certainly is."

It was still sunny with a slight breeze, a seemingly perfect day. The center of the lake below us was deep blue with a light turquoise border rimming the shoreline. Lake of the Clouds was a little larger than I had expected but far more beautiful.

I looked around at the horizon again before descending to the lake. Far in the distance I viewed a large area of dark, nearly black clouds. I pointed to this area and said, "Hey, Bob, look at that." He didn't say much in response. I knew that in the mountain high country, as in the far north, severe storms can be upon you in a short time. Weather can abruptly change in this type of geography, and you can get into real trouble before you know it.

"I don't like the looks of those clouds at all, Bob."

"That's no big deal. It's far away, and if it's coming our way, it won't be here until this evening."

"I don't know about this, Bob. I think we should play it safe and go back to camp and try again tomorrow." I remembered long ago, when I was a boy, that we had failed to heed the advice of our fishing guide in northern Canada and gotten into a real mess with the weather.

"No way! We've hiked up this huge mountain and come all this way to get to this lake. We can fish for an hour or two, and then we'll be out of there."

I felt a little uneasy, but I looked at the beautiful lake again and said,

"OK." Bob was an experienced outdoorsman. But I knew he had been prone to take significant risks in the past, something one should never do in the wilderness.

We started the descent toward the lake. We were less than halfway down when we were suddenly hit by a strong and violent wind. It was strong enough to blow my hat off, tousle my hair, and flip my T-shirt up. I scampered away to retrieve my hat. A gust of wind nearly knocked me down. Suddenly the sky turned almost black, and the temperature dramatically dropped and became terribly cold. The next minute it was snowing so hard I couldn't see two feet ahead of us.

"Let's go back!"

Bob didn't question me now. "OK!"

I couldn't believe how fast the bad weather had blown in and how severe it had gotten within minutes. Neither Bob nor I had ever seen anything quite like this.

When we turned to go back up the mountain, the wind was blowing so hard that we could barely stand. The snow was pelting us in the face so hard that we were barely able to keep our eyes open. Another gust of wind blew me down to my knees as I struggled up the steep and now snow-filled mountain trail. I struggled to my feet.

"It's too windy! I can't see the trail!" Bob said.

"It's going to be a lot worse on the summit. We'll probably be blown off," I said. "Let's go down by the lake and try to find some shelter."

The suddenness and severity of the storm were hard to believe. Reality had violently slapped us in the face, and we were taken completely off guard and unprepared. I remembered an old saying, "Nature does not suffer fools." Now I realized that Bob and I were two fools who had tempted nature and were now going to pay a severe price.

The wind was making so much noise that Bob and I were forced to yell at each other as loudly as we could to hear what the other was saying. We were freezing in our T-shirts. The snow was knee-deep by the time we reached the valley where the lake was. The wind and snow were blowing nearly horizontally, obscuring our vision. We could barely keep our eyes open. It was snowing so hard that we couldn't see the lake, even though we were probably just a few yards from it. Our first thought was to find shelter. There were small, stunted trees around but none large enough to give us any protection from the drastic elements. We continued to walk, although with increasing difficulty. My whole body was shivering from the sudden extreme cold and wind. I was beginning to feel genuinely worried about survival. My teeth were chattering, and my fingers were blue. I was having a real concern about becoming hypothermic or frostbitten. The thought crossed my mind that we might not be able to get out of this alive.

The storm seemed to be increasing in severity as time went on. I tried to think positive thoughts and remove any negativity from my mind. This was getting harder and harder to do, but I was determined to keep fighting for my life and keep walking. Hopefully, we would find shelter of some kind. It seemed that we were walking into nowhere, but I couldn't think of anything else to do. There were no identifiable structures to be seen, not even any large boulders that we could get behind. Even if some kind of shelter was nearby, we wouldn't be able to see it because of the terrible visibility. We resigned ourselves to our only option: to keep going.

A profound fatigue began to set in. It was difficult to walk in the deep snow, which required extra effort just to raise my legs. Now I knew why people wore snowshoes when walking in deep snow. I had the desire to just lie down, curl up in a ball, and go to sleep. I knew that to follow this desire would be a death sentence.

I could barely walk. I fell several times, getting a face full of snow. Every time I fell, it was a shock to my system, being covered with snow with minimal protective clothing. It felt as though I had jumped into a freezing lake. I pulled myself up again with great effort and difficulty. I looked back at Bob, and he was suffering just as badly as I was. I couldn't see more than two yards ahead because of the blinding wind and snow. I wrapped my arms around my torso to combat the freezing temperatures. My head was bent to prevent the wind and snow from directly hitting my face. My whole body was shaking from the bone-chilling cold. I concentrated on putting one foot in front of the other, and then the next. I became mindless, with my only objective being the next step. I was expending enormous amounts of energy with the raising of each leg. I knew this couldn't continue, but I put that thought away and carried on.

I looked back at Bob again and yelled, "We've got to keep going!" He just nodded. Things were looking bleak. Terrible thoughts went through my mind of the grief my parents would have after losing their young son in a freak snowstorm. As I trudged and toiled through the deep snow with my head down, I silently prayed, *Please, Lord, save us! I know you don't hear from me very often, but if you let us out of here with our lives, you'll hear from me every day. I know I'm a sinner, but I'll do my best to do better if you could just save our lives. Amen!*

Just when it looked like all hope was gone, I saw some tracks in the snow. I bent down to take a closer look and brushed the new-fallen snow away for better identification. They were horse tracks. The first thing that came to my mind was that where there were horses, there frequently were people.

I looked back at Bob and pointed. "Let's follow them." This gave us a tiny ray of hope. It also gave us a rush of adrenaline to keep moving—something tangible to make us feel optimistic despite our terrible condition.

We followed the tracks for what seemed an exceedingly long time. I was not going to give up on following this slight ray of hope. Our bodies were running on empty, and we were barely able to walk. Following these tracks was our only hope. We had to keep going! Suddenly right in front of us stood a large canvas tent with a smokestack and smoke coming out of the top. We were stunned. It seemed to appear out of nowhere. Thank God!

"Yo! The tent!" Bob said in his booming voice.

"Come on in!" came a voice. Bob and I looked at each other with the thought of our imminent salvation.

We opened the flaps of the tent. We felt an immediate rush of warm, dry air.

There in front of us were two young cowboys in the middle of playing cards. They were lying on a blanket with cards and poker chips ar-

ranged in stacks. There was a half-empty bottle of Jack Daniel's bourbon in front of them. I quickly looked around the tent and saw that they
had brought their horses inside. This kind of tent is commonly called a
line tent and is frequently used for hunting trips for groups of hunters.
A small propane stove was attached to a stovepipe that passed through
the roof of the tent.

"Howdy! Have a seat, fellas. Do ya feel like a little poker?" said one
of the cowboys.

"Maybe later, but if you have something warm to drink, we'd like
that if you don't mind," I said. Bob and I were both shivering uncon-
trollably with our arms wrapped around our bodies to retain any bit
of heat. We must have been a pitiful sight, but the cowboys didn't say
much about our appearance.

"Why, sure, I'll get you some hot coffee. We've had some brewing all
day." One of the cowboys got up, went over to the stove, and poured

two cups of ready-made hot coffee. He brought the coffee over to Bob and me as we seated ourselves on the poker blanket.

"Here you go; this may help. It might curl your hair a little, though; it's pretty strong."

It wasn't the best coffee in the world, but it was the most needed. It was strong and a bit bitter, but it was hot.

"Oh, man! Thanks, this is great. The coffee hits the spot."

"You can have some Jack Daniel's if you want. We've got plenty."

"No, thanks, coffee is good."

One of the cowboys got up and brought over two blankets for our shivering blue bodies. "By the way, my name is Jim, and this is Maynard."

I introduced myself and Bob. We all shook hands. I noticed that the skin on their hands was thick and callused from years of manual labor. Bob and I made ourselves comfortable on the blanket with the cards, poker chips, and bourbon in front of us. Both Jim and Maynard were lying on their sides, intent on having a good time no matter what the conditions.

They both worked full-time on a ranch on the other side of the mountain. They had the weekend off, so they'd decided to camp in the high country for a little rest and relaxation, possibly with a little fishing on the side. They certainly had no real plans except to have a good time and relax.

Jim said, "We come up here every once in a while to do some fishin. This lake has some big fish in it, and lots of 'em. We're not sure what kind of fish they are, some kind of strange-lookin trout, I would imagine. They're definitely different than any of the standard trout around in other places. Whatever they are, they fight like crazy, and they sure are good eatin. The good thing about this lake is that it's hard to get to, even by horseback. Not many people make it up here. That's why we were so surprised to hear you fellas outside. It looks like we won't be doin any fishin this trip though." I glanced over to the side of the tent, where there were two fly rods rigged up and ready.

We told them that we had intended to go fishing when we were caught in the storm.

"Yep, bad weather can blow up really quick here in the high country, sure enough. Seems like you fellas were pretty lucky to find us."

"I'd say lifesaving, and we appreciate you helping us out."

"Not a problem. I'm only glad you boys found us. Would you like some food?"

"We'd love some!"

"Well, OK, then, I'll just fix somethin up for all of us."

Jim got up and began cooking on the stove while Maynard took another shot of Jack Daniel's. Jim was in his early to mid-twenties, and Maynard seemed around ten years older. They were both nice-look-ing men, although Maynard appeared a little rough around the edges. Neither had an ounce of fat on them. They had a couple days' growth of facial hair. Maynard had a long mustache down to his chin on both sides. Both were wearing broad-brimmed, sweat-stained Western hats that had clearly seen a lot of use. They had outgoing personalities and were quick to smile. They seemed like really nice guys.

"So what line of work are you boys in?"

Bob told them he was a pharmacist in Kansas City.

Maynard said, "I've been to Denver but never K.C. I like K.C.'s baseball team, even though they lose all the time. I like their bright blue-and-white uniforms."

"Yeah, that's the Royals for you," I said.

I told them I had just completed my third year of medical school. With that revelation, Maynard and Jim looked at one another, smiled, and broke out into a song: "Mamas, don't let your babies grow up to be cowboys, let 'em be doctors and lawyers and such!" They then broke into hilarious laughter.

"No offense, when we heard you mention medical school, it brought to mind one of Willie's songs."

It was a verse from a Willie Nelson country and Western song. We found out they loved Willie Nelson and Waylon Jennings. They liked several other country singers, but those two were their favorites. They continued to belt out different songs by the two musicians while Jim was cooking and Maynard slugging away at the Jack Daniel's. The two seemed like something out of a Broadway musical, the way they just spontaneously belted out the songs in unison for whatever reason. They knew the lyrics to nearly every Willie and Waylon song ever written. Bob and I looked at them with amusement while they were totally enjoying themselves, singing away half drunk.

Jim brought over plates of bacon, beans, and bread along with more coffee. It was wonderful. Bob and I were both starving, and we wolfed the food down within minutes. The smell of cooked bacon and coffee permeated the tent. Bob and I were beginning to feel somewhat normal again. Our shivering had stopped, and our energy level had dramatically increased with the food and hot coffee. It felt like a resurrection from the dead.

We began to talk about their line of work, the cowboy life.

Jim began, "I did two years of college and even had a city job for a while, but I was just miserable. Every time I went to work and saw them horses runnin in the pasture and those mountains in the distance, I wanted to rip my tie off and walk out that door. It's good I came to my senses and finally quit. We both know we could make more money sittin behind a desk in an office somewhere, but life isn't about money, now, is it? To me it's about the land, the mountains, good friends, and family."

Jim continued, "I get up in the morning go outside after a good breakfast, breathe clean, fresh mountain air, and look at the snow-capped Rocky Mountains. To me this is the center of the world. It's God's country, if you ask me. It's special to be in the mountains. You might say it's good for your soul. We get to ride and care for our horses every day, which is an important part of our lives. A good horse is like havin an adopted good friend or family member. We get to be around good company and put in an honest day's work. Every once in a while we don't have far to go for good fishin and a hunt for deer or elk. In fact, one of our friends at the ranch is a huntin guide, and he let us borrow this tent."

Maynard responded, "Yes, sir, now that's what I call livin. Sometimes we go into town to eat and have a few beers at our favorite Mexican restaurant. We've been goin there more frequently lately, especially Jim. He's taken a likin to one of the waitresses there. She sure is a cutie."

Jim got up, took another big swig of bourbon, and went over to his horse in the back of the tent. He began brushing its coat with a hand brush. He grabbed a handful of corn from a burlap sack and began feeding both horses.

Jim looked over to Maynard and said, "I was thinkin about asking her to go dancin. Do you think she knows how to do the two-step?"

"I'll bet so. I've seen her brother at Reilly's bar and dance hall a lot," replied Maynard. "It seems that I see him there every time I go. If her brother goes dancin a lot, there's a good chance she knows how to dance or would be inclined to learn if she didn't. Even if she didn't know how, you could have a lot of fun teachin her. Either way I'd move while the fire is still hot and the mood is right, if you know what I mean."

I entered the conversation. "I agree with Maynard. If her brother knows how to dance, she most likely knows as well. Timing to these things is all-important when you're talking about women. She's probably anticipating your call as we speak." Everyone had a good chuckle. Jim gave a big smile and took a swig from the bottle.

Maynard continued, "Usually we leave the horses outside even in bad weather. They're pretty tough, but because we are at such a high altitude and the wind is so strong, we decided to bring 'em in with us, especially since they're our only ticket out of the mountains. Sometimes the horses can be quite helpful when we go fishin. We'll wade out in a lake on horseback so we can cast our lines out further and go deeper in the lake than if we were stuck on the shoreline. Especially if there's a lot of moss and vegetation close to shore. We can get to places to cast our fly that we couldn't reach wearin waders or castin from the bank. It's funny to see the horse look at those fish when we bring 'em in right up to the saddle. They look at you like, *What in the world are you doing? What is that thing you're bringin up to you floppin around?*"

I said, "I've never heard of anyone fishing on horseback, but it makes sense, and it sounds like a fun thing to do."

"We've been fly fishin ever since we were kids. There's lots of high mountain lakes, beautiful rivers, and streams around these parts. Jim and I would love to show you boys some good fishin spots after we get out of here."

"Thanks, we appreciate the offer. We might just take you up on that. How long have you been working on the ranch?"

Jim replied, "Pretty much our entire lives. We both started workin as little kids for our family's ranch. They weren't nearly as big a spread as where we work now, though. Just about everyone in my family is some-how connected to ranch life. My little sister is a better rider than anyone I know. She's a state champion barrel rider with her quarter horse. Her horse is the fastest horse I've ever seen. She can turn so tight around a barrel she can touch the ground with her hand. She gets to ride in parades all fancied up carrying the American flag. It's quite a sight. Her fancy horse blanket has all the colors you can think of. When she rides in parades, she has her saddle all decked out in silver and turquoise. It's a beautiful sight. My folks and our whole family are real proud of her."

Maynard said, "She's a pretty one all right, especially when she gets all decked out. She's got long brown hair down her back and a white Western hat with a turquoise hat band matching her earrings. In those parades she wears so much turquoise and silver you might think she's an Indian. She's a real nice girl too, with a good sense of humor and always a big smile. Everyone in town likes her a lot."

"It's funny these days that the cowboys wear so much silver and turquoise with bright, colorful shirts, they're starting to look like Indians. The Indians are wearing Western hats and boots with big belt buckles, so they're starting to look like cowboys," Jim said. Everyone chuckled at his comment.

Jim went on, "I used to ride broncos in the local rodeo. I traveled around a little with the rodeo circuit, but it never really panned out for me. Plus, rodeo is hard on your body. The amount of money and fun you get out of rodeo wasn't worth the beatin and pain you get from those wild horses. I never could imagine how some guys ride those buckin bulls. That's real risky business if you ask me. I think I would rather take my chances being a matador down in Mexico than to try to ride those crazy things. They have so much power and can do so much damage."

"What do ya mean bein a matador in Mexico? That's the craziest thing I ever heard of," said Maynard.

Jim replied, "I always did like those matador guys. They get to wear those fancy colorful silk and satin outfits, encrusted in jewels and sequins. They strut around like a hotshot rooster gettin cheers from the crowd. After the bull is finished, he walks around the bullring wavin his raised arm, hat in hand, chest out, and smiling at an adorin cheerin crowd. All the while the crowd is throwin flowers at him." Jim was being quite animated, holding his arm in the air, head back, and smiling as if he was in the bullring and enjoying the adulation of the crowd himself.

"All of this to do after just a few passes of the bull through the matador's cape. It's too bad the bull has to die. I think they should let the bull pass by the cape until he gets tired out. Then, the matador can parade around, take a few bows to the crowd, and call it a day after a parade with all the other matadors. That way the matador *and* the bull could claim victory. They both could be celebrated for their bravery."

I could tell Jim was really enjoying his thoughts of being a matador, strutting around the tent with his arms raised, hat in hand as if he were in a Mexican bullring.

Bob, Maynard, and I all broke out laughing at the thought of Jim's fantasy. Maynard was laughing so hard that he lay on his back, holding his chest. After he caught his breath, he sat back up and took another swig of bourbon.

Maynard replied, "That's real good, Jim. You should pick one of them flowers up that the crowd throws at you and put one in your mouth and another in the bull's ear. The bull would be so tired by that time he wouldn't care!"

Everyone started laughing, including Jim. The laughter continued for some time until we wore ourselves out. Bob and I sure needed a good laugh. It was just as important to our revival as food and warm shelter. It definitely improved our spirits. I suspect the purpose of Jim's matador story was to keep things lighthearted.

I asked the two, "How do you manage those thousands of cattle you're responsible for? It sounds nearly impossible."

"The spring and fall are our busiest times. We have to take care of the cattle at the ranch by feedin them and makin sure they don't get themselves in trouble, like wadin too deep into mud they can't get out of, or helpin them with birthin, or identifyin sick cattle. We have to brand any new calves born in the springtime. The herd is then let go to free range on government land during the summer. In the fall we round 'em up and brand any new calves born during the summer. We then herd the cattle that are to be sold and put 'em into holding pens. Hopefully, the cattle fattened up grazin all summer. There are always things you've got to do at the ranch, such as takin care of the horses, all the machinery, and general maintenance of the place."

"How do you find all the cattle scattered over hundreds of square miles of land during roundup in the fall?"

Maynard said, "Cattle like to stay in herds and congregate in certain areas that offer natural protection. We know where these places are. We ride out in the fall and go to the areas they tend to hang out in and then drive 'em back to the ranch. This is where a good horse is essential to get the job done. The horse knows what you want him to do and will act on it before the rider can pull the reins to lead the horse. They seem to know how to get in front of a cow tryin to escape from the herd. It's amazin how the horse and the rider almost become one. You would be surprised at how few cattle we lose. You just have to know the terrain and be familiar with the land you work on."

"Yeah, a good horse can tell your moods too. I know it sounds funny, but it's true. When it's time to get serious and turn on the fire, the horse will step up the pace and do some extraordinary things. When things are loose and you're just havin fun, the horse will act silly too. They know how to chase the cattle out of the brush and the woods without you even tryin to show them. It's really kind of amazin," Jim said.

Jim continued, "We all like roundup. It's always a lot of fun. The whole crew gets up before dawn to ride out into the mountains and chase the cattle out. It takes a long time to learn how to be a cowboy and how to handle a horse and drive the cattle back to the ranch. Sometimes you have to rope a cow that's bein too stubborn. Now that's a skill that takes a long time to learn. Maynard and I grew up with it, so it comes like second nature to us. Bein a cowboy is definitely not for everyone. During roundup we're usually out for several days, sometimes even weeks. We camp out and sleep under the stars. There's somethin special about sleepin out in the open around a campfire. It seems to free your soul. It sounds funny, and it's hard to explain, but needless to say, we love it. The cook fixes up breakfast and dinner. Nothin fancy about the food, but it sticks to your ribs, and you get as much as you want. It's real nice lookin out over the mountains and valleys while you're havin supper. We don't get lunch because we're in the saddle all day. Everyone loves the roundup. We look forward to it all year. We get out in the mountains and do the real work of a cowboy. Although you're workin for the boss, it seems like you have a lot of freedom. You might say we're given a lot of leeway."

"Are you friends with your boss?" I asked.

"I wouldn't call it friends. Don't get me wrong, we like him a lot, and we respect him. We all know when the chips are down, he'll have our backs. However, he can be pretty strict and at times pretty tough. He doesn't mess around when it comes to gettin a job done. He doesn't like slackers. When you show up for work, you had better be on time and get your head into it and work until he tells you to stop. That's what a boss is supposed to do, which is fair. You might call him old school, but that's OK with us. I'm not sure a good leader can be friends with his employees, especially in this line of work. It's a different type of relationship. He's got his own problems. It's hard to be a rancher these days. You have little control over beef and hay prices, and expenses are always going up. Nowadays there are so many federal, state, and county taxes and regulations. The cattle are so dumb they're always gettin in trouble, tryin to kill themselves in a river or tryin to find a hole in a fence and gettin themselves killed on a highway or whatever. No, it's a tough business, and you've got to be smart and tough just to break even. But again, it's not about the money, it's about being independent and free as you can be, and of course livin in these here Rocky Mountains."

"It sounds like you guys work all the time. Do you ever get time off?"

Maynard said, "It's like most jobs. We go home when we're done with work every day."

Jim added, "Except on roundups. After that we're real busy for nearly a month. That's when we sleep over in the bunkhouse occasionally."

"Most of the time we get weekends off, like what we're doin today," Maynard said.

Jim replied, "The boss usually lets everyone off on Sundays. He told us that he likes to keep the sabbath if possible. Like I said, the boss is a real straight arrow, and that includes being religious. I think it's a good thing. My family are real churchgoers. I usually meet my parents and sister at church on Sundays, and then we go out for dinner. It shows them respect. It's one of the ten commandments, you know, to honor your mother and father. Outside of that I don't usually see my family except on holidays and special occasions. I must admit, though, the preacher really makes you think about the big picture sometimes. I think everyone must have some kind of relationship with the creator. To me ridin up high in the mountains and looking out at all the beauty is when I feel the closest to the Great Creator. I guess you might call it inspiration, or maybe it's the Great Creator talkin to my heart. You might say the Rocky Mountains are my church."

Maynard replied, "I grew up a Catholic. You might say I flunked confession. Every week I sinned so much I could read a book to the priest with all the bad things I done. That poor priest just couldn't keep up with me. He told me I was incorrigible, whatever that means. So I stopped goin."

With that comment everyone broke out in laughter.

Jim said, "Maynard, you're just no good!" Everyone broke out in laughter again.

Maynard leaned back and took another big swig of Jack Daniel's. "You sure you boys don't want some?" he asked, offering us the bottle.

"No, thanks, but we appreciate the offer."

They both broke out into another Willie Nelson song, "Whiskey River take my mind, don't let her memory torture me!" We all started laughing again.

After catching his breath Jim looked at Maynard and said, "Speaking of memories of women, what are you goin to do about Delores? It seems that you two have been havin your ups and downs for years but still got it goin on."

Maynard broke into a Waylon Jennings song about a good-hearted woman in love with a good-timing man, and Jim joined in before the first line was finished.

"Yaaahooo!" Jim took his cowboy hat in hand and swung it around.

"Yeah, I know, but gettin hitched is a real big step," said Maynard.

Jim replied, "Well, Maynard, you sure ain't gettin any younger, and Delores is a real fine lady."

"I know, I know. I'm gettin there," Maynard said.

It was comical and even entertaining watching these two cowboys enjoy themselves despite the circumstances.

Maynard took another big swig of Jack Daniel's, let out a deep breath, and shook his head. "Whew! Now that's what I call real good firewater."

Jim replied, "Or maybe real good truth serum."

I looked outside from underneath the edge of the tent and noted that the storm was rapidly improving.

Jim said, "How about some poker?" Bob and I agreed and were given a set amount of different-colored poker chips. These two cowboys really knew how to play well. They were excellent bluffers and played with "stone faces." Before long all of my and Bob's chips were gone, accumulated by Jim and Maynard despite the two being half drunk. The bottle of Jack Daniel's that they had been nursing along was now empty. Jim got up and grabbed another large bottle of bourbon. He opened the bottle, took a big swig, and gave it to Maynard.

"You boys need some lessons in card playin," Maynard said.

Jim responded, "I wonder if they have a course in college, Poker 101. I guess you college boys didn't take that course."

They both broke out laughing again as Maynard leaned back on his elbow. I had no idea how Jim and Maynard were still functioning with as much bourbon as they had both taken in. They seemed to be doing remarkably well, though. They had knocked off a large bottle of bourbon in just a few hours. I had no idea how many bottles they had drunk before that.

While Maynard slowly nursed his own bottle, Jim got another bottle of bourbon for himself, pausing to pat both horses on their necks. The horses seemed to respond favorably, putting their heads against Jim's chest. Jim opened the new bottle, looked at Bob and me, said, "Here's to ya," and took a swig.

Maynard said, "My ancestors helped settle this country with the cattle business and ranch work long ago. They fought off Indians and cattle rustlers, made it through the depression, droughts, and cattle epidemics. They were persistent and stubborn people. They just kept goin. Nobody got rich; they just loved what they were doin and loved the place they were in. I guess this line of work just fit their temperament. They were here to stay and weren't ever gonna give up. You've got to hand it to those folks. They were made of tough stuff. I think that attitude has carried on today—at least I'd like to think so. Just as the song goes," and they both sang in unison, "My heroes have always been cowboys…." They both gave another "Yahoo!" followed by a few more swigs of bourbon.

"You might say we're proud of who we are and where we came from," Maynard said.

I thought there was something uniquely good and American about these two guys that was refreshing to see. They exhibited something most Americans had long since taken for granted: pride in who they were, pride in their family and where they came from, but most of all gratitude for a country where they had freedom to live the life they wanted. They were genuinely good people, sharing their food and shelter with us when we were in dire straits. They were doing the right thing without a second thought.

It had been several hours since we'd entered the tent. I got up and looked outside. The wind was gone. The sun was out, and there had been an increase of probably fifty degrees in temperature. This could be our chance to get out when the getting was good, before the weather got bad again. I told this to Bob, and he agreed.

So we said goodbye to our new friends and thanked them for our lives and the great care they had given us. Both cowboys got to their feet and shook our hands. I was surprised that both could still stand and appear totally sober.

"We sure did enjoy your company," Jim said.

Maynard said, "We had a fine time with you boys. Hope our paths cross again. Look us up sometime if you want to go fishin around here. Good luck to both of you."

We left the large canvas tent and proceeded to march up the mountain to the summit as fast as we could, trudging through the knee-deep snow. When we got to the top, we looked again at the beautiful vista around us. The storm clouds had vanished as quickly as they had appeared. The snow was the only way of telling that there had been a previous violent storm. From this vantage point we could see our camp far away. Emerald and Sapphire Lakes were even more beautiful surrounded by pure white snow. My dad and W.O. seemed like tiny ants walking around the camp.

Although our perilous adventure had taken less than a day, it had seemed like a month. Along with nearly freezing to death, we had gotten a dose of good-natured cowboy hospitality. Although it was a terrible situation, being around Jim and Maynard had been like a breath of fresh air. They were so open about their lives, family, and beliefs. They were devoid of all pretentiousness, which is often hard to find these days. They knew exactly who they were, and they loved what they were doing and why they were doing it. They loved the cowboy life. They shared everything they had with us and went out of their way to make us feel comfortable. Plus, they were hilariously funny and entertaining. We were fortunate to have met such good, generous people. It gave me some faith in our country and humanity in general, knowing that guys like Jim and Maynard were still around.

Bob and I turned to take one last look at Lake of the Clouds. It was unfortunate that we hadn't been able to fish in the lake; however, that would have to wait for another day. We felt thankful and lucky to have escaped with our lives. We could still see the tent far below and Maynard and Jim outside, waving. We waved back at our two good-natured *savior cowboys*.

RENNY'S GARDEN

Nature is not a place to visit. It is home.

GARY SNYDER

D avid Gordon and I were sitting next to each other in expansive soft leather first-class seats in a small private jet, enjoying smoked salmon, cream cheese, and crackers. There was a whole platter of hors d'oeuvres in front of us. The flight attendant offered us some wine. We had not expected such lavish accommodations on the way to a new fishing outpost in northern Saskatchewan, adjacent to the border of the Northwest Territories. Since the fishing lodge was new, the owner was going all-out to impress his new guests. We had booked the flight, but the owner had supplied the food and drinks. Besides me, there were three in our party: David, a classmate of mine from medical school; his brother Mike, who was a teacher in Springfield, Missouri; and Alex, an old high school friend of the two brothers who owned a brokerage firm in Atlanta.

The flight had begun in Winnipeg and was scheduled to land at an intermediary airfield called Points North, where we would pick up a pontoon plane to take us to the lodge. We were enjoying ourselves in the fleeting luxury, knowing that we would be living in fairly spartan conditions for the next two weeks at the fishing camp. The mood was light, and we were all enjoying ourselves. As I glanced out the window, I saw nothing but pine forests and lakes as far as the eye could see. This reminded me of the many fishing adventures of my youth, filling me with a short rush of exhilaration.

I looked over at David and the others, raised my glass of wine, and said, "This is going to be a great adventure, gentlemen!"

They all raised their glasses and gave a toast: "Here's to adventure."

We finally landed and climbed down the ladder of the plane onto the cement runway. This was an unusual place. The airfield was newly made, having been recently cleared out of the bush in the middle of nowhere with military-like efficiency. It looked like an industrial airport with huge earthmoving equipment and helmeted workers in fluorescent yellow safety vests walking around. The airport had been built to support the new mining operations in the area and to transport sportsmen like us to various fishing and hunting lodges. The Canadian government was making it a high priority to develop the newly discovered mineral resources in this area of the far north.

As we walked down the tarmac to the flight office, we could feel a significant drop in temperature from our initial boarding in Winnipeg. I could smell the slight scent of pine permeating the cool, crisp air. We all put on jackets. We definitely were in the North Woods, again giving me the feeling that I was returning to something I had loved and left long ago.

I noticed a group of native women and children on the side of the runway, all in a line watching the activity of the planes and equipment. They looked in awe at all the goings-on as if a circus had come to town. A helicopter revved up its propellers and slowly made a vertical takeoff. When the chopper took off, the native people by the runway began to clap and cheer in excitement. It appeared that these people living deep in the vast Canadian wilderness had little amusement.

After waiting around for an hour, we boarded a pontoon plane located on an adjacent lake close to the runway. As we boarded the cramped plane, I was amazed at how young our pilot looked. I sat in the seat next to the young man. He acted very professionally and seemed to know what he was doing. He gave us the standard safety instructions and checked the instrument panel before taking off. I found out that he was twenty-two years old, and I asked how long he had been flying.

"Since I was sixteen," he said. "It's a way of life up here in the bush. There are few roads and millions of lakes and rivers. The settlements are widely scattered, and hence pontoon planes are used for every kind of transport here. It's like driving across town for someone who lives in a city."

The single-engine propeller pontoon plane was a far cry from the Learjet with wine and hors d'oeuvres. To be honest, I preferred the simplicity and adventure of the pontoon bush plane. It brought back a flood of fond memories of my old fishing guide and friend Jean Broux.

The flight was smooth and uneventful. After we landed and tied the plane to the dock, I saw that the new fishing camp was a no-frills operation, and we were the first clients of the new lodge. We were anticipating good fishing since there had been minimal if any previous fishing pressure. As fishing lodges go, this one was quite small, probably because of the new start-up nature of the place. There were five cabins made of thin plywood. There was a cooking/kitchen cabin and an outhouse, and an outdoor cold-water shower surrounded by a rudimentary plastic curtain adjacent to the outhouse. Two other fishermen from Minneapolis rounded out the new guests. They were quiet and reserved but seemed polite and friendly. They had the most expensive top-of-the-line equipment with them, which was a bit unnecessary for this type of fishing.

Bob, the camp manager, came out with a big smile and welcomed us to the new fishing lodge. Bob was tall, thin, and in his sixties but appeared to be in good physical condition despite his chain smoking. He introduced the native guides, who stood in a row in front of us: Renny, Charlie, Mickey, and Jimmy. It reminded me of a police lineup where the motley crew appeared reluctant to be there. They were all quiet and seemed shy, avoiding direct eye contact. Several were looking at the ground. They acted like a line of schoolboys meeting their elementary school teacher for the first time. I shook hands with all of them. I could tell they thought the handshake was unusual. They shook my hand with a soft grasp, then pumped our clasped hands in an up-and-down motion as if pumping water from an old-fashioned well. This was foreign to me, but I took it as a gesture of goodwill by people with different customs. Jimmy was the only one with a big smile. He had several absent teeth, and the remainder were stained a deep yellow. Jimmy and Mickey were in their early twenties; Renny was in his early forties, roughly my age; and Charlie in his early fifties. I was told that Renny and Charlie had been guiding for years, while Jimmy and Mickey were new to the job. The guides were members of the local Cree tribe. Renny and Charlie were rugged and worn in appearance. They both looked ten to twenty years older than they were from years of hard living in the wilderness.

Charlie was tall with long, greasy black hair streaked with gray. His shoulder-length hair was disheveled and clearly hadn't been washed or combed for weeks, or quite possibly months. He had a gnarled, deformed, large red nose, which in medical terminology is a benign condition called rosacea. His face was pockmarked and scarred from a distant history of severe untreated acne. He moved ploddingly with a slight slouch. His face was totally expressionless, and he was nearly silent with his White clients. I doubted that he knew any English outside of a few words. At first glance, he appeared somewhat intimidating. If you saw him in a major city, you would think he was homeless with a possible mental disorder, but in the present environment, it was not an uncommon look.

Renny, in contrast, was a nice-looking weathered man who was well proportioned. His movements were nimble and athletic. He smiled when he was introduced but otherwise was reserved.

After the initial greetings, we unpacked and placed our gear in the cabins. The guides went to the boats and began preparing for the anticipated fishing. I noticed that the guides were speaking their native tongue and not English. We quickly got our fishing gear together and walked down to the dock. Alex and I had Renny as our guide. Alex took a flask from his coat and took a couple of swigs of whiskey.

"Here's to the morning," he said as he slugged it down. "Do you want a hit?"

"No, thanks, maybe later," I said.

Alex was in his late thirties or early forties. He was probably fifty pounds overweight with a big potbelly. He had a ruddy complexion and a big, round face with rosy cheeks. He had an outgoing personality, in fact, a little too outgoing in that he never stopped talking. He wasn't a bad or malignant person but could at times be a little overbearing. The Gordon brothers had Charlie as their fishing guide in the other boat. One guide was always in camp to do chores and help cook along with Bob the manager.

We motored off in different directions. When we came to a good fishing spot Renny slowed the boat to a slow troll. He then mumbled his instructions to cast toward the shore. I initially had to ask him to repeat what he had said. "Where should we cast?" I could barely understand his soft-spoken voice and thick Cree accent. He pointed toward the shore and said, "There." On our first meeting, Renny had been quiet and reserved. However, in the boat doing his job, he seemed confident and self-assured. When he finally spoke, he did so with an unusual accent and left out many words while speaking in broken English. He pointed at a rocky area of the bank without expression and said, "You fish here. If lucky we get trout."

Renny lit a cigarette and took a deep drag. After smoking the unfiltered cigarette down to a small stub and throwing it into the lake, he filled his cheek with a large wad of Copenhagen chewing tobacco. That was strong stuff, and a lot of it. He continued to smoke his cheap Canadian government cigarettes with a wad of chewing tobacco in his mouth. The cigarettes were different than the ones made in the United States. Canadian cigarettes were managed by the government, and there was only one brand. They were oval and much smaller than American smokes. They burned quickly and were gone in a few drags.

I said, "Renny, those are odd-looking cigarettes you've got there."

"Yeah, they no good, but it's the only smokes we can get up here. I'd love a carton of Marlboros."

"You know smoking is bad for your health." He smiled and looked away. It was obvious that between the cigarettes and the Copenhagen, Renny loved his nicotine.

As we cast our lures to the bank and retrieved them, Alex, my boatmate, as per his nature, talked continuously. I didn't mind him too much. He told a lot of jokes and some good stories, but he could be a little obnoxious. Renny looked at him running his mouth, stone-faced. I could tell that Alex was not Renny's type of guy. Alex had never fished before in his life, not even for bluegill in ponds back in Georgia. Our initial objective was lake trout. They are usually found in the deeper, colder parts of lakes but since the ice was recently out, the water was cold enough that the trout were in shallow water. This lake was too far north for walleye, so our goal was to catch lake trout for lunch and then big northern pike and grayling later in the day.

The fishing was good, and we kept the smaller trout for a shore lunch. I caught most of the trout because Alex did more talking than fishing. While Alex was jabbering away his rod suddenly jerked downward, almost taking it out of his hands.

"Hey, what's going on? What is this?" Alex said.

Renny replied, "Ooohhh, big fish, hold tight!"

I reeled in my lure and stopped fishing, which is a common courtesy if someone else in the boat has a seriously big fish on. It's also fun to watch the fight between the fisherman and the struggling big fish. Alex really had something big on. Renny coached him all the way in a calm, reassuring manner.

"Don't horse him, let him run, don't try to stop him. Let him wear out, then begin to reel him in."

Alex was nervous, intermittently looking fearfully at Renny. Every three minutes or so he would look at Renny and say, "What do I do? What do I do?" Beads of sweat started appearing on his plump red face. He could barely keep his fishing rod still because of his nervous shaking. His jovial attitude became serious as he looked to Renny constantly for instruction. He knew he had a monster on the end of his line, and he knew he was way out of his league.

It was a miracle the fish didn't break the line. I could tell the line was stretched near breaking point multiple times during Alex's battle with the giant fish. When the fish slowly came into eyesight, Alex gave a scream: "It's huge!" I looked down into the crystal-clear water below the boat and saw a large, bright silver trout struggling below us. Alex was right; it was enormous. Thirty minutes later he landed a forty-pound lake trout and then released it after taking photos. Talk about beginner's luck! That trophy trout was the first fish he had ever caught in his life! Renny didn't say much except "That was big fish." By any standards the trout was a trophy and possibly some type of record. Alex pulled a flask of whiskey from his coat pocket and took a couple of big swigs. He then gave a big whooping yell, "Yyaaaa hoooo!" He offered Renny and me a swig, but we both declined. Any of the Native guides caught taking any alcohol for any reason would be immediately fired without exception, and Alex knew this. Since Renny wasn't allowed to drink I felt it was bad manners to drink when he couldn't. Renny just looked away, expressionless. After taking a couple more swigs, Alex let out a loud belch that seemed to reverberate around the lake. He then let out another yell: "Yeah, that's what I'm talking about!"

He did a little dance in the boat, ending with a pelvic thrust like an NFL football player celebrating after scoring a touchdown. Renny remained silent. As a past athlete myself, I've never been a fan of show-boating in sports. It seems arrogant and at times unsportsmanlike. However, maybe I'm just old-fashioned.

"OK, Alex, we know you're happy," I said with a small smile so as not to humiliate him, although I didn't think that was possible with an ego like his. Renny gave me a quick, knowing glance, then turned away silently. I had to remember that Alex was not too bad a guy, and I was going to be in the same boat with him for a week. So I was going to get along with him despite Alex not being my favorite fishing partner.

We met up with the Gordon brothers and Charlie on an island for a shore lunch of fresh trout, fried potatoes, onions, beans, and coffee. It was incredible, and we all had big appetites after a long morning of fishing. Renny and Charlie fixed the entire meal with amazing effi-ciency. After the cooking was done the two guides sat in a separate area of the camp, speaking softly in their Cree language.

I motioned to Renny and Charlie and said, "Why don't you guys come on over and sit with us."

Renny just said, "No, thanks," and resumed talking softly to Charlie.

I offered to help them clean up, but they wouldn't have it. They were being paid to do what they were doing, plus tips, so I didn't press the matter. The lunch was outstanding, as was the beautiful scenery and stories of the morning's fishing. Alex of course was animated in his description of catching his big fish. The way he told the story was hilarious and sounded like Captain Ahab and Moby Dick fighting it out to the death. Everyone had a big laugh, but the guides were quiet. We finished the day with excellent fishing and headed back to the lodge for dinner and an evening of relaxation.

Back in our cabin Alex pulled out another bottle of whiskey and kept talking all night. The last thing I remembered before falling asleep was Alex telling us how to make some fast money with his stock brokerage firm.

The next day I didn't see Renny. Charlie took over for him as our guide, and Mickey went with the Gordon brothers. Apparently Renny wasn't feeling up to par. Charlie didn't say a word all day. He guided us to where the fish were, and we caught a lot. He would pull the boat up to a spot, point, and say, "Fish." Occasionally he remained silent and expressionless and simply pointed to where he wanted us to fish. Alex and I asked him questions about the lake, his family, and hunting, among other things. He looked at us with a blank, expressionless stare with no comment, then looked away. He was a strange-looking character and hard to figure out. Charlie's silence didn't stop Alex from carrying on a one-sided conversation with him that eventually became quite silly.

"Hey, Charlie, have you ever seen Bigfoot around these parts?" No answer.

"Do you have vampires up here?" Again he looked away with no answer.

"Have you ever seen a Chippendales dancer?" Blank stare at Alex with no answer.

"Alex, would you stop it? You're ridiculous!" I finally said.

"Ha ha ha ha, I know," Alex replied.

Still no response from our guide. Charlie just looked away.

Alex took out his flask and drank a big swig of whiskey. He looked at Charlie and said, "Here's to ya," then took another big swig.

A couple of things we knew about Charlie: he did know where to get the fish, and he loved chewing tobacco. He went through three tins of Copenhagen chewing tobacco in a day. This amount of nicotine was beyond comprehension. A tiny pinch of chewing tobacco between my lip and gums was enough to leave me lightheaded and dizzy. Most people would be hospitalized or at least be seriously ill from nicotine poisoning from the amount he was taking in. He must have gradually become accustomed to its effect over many years. This was even more than Renny, but Charlie didn't smoke as much.

I knew some Indian sign language that I had learned in Boy Scouts, and I used a few hand gestures in front of Charlie, but still no response. Charlie was just ignoring us as if we were silly children acting out in front of an adult. No matter how you looked at it, Charlie was a really strange bird.

I concluded that the Native guides were not accustomed to White people. We must have seemed strange and eccentric to them. They probably led a subsistence lifestyle to some degree with minimal outside contact. This entire area of northern Saskatchewan had still been primitive until the new fishing lodge and government mining operations had forced more contact with the outside world. These guides were the most traditional natives I had yet encountered in my many years of fishing in northern Canada.

In Winnipeg airport I had bought several comic books to give my eleven-year-old son when I returned from the fishing trip. I grabbed them out of my duffel bag and gave a few to Renny, Mickey, and Jimmy as a peace offering. I could always get more comic books later. Charlie had no interest. The other three looked at them with amazement. Marvel comic books were completely new to them. They all huddled around and turned each page slowly, all the while laughing hysterically. They really got a charge out of an X-man hero named Wolverine. Jimmy pointed at the comic and said, "Look, half man, half wolverine with steel claws, ha ha ha!" They had experiences with wolverines in their world. They were also enthralled by Superman. "Man can fly! He has fancy outfit, and red cape, ha ha ha ha!"

Even though they may not have been able to read, they could tell the plot of the story with the action-packed colorful pictures. They spent hours looking at those comics. I periodically heard booming laughter from the guides' cabin as they looked over the comics again and again. Jimmy kept the comics in his pocket all day. The other two guests from Minneapolis told us that during shore lunch Jimmy would be looking at one of the comics in the bush, laughing. Needless to say, the comics were a big hit.

That evening after dinner, Renny came up to me and said, "Are you doctor?"

"Yes, I am. What can I do for you, Renny?"

Renny pointed to his upper abdomen and said, "Have great pain here."

I knew that from all the nicotine he was taking, he likely had gastritis or an inflamed stomach, with probable reflux into his esophagus. Nicotine, especially from chewing tobacco, increases acid production in the stomach as well as causing esophageal reflux and severe heartburn.

Now I knew why Renny had taken the day off guiding and stuck us with Charlie. I was going to do everything I could to get Renny back as our guide.

I grabbed my first aid kit and handed Renny some omeprazole, which shuts down acid production in the stomach and heals stomach and esophageal ulcers.

I told him, "Take two now, then one every day for ten days. You need to stop chewing tobacco, at least for a while."

I then gave him some Mylanta. "This will give you some short-term relief before the omeprazole takes effect." I also told him to stop smoking, but I knew this would be a hard order to follow.

"Be sure and don't drink any alcohol. This will make your stomach problems worse." Although I knew they weren't allowed to drink while at the fishing lodge, I said this to be complete in my medical advice.

He responded, "I never drink alcohol, never did, never will. It do bad things to everyone!"

The next day Renny came up to me before breakfast with a big smile on his face. With his thick Cree accent he said, "You good doctor! Pain gone! Renny take you places no one but Renny knows. We catch many big fish!"

That day we caught several trophy pike with Renny as our guide. We got our photos and then released the fish. Later that day we went to a small waterfall with a set of rapids. Here we got out of the boat and fished for arctic grayling from the shore, casting into the small fast-moving river below the falls. Grayling are a beautiful blue-gray fish with a large dorsal fin, like a tiny sailfish. They are usually one to two feet in length. These fish are found only in rivers of the far north, running into the Arctic Ocean or the Bearing Sea. What they lack in size they make up for in fight, especially with ultralight rods. We caught scores of them and had a great time.

Renny seemed like a different person now. He would point and laugh whenever one of the grayling broke the surface of the water and became airborne. He was actively involved with catching and landing each fish with us. Renny ran between Alex and me, netting each fish on our lines like a cobra lunging for its prey. He would then belt out a small yell and give a big smile with each fish he landed in the net. He seemed to be enjoying himself as much as we were. We were now seeing a different side of Renny's personality. It appeared that he had lost his previous inhibitions and become exuberant and even playful.

We broke off fishing to have a shore lunch of lake trout that we had caught earlier that morning. Renny fixed the lunch like a real pro. We asked him to join us, and he sat next to me taking in the delicious trout, fried potatoes, and coffee.

"Not too bad, eh?" Renny said.

"It's perfect, Renny. You're not only a great guide, but you're also a master chef!"

Renny's true personality seemed to be coming out now that he had overcome his stomach issues. He wasn't even smoking anymore. He'd stopped "cold turkey." Renny was quick to smile and laugh. He was expressive and animated when speaking. In short, he was fun to be with and seemed to be having great fun doing something he obviously loved.

I asked him, "I know you're a hunting guide as well. Tell me, do you like fishing or hunting better?"

"Ooohh, hunting by far. I live off the meat from hunting as well as help supply my tribe with meat. Moose is my favorite, followed by caribou. You guys should come up in the fall and we could get a moose. I take one moose in the fall, and that supplies me through the winter. In the late fall or early winter, the tribe and I go on a communal caribou hunt during the annual migration south. In the spring we go on a communal goose and duck hunt. These two hunts usually keep the village stocked with meat for the whole year. The chiefs of the tribe divide the meat among the villagers, mainly to the older people and the ones who can't hunt for themselves. I don't get any meat from the communal hunts because I can hunt for myself. It's my duty to help the tribe in this way. We've been doing this for thousands of years. It's fun for everyone in the tribe. During the winter I have a trap line, and I eat the animals I trap or give the meat away if I have enough. I make good money selling furs. My trap line is over one hundred miles long."

"Where do you do your trapping?" I said.

"Around this area. I change the location somewhat every two years. I grew up around here. This is where all my ancestors hunted, trapped, and fished for centuries. I use a snowmachine now, but my dad used sled dogs, and I did too when I was younger. There are advantages and disadvantages to each. If you have a snowmobile, you must be a good mechanic. If you have a mechanical breakdown in the bush, you're in real trouble unless you know how to fix the problem. However, at least you don't have to train and feed sled dogs, which takes a lot of time and effort."

Alex, who was always talking and always trying to get a rise out of someone, told Renny, "I'll bet you're not that good of a shot."

"Ooohhh, no, I'm a good shot!" I could tell Alex was just kidding him, but Renny took him seriously.

"Renny, don't listen to him; he's just giving you grief."

Renny stood up and looked far out over the lake. He pointed and said, "Do you see that seagull way out on that rock?"

I could see a little white dot on a rock in the middle of the lake that I took for the seagull. It must have been a half mile or more away. Renny walked over to the boat and grabbed a .222-caliber semiautomatic rifle and brought it back.

Renny said, "Watch this." He put the rifle to his shoulder, took a wind and distance adjustment, and aimed at the bird. He didn't have a scope on the rifle.

I thought, *No way.*

He was steady as a rock and then fired. Suddenly I could see an explosion of white feathers fly up like a small cloud over the rock where the bird had been. Renny put the rifle down and started laughing.

"I should have bet money, ha ha ha ha!"

I thought that was an impossible shot. I guess Renny proved his point. Alex's mouth was wide open, barely believing what he had just witnessed. For a rare moment Alex was silent.

Then he took his flask out again and had a big swig of whiskey. "I'll drink to that shot!" He again offered it to Renny but again was declined. I didn't know why Alex kept tempting Renny that way.

We proceeded to have a wonderful shore lunch of trout, fried potatoes, onions, beans, and coffee. We were about to clean up when Alex demanded more food. The amount we had already consumed was quite large by any standard. I considered it a lakeside feast!

Renny said, "We ate all the fish and potatoes, but I can fix some more beans if you wish?"

"Fix the beans, Renny. I'm still hungry."

Renny proceeded to cook two extra cans of beans to satisfy Alex. He gobbled up the extra beans within minutes.

"That was great, Renny. I've never had such delicious beans, by golly!"

Renny smiled and was silent.

Alex put his plate down and got up. He walked a few feet, raised one leg in the air, bent over, and passed an enormously loud fart.

"There, you see, I told you the beans were good. Ha ha ha!"

"Alex, you're disgusting," I said indignantly.

Renny remained silent as if nothing had happened.

As we were helping clean up the lunch, Alex kept jabbering away. "Hey, Renny, are you married?"

"Nope."

Alex, always trying to stir the pot by asking ridiculous questions, asked Renny, "Have you ever dated an Eskimo woman?"

"Alex, would you stop!" I said, showing Renny some deserved respect.

Renny, always taking things seriously, replied, "Ooohhh, yea, I like Eskimo women. I dated one lady who lived in Churchill for a while. The only problem was she lived so far away. I had to get on the bush train for several hours to see her. That got a little old. I sell my furs in Churchill after trapping season. I see her occasionally then."

The Canadian railroad travels through the dense, sparsely inhabited forest areas of the north. If you just stand by the railroad tracks in an area where the locomotive engineer can see you, the train is obligated to stop and pick anyone up since there are no roads. It's often the only way for the Indigenous people to get to civilization. Churchill is located on the tundra adjacent to Hudson Bay. The small town is known for its resident polar bears, which wait until the bay freezes and then leave for the pack ice. It is also the destination for the Indigenous people to sell furs after trapping season. This has been a steady source of income for the town for over 350 years. These days one of the main sources of income for the town is ecotourism. Tourists are taken in large buses to view the bears, other arctic wildlife, and the tundra along Hudson Bay. Churchill was the largest town Renny had ever been to.

"Eskimo girls like to go round and round, ha ha ha!" he said, making a circular movement with his hands while belting out a big laugh. I wasn't sure what Renny was talking about, and I wasn't sure I wanted to know, but he sure extrapolated on Alex's silly question.

I think Renny finally came to realize that Alex's Eskimo question was not a serious one but was asked only to make fun of him. I don't think Renny was used to this kind of sarcastic humor.

As we were packing our gear and placing it in the boat, Alex and I looked around and didn't see Renny. We called out but got no answer and then started walking around the area where we had eaten our shore lunch. Renny had vanished like a ghost in the night without a sound. One minute he was right in front of us, and the next minute it seemed as if he had evaporated into thin air. Just as Alex walked under a tree, he heard a loud screech not two feet behind him and felt a hard slap on the back. This scared the wits out of Alex, who was almost hyperventilating. Renny had stealthily climbed the tree and waited for Alex to pass under him, then jumped out of the tree without a sound right behind Alex. Renny laughed so hard that he had to bend over with his hands on his knees, slapping his thighs.

Alex regained his breath and said, "Renny, you scared the heck out of me." Alex just shook his head. This was Renny's payback for Alex always stirring the pot.

"That deserves another hit," Alex said as he pulled out his flask and took a big swig of whiskey.

On our way back to the lodge in the boat, I asked Renny, "Do you know where Charlie and the Gordon brothers are?"

He stood up and looked back, all the while keeping his hand on the throttle. "There they are," he said, pointing to the horizon of the large lake. Neither Alex nor I saw anything.

"What do you mean? I don't see a thing. How can you see them when we can't?"

"Look just above the surface of the water at the most distant horizon. You can see a movement or a shimmering of the sky just above the water where you don't see it elsewhere."

"Oh, yeah, I see that. It's very subtle, but I definitely see a difference."

Renny said, "You'll see that disturbance in the air long before you see the object on the water."

Renny knew things that we who live in urban environments had no idea of. We were amazed. He just smiled like a teacher explaining a new lesson to a student.

When we got back to the lodge, we unpacked our gear from the boat and brought it up to our flimsy plywood cabin. Just as Renny had predicted, Charlie and the Gordon brothers were right behind us. Everyone had had a great day fishing.

Later I walked back to the dock to take in the beautiful vista of the lake. Renny was still on the dock, fixing some things on the boat. I sat down on the dock next to Renny and asked him about his life and his tribe. He was quite open and expressive. He seemed thrilled that I had asked about his world. We had a long and interesting conversation. I think he appreciated my interest in him as a person opposed to just an employee doing a job for me and the lodge.

I told Renny, "We had a good day today."

Renny looked at me and said, "Every day is a good day when you're in the bush."

"I can see what you mean. You certainly have a lot of freedom up here."

"Yeah, isn't that what life should be about?"

I was momentarily taken off guard at the philosophical depth of thought Renny had just expressed. He momentarily looked at me and then turned his glance out onto the lake in a subdued and serious manner.

"I guess you're right, Renny. I guess you're right."

That evening I happened to be wearing a Kansas City Royals baseball cap.

"That sure is a pretty blue hat you have on."

"It's a baseball cap from a team where I come from."

"What's baseball?"

"It's a game played in the summer where I live. It involves hitting a ball with a wooden stick. After you hit the ball, you run as fast as you can."

"Sounds like fun."

"It is fun. Here, take the hat, it's yours. I've got plenty of other hats." I removed the blue KC Royals cap and handed it to Renny.

Renny looked at me as if I had given him a thousand dollars. He was not expecting the gift. He was just complimenting me on the hat. He gently stroked it, as if it were a valuable mink fur. He put the cap on and gave me a big smile.

"Looks pretty good, eh?" he said as he tipped the brim over his forehead.

"Yeah, it looks good. You look good in blue."

"Ha ha ha, blue, eh. You're a good man. You have a good heart." He placed his hand over his chest and then made a spiral movement with it, culminating by pointing his finger to the sky. I wasn't sure what the sign language meant, but I think it was more than simply thank you.

The native people here were not experienced in our urban ways and customs. They seemed innocent, honest, and even childlike in some ways. They didn't pick up on subtleties and inuendo in our conversations, which was almost refreshing. They took things a person said at face value. However, they seemed to be good judges of individual character. I could tell Renny could assess people and quickly determine what made that person tick.

That evening we had a big steak dinner cooked by Bob, the camp manager, and Mickey. It was delicious. The steaks were so large that they overlapped the plate on each side. They probably were over seventy-two ounces each. Renny and Jimmy didn't finish their whole portions. Alex spied the leftovers after he had finished his steak. He got up with his plate in hand and asked the two guides if he could have theirs if they were done with them. Both guides agreed, Alex then quickly stabbed both large unfinished pieces of meat before they could run away and plopped them on his plate. The leftover steaks combined were probably at least another fifty ounces. He quickly devoured both pieces. Renny looked at him with a subtle silent disdain as Alex stuffed his mouth with oversized portions that necessitated chewing each huge meat bolus with his mouth open. Renny said something softly in the Cree language to the other guides, which I later found out meant "glutton."

After dinner David Gordon, Renny, and I walked out of the kitchen cabin and strolled down by the dock. David and I were discussing family heritage. Both of our last names were Scottish in origin.

Renny's eyes lit up and he faced us, stopping our stroll. "A man from Scotland saved my grandfather's life after being attacked by wolves! His name was Angus McDonald, and he came from Scotland. He was an important man in my village even though he was a White man. He even spoke our language. People from Scotland must be good people, eh?"

"I think they must be good people since many of David's and my people came from there." We both laughed.

"Ooohh, yes, they must be good people! Just like us Indians, you White people have different tribes with different customs and languages. Some friendly and some not so friendly, eh? I know that White people in Quebec speak French. They must be from a different tribe, eh?"

"I guess you're right, Renny; in the beginning we all came from different tribes. David and I were from the Scottish tribe. With a name like Angus McDonald, you can't get more Scottish than that."

"Yeah, Angus brought in many things to help the people of my tribe to make life easier for us. He was a doctor too and saved many people's lives. He and my grandfather were good friends."

I could tell from the way Renny had reacted to the mention of Scotland that there must be a long and interesting story behind Angus and his grandfather. I could tell Renny really wanted to tell me the story.

"I'll tell you the whole story later since it's a long one, but a very important story of my family and my tribe. Angus McDonald was revered in my tribe as a brother and a leader, even though he was a White man. People in my tribe still tell stories of Angus and my grandfather Isha. Angus has long since passed into the spirit world, but I wonder if you know any of his family?"

It seemed that the story of Angus and his grandfather was an important part of his and his family's life. Renny thought that I might be distantly connected to this story because of my Scottish family name.

"I'm afraid not, Renny. There are a lot of people with Scottish ancestry in Canada and America."

I don't think Renny had a concept of how big the world is and how many people are in it. Renny knew or had heard of nearly everyone in his tribe in this vast region of Canada. In his mind it wouldn't be too far a stretch for me to have heard of Angus McDonald or his family because we were from the same "Scottish tribe." Renny had lived in the bush all his life, like his ancestors before him for thousands of years. This minor interaction with Renny reminded me of what a remote place we were in, and what little contact with "civilization" the people in this region of northern Saskatchewan and Northwest Territories had had until quite recently.

The Gordon brothers, Alex, and I took chairs by the dock and watched the sun slowly descend over the beautiful lake, at the same time having a few drinks and some cigars. We had a lively and enjoyable conversation and sang a few old songs we all knew from our younger days. The sun never totally set since we were so far north. Alex had more than a few drinks, polishing off an entire bottle of whiskey by himself. He began cutting off pieces of a large salami and chewing them between drinks. How he was able to stuff in any more food and drink was unimaginable.

He began slurring his rapid-fire speech while spewing out small pieces of salami, spittle, and liquor. He let out several large, reverberating belches. They were so loud I was expecting to see ripples form on the placid lake. After each loud belch he would yell out, "Yeah!" quite proud of himself for having produced such a loud sound.

After our get-together by the lake, our cigars smoked down to stubs, Alex became even more boisterous. He got up from his chair and began staggering around the camp, singing "Stairway to Heaven" by Led Zeppelin, including the guitar instrumental solo part while playing his "air guitar." Alex fell down several times and vomited with each fall. I was amazed at the volume coming out of him with each eructation and how he was able to get back up again. His huge steak dinner was now gone. Each time he fell he slowly arose and continued singing. Finally he fell to his knees and then rolled onto his back, still singing the end of the song.

Renny looked at him again disdainfully and shook his head. I was fully aware that Renny must have had firsthand experience of the terrible effects of alcohol and drugs on his people. Although alcohol and drugs are technically illegal on Canadian native reserves, they are commonly smuggled in. The more exposure to White people, the more exposure to their vices as well. There are extremely high rates of alcoholism, depression, and suicide among the First Nations peoples of Canada, which has severely damaged tribal and family structures.

Alex was now down for good. With a significant amount of effort,

I picked him up from his last fall and put his arm around my shoulder. We then stumbled back to the cabin. It was like carrying a 240-pound sack of potatoes with minimal assistance. I helped Alex into his bunk and put his sleeping bag over him. Eventually we all called it a night and quickly fell asleep.

I was suddenly awakened by a loud crashing sound just outside the cabin. I sat up abruptly and saw both Gordon brothers sitting, fully awake as well. Alex was sleeping soundly, snoring away. The brothers glanced at me with puzzled looks. They had been awakened by the same noise.

We got up and went to the window. It was partially dark but light enough that we could see around the camp without too much difficulty. To my horror the biggest bear I had ever seen was wreaking havoc on the camp. He was brown and had a shaggy coat. His head was quite large, and his girth reminded me of a hippopotamus with long, sharp claws. He had overturned the outhouse and torn off the screen door of the kitchen cabin, leaving deep claw marks in the door and scraping the paint off to the bare wood. He had dug up the plastic pipes leading from the shower. The bear crushed the pipes open and licked the soap residue out of them. he then headed for our cabin. The bear looked at the window and clearly saw me there.

The Gordon brothers and I started yelling at the tops of our voices, "Get out of here bear, go away! Git! Get out of here!"

Usually bears when confronted with humans will run away if given a chance. But this bear was totally undeterred by our noise making. In fact, we seemed to be drawing him closer to us. The bear and I made definite eye contact again, and I suddenly felt like I was prey for this huge, hungry predator. As he walked toward the cabin, the bear continued to stare at me as if I were what he was after. I suddenly began to fear for my life. There was nowhere to run since the huge bear would see me come out the door. I also knew bears are extraordinarily fast and could certainly outrun me.

I asked the Gordon brothers, "Do we have any food in this cabin that would give him an incentive?" We quickly looked around and saw the large salami lying on Alex's pack. We had been told not to keep any food in the cabin because of the possibility of drawing bears. Of course, Alex didn't think that was necessary. But bears can smell the smallest food item from miles away. Their sense of smell is three times greater than that of a bloodhound. The scent of the steak dinners and the grease from the previous night may have been the stimulus that had drawn the ravenous bear, recently out of a long winter of hibernation, to the camp.

Now the bear was coming for Alex's salami—or quite possibly me! That dreaded thought filled me with further anxiety since the bear was still looking at me as he continued on his slow but relentless path toward the cabin. I started looking around the cabin for a weapon. Nothing was around but fishing poles and some chairs. I thought that I could temporarily keep the bear at bay with a chair with the legs facing toward him. I knew this would be only a temporary solution if he wanted one of us for a meal. He could quickly knock away a chair with a minor swing of his massive paw. Maybe he would go after Alex and his salami first while Alex was still sleeping.

Our cabin was made of flimsy plywood, much less strong than the kitchen cabin that the bear had unsuccessfully tried to enter. We continued to yell at the bear. It just didn't care. It was on a mission and not to be deterred. It was heading straight for us. We all knew this thing had the capability to tear down the plywood cabin with ease. The bear was now just a few feet from our flimsy plywood front porch. Fortunately, Alex's vomit was still on the ground, temporarily delaying the bear as he paused to make a quick snack of it. Fortunately, Alex had vomited multiple times, delaying the bear a bit longer. The bear was relishing the partially digested steak dinner and salami mixed with whiskey as an hors d'oeuvre before coming to get us.

Out of nowhere Renny appeared on the front porch of our cabin in a determined, no-nonsense manner. In his hand. he held his .222-caliber rifle. This type of rifle is high velocity but low in caliber. It's usually used for smaller game, such as coyotes, groundhogs, or beavers. It's not noted for its stopping power for larger animals.

I quickly looked at Renny and said, "You're not going to shoot that bear with that, are you?"

He didn't even look at me. Before I could complete my sentence, Renny rapidly raised his gun to his shoulder, aimed, and fired three rounds at the bear. The bear seemed startled and quickly turned his huge head to look down at his torso as if he had been stung by a large bee. Suddenly he jumped into the air with all four legs and lurched forward, then turned and ran out of the camp like a rampaging bull. I was shocked at how fast he could run. I could hear him crashing through

the bush long after he went out of sight. By now the remainder of the guides were on our cabin porch. Renny said something to them in Cree, and they all ran off into the twilight, deep into the bush. All the while Renny never even turned his head toward me. He knew exactly what he wanted to do and didn't ask me any questions.

Now we had a wounded bear that could terrorize our camp at will, not to mention Renny and the other guides out there in the bush, who could be ambushed anytime in the dark.

I grabbed Alex's salami, went outside, and heaved it into the lake. Alex was still snoring away. The whiskey the night before had conked him out. The Gordon brothers were silent and pale. It appeared that all the blood had been drained from them. Their eyes were wide open. It seemed that they were in shock and were still coming to grips with what had just happened. I reassured them that we were fine now that the danger was gone. However, I was thinking that maybe I was premature in that prediction, with a wounded, enraged bear somewhere nearby in the bush, ready to take revenge.

Thirty minutes later I heard a loud yell deep in the bush. *Oh no!* I thought. *Now we've got a casualty.* This wounded bear when he attacked was not going to hold back until his victim was in pieces.

My mind was racing. I hoped that it wasn't Renny whom I'd heard. My thoughts ran through possibilities. *There is little I'll be able to do. We will need a level-one trauma center for injuries sustained by a bear attack, if not a morgue.* I kept thinking, *Whatever the situation, this is not going to end well.* I waited for the guides to bring back one or more terribly mauled or possibly dead individuals. And then, what about the bear? Would he follow them into camp to wreak more revenge?

I'm a surgeon, but without equipment or appropriate medical facilities, there would be little I could do to help. David Gordon was a specialist in infectious disease and wouldn't be expected to add much to the present situation. I hadn't heard any shots fired. Maybe the bear had been drawn to Charlie because of his strong scent. I chuckled briefly at the thought. All was silent after the one yell we had heard. It seemed like hours had passed since the solitary scream deep in the bush.

After thirty minutes I heard something in the forest close by, rumbling through the brush. I couldn't see anything yet, and I was not about to go out of camp into the bush to investigate. I began gathering a large number of towels to use as bandages or a tourniquet. I grabbed one of Alex's whiskey bottles to help sterilize any wound. I quickly rummaged through my tackle box and retrieved a surgical hemostat that I used to remove barbed hooks from the mouths of fish. I intended to sterilize the instrument with alcohol and use it to quickly clamp any actively bleeding vessels.

I began to prepare a primitive trauma room on the front porch of the cabin. I laid out one of the towels and placed the alcohol, hemostat, gauze, tape, antibiotic ointment, a knife, and some braided fishing line to suture a bleeding vessel. I knew this was grossly inadequate, but I was hoping to stop emergent blood loss to temporarily stabilize the victim until we could arrange for some type of plane transfer out. I did have some broad-spectrum antibiotics and some painkillers in my first aid kit. However, I knew all of this would be woefully inadequate for the type of injuries I was expecting.

I heard more noise in the forest, with sticks breaking and rustling leaves. I didn't know what was there. If it was the bear, I considered running to the lake to jump into a boat. My body was frozen in place as I focused all my attention on the edge of the camp and forest where the noise was coming from. I then began to hear voices in the distance. Was it the guides bringing back the wounded or dead? Were they being followed by the bear? I certainly didn't hear any further gunshots. The sound of the voices became louder. It didn't seem there was any urgency or yelling, as I would expect if someone was injured or being chased by the bear.

I was in total shock when I saw all four guides dragging an enormous dead bear into camp. "Hey, hey, hey, look what we got" said Renny. They dragged the bear into the middle of the camp with some significant effort because of its size.

"I shot him three times in the heart, and he just didn't want to die. He was a strong bear. He ran for fifty yards in the bush before he collapsed."

The yell that I'd heard in the bush was Renny giving a victory war whoop when he found the bear. Renny looked at all the towels, primitive equipment, and bottle of whiskey on the porch of the cabin and said, "What's all this for?"

"This was to attempt to fix your mangled body, not that I could've done much good."

"Aw, that's really nice of you Doc, to think of us. Were you going to get us drunk too?" as he viewed the whiskey bottle.

"If I had to, but mainly to sterilize any wounds."

Then something strange happened. The guides knelt around the bear and placed their hands on its gigantic, motionless body. Renny began a chant in Cree. They were thanking the spirit of the bear for giving his life so they could live. I was amazed that these guides still retained their ancient customs.

After this small ceremony, they dragged the bear to the dock, where they put him into one of the boats and motored off to a small island far from the main camp. All four guides went with tools to skin and prepare the bear. They did this away from camp to avoid blood and tissue around the camp and prevent any further attraction of predators.

Within an hour Renny and the guides came back with the bearskin and a large amount of quartered meat along with the liver, heart, and brain. They put the meat in the freezer to be divided among themselves later when they went home. Renny also had the claws of the bear as a totem to give him strength. They quickly made a wooden rack to stretch the hide and tied it to the edges. The skin was scraped clean of further tissue. The brain was rubbed into the hide to make it soft and pliable. The bearskin was then left in the sun to dry. I was amazed at the quickness and efficiency with which all this was done. This was obviously something they had done frequently in the past. It seemed routine for them.

I asked Renny if he liked bear meat.

"It's not as good as moose or caribou but not bad. It's rare that we eat bear, though. We look at them as a kindred spirit to man. Man and bear eat the same things, both plants and animals, but unlike man, they are solitary and have a more courageous spirit. They don't need to be among other bears for strength like humans do with each other. We are weaker animals, both physically and in spirit. In fact, I belong to the Bear Clan of the Cree tribe. I didn't want to shoot the bear, but he forced me to do it. Just as with humans, there are good and bad individuals, the same is true for bears. That bear knew he shouldn't have been where he was. Most of the time if you just yell at the bear and give warning, they will respect that and run away. That bear was different. He didn't respect human beings, and he would have been a continued threat to us unless he was killed. He was a bad bear."

That morning at breakfast Bob, the camp manager, congratulated the guides on a job well done. He could ill afford bear trouble with his new clientele. Alex woke up late and eventually slowly walked into the kitchen cabin, looking disheveled. His hair was sticking up in strange directions, and his eyes were bloodshot. All of us had already eaten breakfast, but Mickey and Bob were good enough to fix another for Alex. He had slept through the entire ordeal overnight. Alex sat down at the kitchen table and shook his head to wake up.

"What happened last night?"

"Oh, just a little drama," I said. With that everyone broke out in laughter. Alex was clearly hungover in a big way.

"Hey, I can't find my salami. Do you know where I put it?"

Renny smiled and said, "I think the bear ate it." I looked at Renny as I gave a slight chuckle. Renny knew exactly what I had done to the salami. I think it was Renny's first use of sarcasm. He had picked up some bad things from the White man already.

Alex just shook his head, looking down at the plate in front of him, and began digging into the bacon, eggs, hash browns, and coffee.

"I'm not going fishing today; I'm going to sleep in and take it easy."

"That's OK, suit yourself, Renny and I will go without you. We'll be fine but let me know if you change your mind."

I could tell that Renny was pleased to be rid of Alex for a day.

There was a huge, crazy looking fishing lure about a foot long hanging on the wall in the dining cabin. It was brightly colored hot pink, yellow, and chartreuse. It had two big bulging glass eyes and a big propeller on its tail to agitate the water.

I asked Bob, "What's with that crazy lure?"

"I've caught some pretty big pike with that lure."

I looked closer at it, and there were teeth marks and scratches over its torso, indicating that Bob wasn't lying. One thing for sure, you weren't going to catch anything small with that thing. It was so bizarre in appearance that I couldn't imagine how any fish would want to eat it. It looked like a child's bath toy.

"You can use it today if you want."

"OK, I'll give it a try."

Renny and I got in the boat, and we were off.

"I'm going to take you to a place today that nobody has ever fished before. The lake isn't on any maps. We're going to have to walk into the lake for about a half mile. It's a steep climb, but you should be fine. There should be some monster pike there. This place is close to where I grew up. It is sacred ground for the Cree people."

"That sounds like a good plan, Renny; let's go for it. Will it be a problem for me entering a sacred place?"

"Not if I take you."

As we traveled in the boat to our destination, Renny said, "I would like to see your Kansas City sometime. I know Bob has a booth to promote the lodge at the K.C. sports show every year. Maybe he could take me with him."

"You can stay at my house anytime, Renny. We would love to have you and Bob."

"That would be too much to ask. I would like to camp by a river or lake close to your house. Maybe I could fish and cook my own meals."

"The only body of water that is anywhere close to me is the Missouri and Kansas Rivers, and they're muddy. You definitely couldn't drink the water from those rivers like you do up here where you live."

"Do those rivers have pike or trout in them?"

"No, only carp and catfish mainly."

"I've heard of catfish but have never seen one. Do they have sharp teeth like pike?"

"No, you can barely see their teeth. They have long whiskers and usually feed off the bottom."

"Whiskers like cat?"

"Kind of, but more sensitive and longer. They mainly feed by sense of smell and feel from the whiskers. Catfish don't have scales; they have skin instead."

"What a strange fish! Is Kansas City larger than Churchill?"

"Oh, yes, very much larger."

We motored the boat much farther than we had ever gone before on the big lake. We finally turned between two islands, and a small waterfall came into view, flowing down a steep, rocky incline to the shore. We beached the boat, and I followed Renny up the incline next to the waterfall. We climbed to the top of a small mountain by way of a small trail that was clearly not traveled frequently because of the overgrowth of vegetation. At the top of the small mountain was a huge black rock, nearly thirty feet long and ten feet high. This rock seemed dramatically out of place from the surrounding rocks, as if someone had placed it in an area where it didn't belong. The rock stood out from the surrounding light gray granite rocks of the surrounding area.

Renny said, "I'll tell you about the rock later, but for now let's go fishing."

About fifty yards from the top of the mountain we came upon Renny's lake. It was a beautiful but shallow lake with lots of vegetation along the shore and lily pads around the edges, the perfect habitat for big northern pike. Renny had brought his fishing rod for the first time. He had shed his position as fishing guide, and we were now fishing together as friends. We both began to cast our lures into the lake. In no time we caught several trophy pike, one after another. We lost count after fifteen. This wasn't fishing, it was catching.

We were having a great time. Renny laughed every time he hooked a pike. He was enjoying himself immensely. Every time I hooked a big pike I yelled, "Fire in the hole!" to let him know I had a fish on.

He looked at me and said, "What does this mean, 'fire in the hole'?"

"I don't know, Renny, I just recall my dad saying that whenever he had a big fish on."

"Oh, yes, I understand that. I say and do many things I learned from my father and family that I do not know the meaning of, but I do them as an honored tradition."

"Yeah, I guess it's something like that."

The fish put up a big fight, splashing the surface with their fins, jumping in the air, and attempting to throw the hook. It was an exciting sight. Renny and I were laughing and having great fun.

After over an hour had passed, Renny came over to where I was fishing by the bank. I told him, "I'm going to try out the crazy lure Bob gave me just for fun."

Renny laughed and said, "That should be fun to watch. I'd like to see how it moves in the water."

I tied the lure onto the steel leader and let it fly far out into the middle of a small bay. It was a heavy lure, so I was able to throw it extra far. I began the retrieve of the lure. It created a real commotion on top of the water. The water was churning and bubbling around the lure. Both Renny and I started laughing at the absurd splashing lure with its small propeller, big protruding eyeballs, and fantastic bright colors. It seemed a joke to use this crazy thing, but it was worth a good laugh.

I said, "This kind of lure is more effective catching fishermen than fish."

Suddenly Renny stopped laughing and said, "Ooohh, look there!" He pointed to an area of water close to a patch of reeds.

Something very large was just under the surface of the water, making a wake like a torpedo on a direct intercept course with my crazy lure. I kept up a slow, steady retrieve. Both of us watched as the giant pike gained on the lure, opened its mouth, and then took it under. My line screamed out of my reel. The huge fish was taking out yards of my line on a big run. When it finished, I began reeling back. The fish made multiple runs, and I could feel real power and a lot of weight at the end of my line. I eventually brought the pike close to the shore. I suddenly realized we hadn't brought a fishing net to land the fish. Without saying a word Renny jumped in the water, underhooked the fish with both arms, and brought it to shore as if carrying a load of firewood. It was huge, the biggest pike I had ever caught. Northern pike don't get much larger than this. After a photo we returned the fish to the lake unharmed. Renny let out a big yell, the same sound I had heard when he had found the carcass of the dead bear deep in the bush on that eventful night. Renny and I looked at one another and laughed. I taught Renny how to give a high five in celebration. He liked the gesture a lot. Renny got as much enjoyment watching me land these big pike as if he were pulling them in himself.

I said, "Renny, what do you say we call it a day? We're not going to beat a fish like that one."

Renny and I walked back to the top of the small mountain where the big black rock was. We climbed on top of it and looked around at an amazing vista. We could see for miles. The main lake was far below, and Renny's lake was behind us. Adjacent to us was a beautiful waterfall. Renny told me that the two rock walls at the top of the waterfall had collapsed eight years before, partially occluding the outflow of a small lake where the waterfall began. This had caused a backup of water to make the much larger lake that we could see now. Beavers had made the backup of water more substantial by building their own dam to obstruct even more of the outflowing water.

He said, "This lake now attracts moose, which feed on water plants. Shallow lakes like this attract many other animals as well, mink, martin, lynx, just to name a few. The area is rich in animal life. I don't have to go too far to trap a lot of fur. The aerial maps of this area were taken before the lake had formed in its present size, so there is no record of it. The map shows only a swampy area instead of a true lake."

"What about this big black rock?"

Renny began to tell me the story of the large black rock that looked so out of place with its environment. "Long ago, the Indian people in this area were being terrorized by a monster called the Wendigo. It was over fifteen feet tall and walked on two hoofed legs. It had horns on its head and scales for skin. It had large teeth that were poisonous. Its eyes bulged out and were red. This beast would kill any creature that it saw. Not for food but just to kill and mutilate the body because it liked to see humans and other animals in fear and die. It killed a lot of Indian people, including young children. It lurked around the edge of the village, where it could pounce on any unsuspecting person. This beast was made by the devil, the great evil spirit. Many hunters from the tribe tried to kill the beast with spears and arrows, but they always failed. The Wendigo was too quick and too clever to be killed by human beings alone. The hunters became the hunted as the Wendigo stalked anyone who ventured out too far from the village.

"Finally, when all the humans' efforts failed to kill the beast, the chief of the tribe went to the cave of a great bear. He talked to the bear, saying, 'Humans are not strong enough to kill this monster who threatens our existence. Will you help us?' Since the monster was killing all animals, it was affecting the bear's ability to hunt food. The great bear agreed to help the people rid the land of the monster.

"The people set up an ambush. They showed themselves to the monster and started running away as if in fear. The monster ran after them. The Wendigo was much faster than humans and was about to catch them. The great bear lay hiding behind a large rock. When the monster passed by, the great bear pounced on the monster's back and bit him in the neck, killing him. Before the monster died it bit the great bear in the foot, poisoning him. The great bear knew he was slowly dying, so he wanted to go to a beautiful place to lie down. The great bear came here above the waterfall overlooking the lake. He then lay down and died. The Indian people thanked the spirit of the great bear. They prayed to the Great Spirit to preserve the great bear so no one would forget his bravery and the help the bear had given to the people.

"The Great Spirit heard the prayers of the people and turned the great black bear into the large black stone that we are now sitting on. This is a sacred spot. People sit here to gain the strength and power of the great bear spirit. The Great Spirit saw the good things the great bear had done for humans and therefore populated the world with smaller versions of the great bear so humans and the bears could easily coexist with one another. This is the reason my clan in the Cree tribe is called the Bear Clan, because we live in this area. This rock and this whole area are revered by all Cree peoples as sacred and a special place to gain strength.

"I grew up around two miles from here. We built our cabin and lived off the land, hunting, fishing, and trapping."

Renny pointed to a clearing across the waterfall with several stone markers. "That's where all my ancestors are buried, facing the east, looking over the waterfall and the big lake. They are greeted by the first rays of the sun when it rises. Like rising from the dead of night." He pointed at a large granite stone with colorful symbols painted on it. "That's where my grandfather Isha is buried. He was a great hunter and a good man. He was very brave. Would you like to hear his story? It's a long one, though."

"Sure. I can't imagine a more beautiful place to spend the afternoon with such a fine person. We've got all the time in the world."

Renny went on to tell me the long story of his grandfather Isha, who had been attacked by wolves and saved by his sled dog Atu and an old Scotsman, Angus McDonald. He told the story in such vivid and exquisite detail that he mesmerized me. While telling the story he would frequently stand up, jump, and become quite animated, using

his arms and legs and letting out yells and growls. He imitated various animals, bears, wolves, moose, and others, as he stooped, crouched, and walked on all fours. His movements were exaggerated to make more of a dramatic and emotional effect on the audience, which was me. Renny made his grandfather and the animals come alive, almost as if I had been there as a witness. It was an incredible performance that had probably been passed down from one generation to the next. I could imagine Renny performing this story by a campfire, which would make it even more effective.

When Renny finished I asked him, "Do you have any more stories like that?"

"Ooohh, yes. Many, many more about many things! I thought you would be interested in this story because Angus McDonald was from the same Scottish tribe as you."

Without the written word and books, oral storytelling like this was the way one generation passed on its history and life stories to the next.

I would have loved to hear more stories from Renny and document them, but I was leaving Canada and my great adventure the next day.

I felt honored that Renny would tell me the stories of his people and show me his sacred area. He opened his heart to me. He showed me what was important in his life without hesitation. It revealed real trust between two new friends. Possibly he sensed a kindred spirit in me.

"I come here whenever I need strength. This area not only sustains me with food and furs but also gives me peace of mind. I am strengthened by the great bear spirit, and I am supported by my nearby ancestors. I know the stories of each of my ancestors, what their strengths and weaknesses were. They serve as great lessons of life. Many I never knew personally because they lived before I was born. However, they are always alive to me now because of the stories my parents and grandparents passed down to me. My ancestors are now protectors and guides for me. You must know how to listen to them. They speak to your heart when you're alone and searching for answers, especially when sitting where we are, on the great bear rock."

Although Renny had limited formal education, he was highly intelligent and spiritual. We came from entirely different worlds, with different customs and different life experiences. However, we were able to communicate on a basic human level. On that level we had a great deal in common.

"The good thing about being self-sufficient is freedom, and that is of great importance to me. Here I have everything I need. I will never leave this place. It is the center of my world that gives me strength. This is a place of bounty and beauty for me. *This is my garden.*"

HALF IN AND HALF OUT

Everything in nature invites us constantly to be what we are.

GRETEL EHRLICH

My good friend Dallas, his son, Zack, and I were planning a fishing trip to Big Rock Lake in northern Manitoba. We had been planning the trip for some time. The day before the trip, Dallas had a business emergency come up and had to cancel. It was a big disappointment to me as well as to Zack. I told Dallas I would be willing to take Zack on the trip if he couldn't go. At the time Zack was in his midtwenties and more than anxious to go fishing. I just didn't have the heart to see him cancel as well. There was never a friendlier, more lighthearted and amiable person than Zack. He was always happy and got along with everyone. He was wonderful in conversation, and he kept things from ever getting dull or boring. This was in addition to his wonderful sense of humor. Zack was a giant of a young man. He was six foot eight and weighed over three hundred pounds. He had a large, round face with what seemed like a perpetual smile. He wasn't fat; he was just plain big. I cannot recall a better fishing companion than Zack.

I had never been to Big Rock Lake before. It had been highly recommended by a doctor friend of mine who said he'd had the best fishing of his life there. I didn't know how extensive his experience in fishing was, but otherwise he was an exceptionally reliable person. He had been there several years in a row and loved the place. After taking a jet airliner to Winnipeg, we took a large charter propeller plane to the lodge at Big Rock Lake. The plane carried nearly thirty fishermen. I wasn't expecting the large number of people going to the same place. This was a huge departure from all my previous fishing experiences, which had usually been bare-bones wilderness adventures with limited amenities and few other guests. In all honesty, when I saw the number of people on the plane, I was apprehensive about our upcoming fishing experience. Big Rock Lodge had its own airstrip made of packed dirt. The lodge, as it turned out, was a highly sophisticated big operation.

After we landed, we were met by the entire crew of fishing guides, waiting next to the plane, all wearing red T-shirts with the Big Rock Lodge logo on the left chest. The manager called them the "red army," which was a little odd since they were all Native Americans mostly of the Cree tribe. The red shirts were basically uniforms, again something much different than I had seen before. They were there to pick up our bags and take us to our individual cabins. A tractor pulling a large open trailer carried all the fishermen's luggage and gear. I had never seen such service before.

The lodge was a large structure made of huge logs. The dining room looked out on the lake from a giant picture window. It reminded me of a large theater with a huge screen showing a view of a beautiful lake and a picturesque northern wilderness. The lodge was immaculate and exceptionally clean. It had a large kitchen with a full-time chef and staff as well as a well-stocked bar and bartender. They even had a fishing tackle shop for any last-minute fishing needs. The individual cabins were placed on a hill overlooking the lake, each with a beautiful porch. There was full-time hot water and electricity as well as daily linen changes. There was a woodburning stove in each cabin. This place was like a high-end hotel in the middle of nowhere. It was not much more expensive than most other remote Canadian fishing lodges, but with all the perks and more. I would say this place was for the gentleman sportsman. If I was able to catch a lot of big fish, it didn't matter to me. I thought, *Why not? A little luxury occasionally can sure be nice.* The lodge was the only one on this remote lake and was far from any civilization.

After placing their gear in the cabins, the fishermen met at the main lodge for a welcome and briefing given by the manager. He was friendly, informative, articulate, and aiming to please. This place was a real professionally run operation. Usually in places like this, the fishing is not as good as it is at the smaller lodges because of the fishing pressure, and the fishing guides can be hit-or-miss. However, this was yet to be determined. The lake was large, and their policy was catch and release, so hopefully the fishing pressure wouldn't be too great a factor. Our main objectives were big northern pike and walleye as well as lake trout.

It was a beautiful day, and we wasted no time in preparing to go fishing. After our briefing at the main lodge, Zack and I walked down a dirt road toward our cabin. Enormous pine trees towered over the road. The air was cool and damp with a strong scent of pine. It felt good to be in the north country again. Our cabin didn't disappoint. It was made from sturdy logs and, like the main lodge, was immaculate and had all the amenities of a major hotel.

We were setting up our fishing gear in our cabin when we heard knocking at the door. I went to the door and opened it, having no idea who it could be. I thought it was possibly room service. At the door was a young man in the red T-shirt lodge uniform and a baseball hat.

In a soft voice, the young man said, "Hi, I'm your fishing guide."

I introduced myself and Zack. "I wasn't expecting you so soon.

Come on in." Our guide slowly and somewhat reluctantly entered the cabin. "What's your name?"

"Murdock"

"What's your first name?"

"I go by just Murdock."

"Well, OK, Murdock, pleased to meet you." We shook hands. It was a tentative, light-handed handshake that I had frequently noted among many Native American fishing guides in the past.

He was around five foot eight with broad shoulders and seemed to be in excellent condition. Although he was clearly Indigenous, he looked more Mongolian than any other ethnicity. His eyes were slightly slanted, and he had a broad face with high cheekbones. He was deeply tanned from the sun and wind exposure, as was standard for most fishing guides. His slight Fu Manchu mustache accentuated his Asian appearance. He looked for all the world like Genghis Khan—tough, thick, and muscular, someone you wouldn't want to mess with. However, he seemed quite reserved and soft-spoken. He showed no expression on his face on our first meeting.

"Well, Murdock, what do you say we go fishing!"

He looked down and away and said softly, "I'm OK with that."

Zack and I picked up our fishing gear and followed Murdock down to the dock. After we stepped into the boat, Zack untied it from the dock and pushed off. Murdock put on a pair of wraparound shades, turned his baseball cap backward, and started the engine.

"What kind of fish you guys after?"

I said, "Let's go for big pike today." Without another word we sped off.

We traveled for around fifteen minutes and motored into a big, secluded bay filled with underwater weeds, a perfect habitat for big northern pike.

I looked at Murdock and said, "It looks really good!" He nodded in acknowledgment. Zack and I started fishing with the standard five of diamonds fishing lure, which was always my initial go-to lure for pike.

"Hey, Murdock, do you like this lure?" I asked, trying to start a little conversation.

"Yep," he responded, still expressionless.

Within a few minutes we caught some big trophy pike. Murdock didn't say a word while he netted the fish and helped remove the lures from the pikes' sharp-toothed mouths.

"What do you think, Murdock?"

"Big fish," he said in a low monotoned voice.

We caught several more pike. After photos were taken and the fish were released, Murdock said, "Let's get some walleye for a shore lunch."

It was nearly noon, and Zack and I were getting hungry. We motored off to a nearby rocky point, switched lures to black jigs, and within thirty minutes had a whole stringer of walleye. In my opinion, walleye is the best-tasting fish on the planet. Our ability to catch a whole stringer of walleye within thirty minutes testified to the productive capacity of the lake. I was amazed.

I asked Murdock, "Is it always this easy to catch this many walleye in such a short time?"

"Usually."

After catching the fish, we headed for a good location for a shore lunch. Murdock knew right where to go. The shore lunch is almost a ritual of fishing in the north country and one of the most enjoyable aspects of the fishing adventure. It is usually planned for the early afternoon, when the fishing has slowed down. One can have an excellent meal of freshly cooked fish in a beautiful setting, viewing the lake and surrounding forest.

We beached the boat on a sandy area, and Murdock went straight to work silently making a fire and preparing lunch: fresh walleye, fried potatoes, onions, beans, and coffee. I had had literally hundreds of shore lunches before, but I could not remember a more delicious meal. Murdock really did it right.

Zack and I kept talking to Murdock, but he seemed to intentionally avoid eye contact. He was not much of a conversationalist, responding only to direct questions. We invited him to have a seat with us and enjoy the meal, but he just shook his head. I thought possibly he was just maintaining a professional relationship. I surely couldn't blame him for that. I just wanted to be friendly since Zack and I would be spending all day with him every day for the next week. Fishing guides always seem to try harder to get their clients good fishing if they like them. It was not as if he didn't speak much English. He was just quiet. Yet there was more to him under the surface that intrigued me. There was a mystery about him that I couldn't put my finger on. It seemed that he had a lot of mental activity going on even though he remained silent.

Murdock ate quickly after we had finished and were relaxing on the beach, drinking some of the best coffee I had ever had. The expressionless face and the wraparound shades added to the mystery of our new fishing guide. It seemed to me that he was holding something in that wanted to come out. I thought, *Maybe I'm reading too much into this guy*, but he began to fascinate me.

After the first day we continued to catch a lot of fish. It was more than successful by any standards. There were not only large quantities of fish but several trophy pike as well. Murdock did a great job of putting us on the fish. He was an excellent fishing guide but remained quite reserved, to say the least.

That first evening it was cool and crisp, so Zack and I stoked up the woodburning stove in the cabin, making a comfortable night in the Canadian far north.

Early the next day Zack and I woke up early and went up to the main lodge, where they were serving a huge all-you-could-eat breakfast: bacon, eggs, pancakes, coffee, sausage, and oatmeal along with toast and jelly. This was a breakfast made for hearty lumberjacks. While all the fishermen were eating, the manager gave us a report on what had been caught, the location, and with what lures the previous day. I continued to be impressed with the professionalism of this lodge. After eating our fill, we went back to the cabin. No sooner had we shut the door than we heard knocking. I yelled, "Come on in." The door opened, and in walked Murdock.

"You boys ready to go fishing?"

"You bet! Let's go."

I was impressed with Murdock's on-the-dot punctuality, which is an issue with some fishing guides. He was right on time to the minute. He had probably been waiting just outside, looking at his watch to knock on the door at the exact minute we had agreed on.

Just like the previous day, we walked down to the dock and jumped into the boat. Again Murdock turned his ball cap backward and dawned his wraparound dark shades, and we were off. After about twenty minutes, we motored into a large, shallow bay. At the far end of the bay, we saw a female moose and her calf wade out of the water. Murdock silently pointed skyward at a bald eagle soaring above. There was certainly a lot of wildlife around. This lake was in a remote area away from civilization except for the state-of-the-art lodge.

Looking down at the water, I could see large shadows of big pike lying motionless like big logs on the sandy bottom. I had seen this before in big pike when I was young while fishing in the Churchill River. Murdock suggested that we switch lures to a top-water type. We cast out our "spooks," a lure that takes the appearance of a large, wounded minnow on the surface of the water. Sure enough, this new lure triggered strike after strike. It was a thrill to see these large predatory fish dart up from the shallow, sandy bottom, inhale the lures in their gaping mouths filled with teeth, and then dive for the bottom. A big northern pike flew into the air, breaking the surface. As it came down it slapped the water, making a loud sound that reverberated like an echo. Its broad tailfin created a genuinely exciting sporting show.

Murdock again remained reserved and professional despite the exciting fishing. He didn't speak unless he was spoken to and was matter of fact and expressionless. He was doing an excellent job as a guide, and as a cook, I had never had better.

Later that afternoon, as we were fishing not twenty yards from the shore, I could see bushes moving and hear twigs and small branches snapping. By the sound and movement of the nearly eight-foot high bushes, I could tell there was something quite large hidden from view. I thought a moose might eventually show itself. I stopped the retrieve of my lure and focused my attention on the commotion in the bush. Suddenly a large male black bear emerged from the bushes. It was a shock, to say the least.

We stopped fishing for a while to observe this unusual sight. The bear saw us and clearly knew we were there. He looked right at us. After staring at us for several minutes, he began swatting the ground with his huge paws and growling. He was tearing up pieces of dirt and sod in an aggressive display of anger. He then stared at us and began to rock between his front and back legs. He made a chomping sound with his teeth with his head raised in the air.

I looked at Murdock and said, "What's with this bear?"

"This bear is angry that we're in his territory. It's extremely rare for a bear to do this; even mean ones don't do this. When bears rock back and forth on their legs and bite in the air with their teeth, it signifies extreme agitation and aggression. He wants to kill us if he could get at us. We're lucky we're in this boat instead of on land. We would have a real problem if we were."

"We're in the lake on a boat. Does he consider the lake his territory?"

"I guess so. I've seen a lot of bears, but never anything like this. Most bears, even big males, will leave quickly when there is any sign of man. They usually are quite timid unless provoked, startled, or protecting cubs or a valued food source," Murdock said.

I wondered if the bear had rabies and was out of his mind. Murdock said he had never encountered a rabid animal before or heard of rabies in this region, but he said it was possible based on the crazy actions of this bear.

The bear continued to swipe at bushes with his huge paws and tear up sod as long as we were there. He was not going away. He paced back and forth along the shoreline, making heavy growling and huffing sounds. We began to yell at him and wave our arms in the air. But the more we yelled and moved our arms, the more agitated he seemed to become. He even rose up on two legs and began swatting the tops of bushes close to the lakeshore. The constant harassment of the bear, even though he was on land, and we were in no immediate danger, became unnerving. It was creepy to have this bear constantly growling at us from just a few yards away while we were busy fishing.

We decided to move out of the bear's territory, so we motored around the other side of the peninsula until the bear was out of our sight. We were temporarily relieved from the annoying crazy beast. While we were casting our lures toward the bank, the bear again emerged from the bushes. We were on the other side of the peninsula from where we had first encountered him and were shocked that he had followed us. The bear stopped and again glared at us menacingly. He gave a loud snort and a growl. He was stalking us! He was going out of his way to harass us.

I looked at Murdock and said, "Have you ever seen anything like this before?"

"No, he's a real bad boy. I think he is mentally unhinged."

The bear never left. We tried to ignore him as we fished while he continued to display his aggressive behavior on the bank. He wanted us gone now!

When Murdock suggested that we find another fishing spot, we agreed. So Murdock turned the boat around and motored out of the bay into the main lake. We called this place "Bad Bear Bay."

On our way back to the lodge, we spied something large swimming in the middle of the lake. I pointed and asked Murdock, "Do you see that?"

He exuberantly replied, "Moose!" This was the most emotion that Murdock had shown yet.

Without any further discussion he opened the throttle and headed for the moose, which was swimming across the large body of water. I was not sure what his intention was, but I imagined it was just plain curiosity. We motored next to the large bull moose with its huge, broad antlers standing erect out of the water with multiple points, almost like masts on a sailing ship. It was an arm's length from the side of the boat. I could have touched its head if I had wanted to. I had heard a story about Theodore Roosevelt jumping on a moose's back while it was crossing a lake when presented with a similar situation. I never knew whether the story was fiction, but it seemed to fit Teddy's character. I knew it was feasible, but I certainly wasn't going to be a Teddy Roosevelt and jump on the moose.

I turned toward Murdock and said, "Do you want me to jump on its back?" He finally cracked a smile. Both he and I knew I wasn't going to do it, but the crazy thought was certainly humorous. Murdock showed a new side of his hidden personality, being amused at the sense of absurdity.

"Teddy Roosevelt rode a moose once like this in the middle of a lake," I said.

"Well, he was the president of the United States with armed guards, and you're not. He was also a bit crazy. Maybe Andrew Jackson might have done something like that. You know he shot a guy in a duel once. He was a real badass. I think the most likely person to ride a moose in the middle of a lake would have been Ernest Hemingway." I turned to look at Murdock and smiled in acknowledgment. He was still expressionless, staring straight ahead.

I turned back around to look at the moose flexing its enormous muscles swimming away, startled at this revelation that an Indigenous fishing guide in northern Canada would have any idea who Teddy Roosevelt, Andrew Jackson, or for that matter Ernest Hemingway were, let alone their peculiar personalities. This implied an unusual depth of general knowledge and education, not only of American history but of literature. I was intrigued to find out more about our enigmatic, fierce-looking fishing guide.

The remainder of the day brought excellent fishing. Murdock remained silent despite the continued banter between Zack and me. He reminded me of the old saying "Still waters run deep." It crossed my mind that he might be hiding deep-seated anger, or for that matter depression. Or maybe he was just a quiet guy. However, I felt that something more complex was going on with Murdock, and it intrigued me.

The next day in the early afternoon we again caught a whole stringer of large walleye. We pulled up onto another sandy beach about a mile across the lake from "Bad Bear Bay." There we set up a shore lunch, cooking the freshly caught fish along with the other fixings. It again was superb.

Murdock was silent as usual and ate alone. After finishing the meal, he began to clean up. Zack and I were sitting on the beach, looking out at the pristine lake and drinking coffee. The sand of the beach was warm and felt good in contrast to the mildly cool air temperature. We were enjoying nature's luxury, relaxing while our thoughts drifted far away into the spaciousness of the lake.

Suddenly Murdock abruptly stood straight up and looked toward the bush in a serious and urgent manner. He motioned with his hands for us to be silent. Neither Zack nor I heard or saw anything out of the ordinary. We sat there and looked at each other quizzically while Murdock remained transfixed like a silent statue, peering into the dense forest. We had no idea what was going on. We were relying on our guide's knowledge of the wilderness for further instructions.

In a barely audible urgent whisper, he told us to pack up the boat, now!

I whispered, "What's going on?"

Murdock didn't answer. He kept intently peering into the bush. He motioned with his hands to get busy packing and get in the boat. We followed his commands, putting all the cooking equipment into the boat. Murdock had already poured the spent cooking grease into the sand. Zack and I got into the boat and intently watched as Murdock slowly and carefully walked toward the bush. We still didn't see or hear anything. At the edge of the underbrush, he stopped. He was standing silent and motionless, staring into the bush, transfixed. For several minutes, which seemed like hours, he stood frozen in his position of intense awareness.

Then he abruptly about-faced and bolted toward the boat. I have rarely seen such quick movements, even from a professional athlete. He ran like an antelope in Africa being chased by a lion. I'm sure he could have set some type of Olympic record for a fifty-yard dash if they had such an event. We heard a loud commotion from the bush behind

Murdock. Bushes were rustling, branches cracking, and leaves being loudly crushed.

A large bear suddenly emerged from the underbrush, galloping rapidly right behind him. The bear was seriously intent on getting Murdock. This was no half-hearted feigned attack, no attempt to simply move Murdock out of its territory. The bear was bolting after Murdock as fast as he could run and was rapidly gaining on our guide. We could tell this was the same large male bear we had encountered the previous day. Seeing this dangerous animal so close and rapidly advancing struck dread into our hearts. There was no protective lake between us now. I thought of jumping into the water if it came too close.

What if this bear got Murdock? What would I do then? I quickly looked around for any weapons. The only thing I could see was the

large frying pan we had cooked the fish in. Maybe I could throw it at the animal if it caught Murdock. However, I knew this would only distract him for a moment. Murdock leaped into the boat. With lightning-like speed, he started the motor and drove away from the shore.

The bear immediately veered off from the chase toward where we had dumped the cooking grease into the sand. Fifty yards away, Murdock stopped the boat, putting it in neutral. We all looked back at the bear as Murdock opened a small storage bin in the boat. He pulled out a pack of cigarettes and lit up, taking a deep, long drag. He looked at the bear and just shook his head in relief. He then looked at us and said, "Damn!" Murdock appeared obviously shaken as he puffed his cigarette.

"I didn't think you smoked, Murdock."

"I don't. These belong to a friend of mine who left them in the boat the other day. I don't think he'll mind if I borrow one after being chased by a crazy bear."

Zack and I started to laugh. We saw the bear digging in the sand where the cooking grease had been dumped. The bear was swallowing large lumps of the grease-soaked sand! I couldn't imagine how he was going to digest this. Murdock said, "Bears have an extraordinarily strong intestinal tract. They can eat just about anything." After three big drags on the cigarette, Murdock pitched the unused remainder into the lake. "I've never been chased by a bear before. That bear was serious! That was crazy." The bear had scared the wits out of us all.

Zack said, "I hope the sand gives that bear a bad bellyache."

This lunch site was on the opposite side of the lake from "Bad Bear Bay," where we had seen the bear the day before. Bears have an extraordinary sense of smell, and he had probably picked up the scent of the lunch from across the lake, which was over a mile. Bears are noted to be excellent swimmers. Still, he must have been very hungry and incredibly determined to swim across the lake from such a distance to our present lunch site.

Murdock had sensed the bear's presence long before Zack or I saw it. It has been my experience that Indigenous people who live all their lives in the bush have a heightened sense of the natural world around them, far beyond the abilities of outsiders from urban environments. I was grateful for Murdock's awareness because without him, the bear would have been on us without any notice.

While finishing out the day fishing, I thanked Murdock for his alertness regarding the bear. Zack said, "Yeah, you probably saved our hides from that crazy bear." Murdock simply shook his head affirmatively without expression, still wearing his backward ball cap and wraparound shades.

The next day, while Murdock was driving the boat to our next fishing location, I couldn't help but notice that he had a slight bend and scar at the apex of his nose. This was a classic sign of an old boxing injury. "Hey, Murdock, did you used to box?"

"Oh, yeah, you must have noticed my nose, eh?" he said, still without any facial expression.

I replied, "I had the same injury when I was a kid but got it fixed on the spot since my dad was a doctor."

"Yeah, I used to box for my high school team and for a private club as well. It's a popular sport where I come from. We had boxing matches with other towns, both on and off the reserve. Yeah, I did fairly well, I was the regional provincial champion in northern Manitoba for my weight division."

"What was your favorite go-to knockout punch?"

"A left hook."

"Oh, so you were a good counterpuncher." I knew from my history of boxing that the best time to throw an effective left hook is when your opponent throws a right cross punch and misses, which exposes him to a devastating left hook to the side of the head or to the body.

"Yeah, how did you know? Did you use to box?"

"Yeah, a long, long, ago," I said, smiling and bringing both fists in front of my face.

Murdock cracked a big smile and said, "All right!" I felt Murdock was starting to loosen up a bit.

We seemed to have touched on a common experience that was unique. Win or lose, it takes courage to get into a boxing ring, in front of a lot of people, and fight another guy. To be successful in boxing requires intense training and commitment to the sport. It also requires a competitive personality. We gained a mutual respect that was not verbalized but sensed between us.

"I was mainly a wrestler; however, I boxed a lot as well when I was a young man. All the men in my family were boxers," I said.

Murdock nodded in acknowledgment as his smile quickly vanished.

That evening we were served a large prime-rib dinner and banana-cream pie for dessert. There were the usual white tablecloths on each table. The chef came out and inquired at each table how the food was. This was like a high-end restaurant in an idyllic North Woods setting! I still had a hard time believing it. It was almost surreal having been chased by a bad bear earlier in the day and then having fine dining at a four-star restaurant in the evening. This was certainly not something I was used to; however, I was not about to complain about the luxury.

The next day was cloudy with intermittent rain showers. We put on our rain gear and decided to fish for lake trout. Lake trout thrive in cold temperatures, which are in deep water, frequently in the middle of the lake and farthest from shore. This was a large lake, and the distance from shore at times could be considerable.

We caught a few nice lake trout, but not the volume or size we were hoping for. We were slowly trolling our deep running lures when Zack asked, "Why does my fishing line make noise? It's vibrating like a violin string."

Murdock and I inspected Zack's monofilament fishing line, and sure enough, it was humming like a stringed instrument. Some unknown force was causing it to vibrate and make a sound. We didn't know what to make of this unusual phenomenon. None of us had ever seen anything like it before. Murdock even took off his wraparound shades to closely inspect the unusual vibration of the fishing line.

Then my line started to vibrate, making a low sound like Zack's. We all looked at each other quizzically. I had the sensation of the fine hair on my arms standing up. My exposed skin felt like it was being poked by tiny needles. I looked at Murdock and noticed that he was rubbing his arms and was obviously experiencing the same sensation. I then felt a subtle increased tingling sensation on my skin, especially over my head and neck. Murdock had taken his hat off and was scratching his head.

Zack said, "Have we just entered the twilight zone?"

I repositioned my body and touched the side of the aluminum boat. I received a minute but definite electric shock. I quickly drew my hand away. I looked at Murdock, who was rapidly removing his hand from the motor, having received the same shock that I had experienced. We were all silent, just looking at each other. None of us knew what was going on. Maybe Zack was right. Maybe we had entered the twilight zone!

On the horizon we suddenly saw a bolt of lightning in the distance. Murdock yelled, "Get your lines in now!" Murdock opened the throttle, and we began speeding away. We all immediately came to the same conclusion about the cause of the unusual physical phenomenon

as soon as we saw the lightning. Static electricity was steadily building around us. We were in imminent danger of being struck by lightning!

My thoughts quickly went to a good friend of mine who had been
killed by lightning in high school while sitting under a tree during a
vacation. In the burn unit as a surgical resident, I had treated light-
ning-strike injuries on those who had survived. These types of injuries were severe, leaving large portions of the body burned as well as
cardiac damage with arrythmias that could be permanent—that is,
if you were lucky enough survive after a lightning strike, which was
uncommon.

Murdock was grimacing while being continually shocked by the
electrical force as he held on to the throttle of the outboard engine.
He had no choice but to endure the painful electric current constantly
shocking him. I again touched the side of the aluminum boat, and the
electric shock was much greater now. I jerked my hand away from the
side of the boat.

Murdock knew we had to get out of the vicinity fast or risk being
struck by lightning. We all knew the strike could occur at any time, depending on the buildup of electric charge in the atmosphere around the
aluminum boat. His face was contorted, and his teeth were clenched.
He never said a word, all the while being shocked by electricity from
the throttle. His mind was focused on keeping his hand on the throttle
and propelling the boat away from the electric charge and to the nearest
land as quickly as possible. We were truly in fear for our lives, expecting
to be hit by millions of volts of electricity at any moment. I closed my
eyes and said a quick prayer to save us all. We saw several more bolts of
lightning in the distance, making us even more anxious.

After ten minutes, which seemed like ten hours, the electrical shocks
and the other electrical phenomena stopped. We all sighed in relief at

being out of imminent danger. Murdock switched hands on the throttle and shook his now free hand.

We arrived at the dock below the fishing lodge unscathed and grateful to be alive. I said to Murdock, "You did a great job today, my friend. I knew you had to take it and fight through the pain to get us out of there."

Murdock just smiled and said, "I've never seen anything like that. I've heard of lightning strikes in boats before, but it's extremely rare. I didn't want to be one of those rare incidents people talk about."

Later that evening during "happy hour," before dinner, I talked to the manager of the lodge. I told him what a great job Murdock had done saving us from an aggressive bear and then avoiding a lightning strike. Plus, he was guiding us to a lot of great fishing, not to mention his skills as a shore lunch cook.

The manager said, "Murdock is one of our best and most reliable guides. He's also good at fixing boat motors when we need a mechanic. He saves us a lot of money on repairs. The other guides seem to look up to Murdock as a leader. He's a spokesman if any of the fellows need something. Sometimes they're a little hesitant to ask for things themselves. Murdock's father is one of the tribal leaders on their reserve. Some people say that Murdock may fill that leadership position one day. Murdock's entire family are good and respected people."

The manager went on, "I know Murdock got into some trouble in Winnipeg last year. I'm not sure exactly what happened, but I think he might have done some jail time. However, I find that hard to imagine. Sometimes it's best to ignore rumors about people who you know are good." I was impressed with the manager's last comment, which I thought exhibited great wisdom.

"Thanks for the feedback on Murdock," the manager continued. "We always like to hear from our guests about how our guides are doing or if there's anything we can improve on to enhance your stay with us. Oh, and by the way, we'll plan on sending out a hunting party for that crazy bear. We can't have something like that running around endangering our guests. I'm sure our boys will find that bear and be done with him." Again, I was impressed with the manager's professionalism and courtesy.

The next day I told Murdock that I had told the lodge manager what a great job he was doing. "I believe that a job well done should always be acknowledged." Murdock's eyes opened wide as he looked at me with surprise. I could tell that Murdock appreciated the comment to his boss.

During the day of fishing Murdock was more talkative. He seemed to be loosening up. He now made eye contact more frequently and smiled more. Overall, he appeared to be enjoying our company. He even began kidding Zack. He pointed at Zack and said jokingly, "Hey, Bigfoot."

Zack turned and replied, "Yes, Murdock," with his usual big smile. This, of course, was not the first time he had been called "Bigfoot." For the remainder of the trip, many of the other fishing guides would wave at Zack and say, "Hey, Bigfoot" in a lighthearted manner. Zack, being his happy and gregarious self, struck up friendships with the local guides and other fishermen. The name "Bigfoot" stuck, and he was affectionately called this throughout the trip.

Murdock continued to intrigue me. There was something beneath the surface that was different than any fishing guide I had worked with before. It seemed that he had a deep need for something that was unfulfilled. I recognized that feeling since I had initially been rejected from medical school twice, despite being well qualified, before finally being accepted. This was something I wanted more than anything in the world. During this time, I felt my life was in limbo. At the time I was discouraged and disheartened. I sensed something like that in Murdock. Although Murdock was an excellent fishing guide, in fact one of the best I'd ever had, I had the feeling he wanted something more in life. I remained curious about this unique and mysterious young Cree guide.

We caught a lot of big pike that morning and then a stringer of walleye within thirty minutes just before our shore lunch. It again truly amazed me that we could catch so many walleye at will in such a short period. We again prepared our shore lunch. This time Murdock sat beside us on a large log overlooking the lake. We ate another fresh walleye dinner with all the side dishes together. Murdock previously had eaten in silence and apart from Zack and me. It felt good to all eat together, having a good conversation with a few laughs. It seemed that we were now friends. There was a definite change in Murdock's demeanor, and Zack and I enjoyed his company.

In his usual congenial way, Zack asked Murdock, "So, Murdock, what was the craziest guest you ever had to guide?"

"Oh, that's easy. Crazy Charlie!

"It's always a bad sign when someone shows up at eight in the morning to go fishing and is so drunk he can barely walk. We did very little fishing that day. Crazy Charlie kept drinking from a bottle of whiskey he brought. Since he wasn't going to fish, I was going to catch shore lunch. I did the fishing, and he did the drinking. He even started taking his fishing lures out of his tackle box and throwing the lures into the lake while he was rolling around in the boat laughing. I'm not sure what he was laughing about or why he was throwing his expensive lures into the lake. During the shore lunch he told me that he was recently divorced and was angry at his former wife. He said that she really took him to the cleaners and made his life a living hell. He showed me some X-rated photos of her and called her all sorts of terrible names. I guess he came on the fishing trip to let off some steam and frustrations. As it turned out, he had a little too much steam and frustration. I realize some men when they go on a fishing vacation, they may have a little too much to drink when they usually are not that way at home. However, crazy Charlie was far beyond that.

"Later when Charlie was back at the lodge, still drunk, he got bored and took a long walk in the bush. He got lost for several hours. Just when we were going to organize a search party, he strolled back into camp. He asked me what's up with all the mangy-looking big dogs around here. They were following him while he was lost in the bush. I told him there are no dogs up here! He was being followed by a wolf pack. Wolves can sense weakened or impaired animals and usually quickly take advantage of them. He was lucky to survive without being torn to pieces and eaten.

"One time at three in the morning he wandered through the guides' cabin area, screaming and yelling my name to go fishing. He woke the whole camp up. I guess when he got sleepy from the whiskey, he started doing crack cocaine, making him act even more crazy. In the dining room he threw his plate across the room because he didn't like what he got. He then got into a scuffle with one of the other guests. He caused such a continued disturbance that the management kicked him out of the lodge and sent him back to Winnipeg on a special plane, which he had to pay for. I'll bet that cost him a pretty penny."

Zack and I started laughing at the crazy Charlie story. We were laughing so hard that we had to stop fishing for a while. It was the first time I'd seen Murdock with a wide smile while reliving that experience.

Later the fishing had slowed down when Murdock asked if we would like to see an old, abandoned cabin close to where we were. I said sure, it would be interesting. We pulled up to the shoreline and roped the boat to a nearby tree. We followed Murdock into the bush for about thirty yards. There lay an old cabin that had clearly not been used for some time. The roof had caved in, and there were still utensils of everyday living scattered around the area. Although the cabin had deteriorated significantly, I could tell that it had been poorly built to begin with. The roof was improperly made. The logs making up the walls were not cut so they would lock together as they should. There was no packing between the logs for insulation. The cabin was small by any standard and consisted of only one small room. Some poorly made rustic furniture was scattered about.

Murdock told us the story behind the abandoned ramshackle cabin. "Two White guys from the city came up here to live on a subsistence level. They wanted to get closer to nature, I guess. I think they had an unrealistic idea of what living in the wilderness was about. They came in by canoe during the warm months and then got snowed in during the winter. They ran out of supplies and couldn't get out. They were inexperienced and didn't know what they were doing. You can tell by the way they built their cabin they weren't going to make it through the winter, and they didn't. Their bodies were found the next spring. It wasn't clear if they starved or froze to death, or maybe a little of both. Nature can be dangerous in more ways than one if you don't know what you're doing. The wilderness is no joke. It can be beautiful and bountiful, or it can be cruel and unforgiving. Those guys learned the hard way.

"I kind of know how they felt in an opposite way. I tried to make it in the White world in Winnipeg. It was just as foreign and different to me as the bush was to those two dead guys. Just like those two, I was totally unprepared and didn't know what I was doing. I was determined to get off the reserve and make a life for myself in the White world, but it didn't work out. I felt alone and out of place."

"So why did you go to Winnipeg?"

"I got a job doing construction with some other guys. The job paid well. We all had an apartment. I was hoping to get enough money to go to college and get a business and management degree. My parents are good people and were supportive, especially my father. They encouraged me, but they didn't have the funds to send me to school. I knew I didn't want to be a guide or a boat mechanic on the reserve. I wanted more, and I thought I had the ability, since I did well in school. After a year or two I would have enough money for college. Things were going well with my job. However, socially I felt overwhelmed and out of place in the big city. The people in the city acted so differently than what I was used to on the reserve. I didn't know how to take them. Although I speak English, it seemed we spoke a different language.

"One Friday night after work, my roommates had a big party. There were lots of people there I didn't know. There was a lot of drinking, and people started getting rowdy. Eventually several fights broke out, and the police were called. I tried to leave, but someone grabbed me from behind. I quickly turned and hit the guy. It was a reflex you learn if you're a trained boxer. I did it without thinking. Sort of an instinct of self-preservation, I guess. It happened so quickly, almost in a flash. When I got a look at the guy on the floor, I realized I had just decked a policeman. The next thing you know, I was handcuffed and taken to jail. I didn't have enough money to pay the fine, so I spent a few weeks in jail. I lost my job, and my dreams of a better life seemed to implode in front of me. When I returned to the reserve, I felt that I had let my family down. Other people in town would talk, saying, 'He thought he was better than the rest of us, and now he's back after failing in his high-minded dreams in the White world.' Most people on the reserve have no ambition, and I think they were jealous of me trying to better myself. My parents were still supportive and understanding. They told me not to listen to people, that things would work out. However, I was still unhappy. I felt that I had dishonored my family. At present, my life feels like I've hit a brick wall with no clear direction. It has affected everything, including my social life.

"So now it seems that I'm not in either world, Indian or White, half in and half out, in both worlds."

Murdock looked down at the ground and picked up a rock. He threw the rock into the bush and stared pensively into the distance.

After a moment of silence, I responded to his story.

"I'm still optimistic for you. How many times have you lost the first round of a boxing match and gone on to win the fight? I'll bet quite a few. For that matter, how many times have you been knocked down and then got up to win? No, my friend, I think this is just the first round for you. A determined spirit usually cannot be contained. Many times, you may wind up in a different position than what you were wishing for but nonetheless successful and happy in the end, even though it was not your initial goal. As the lyrics to an old song go, 'You can't always get what you want, but if you try sometimes, well you might find, you get what you need!' I have found this frequently to be true. One door may shut on you, but another door may open for a new opportunity. The key is to keep optimistic and not get down on yourself. If there is persistence and a will to improve yourself, success is usually inevitable. If you truly wish to be successful in the White world, I'll give you some tips that I think will make a big difference. I believe you're made of the right stuff if you truly wish to proceed with this."

"Oh, yes! I would appreciate any suggestions that you may have that would be helpful to me."

"OK, then, let's talk after dinner tonight."

"OK, I'll see you then."

Murdock seemed interested and open to advice. He didn't avoid eye contact with me anymore, and he was more outspoken. He didn't seem so mysterious or threatening.

We walked away from the rundown cabin and jumped into the boat. After a few more hours of fishing, we motored back to the lodge.

By the time we got back to the lodge, I wasn't feeling well. I had an upset stomach and slight nausea. I was going to skip dinner. Zack went to dinner without me. After an hour or two had passed, I heard a knock on the door. I yelled, "Come in." In walked Murdock with a teapot.

"Zack told me you weren't feeling well."

"Probably a minor virus. I'll likely be OK tomorrow."

"I brought some Labrador tea. It's a Cree Indian remedy for stomachache and nausea. It has worked for me in the past. The Labrador plant is all over the place up here, and the leaves when boiled in a tea are medicinal. I picked some leaves and had the cook brew some for the tea. Here, have some."

He poured the steaming tea into a mug he had brought and handed it to me. It tasted good, almost like a hint of peppermint in chamomile tea. After a few big sips, my stomach felt better right away.

"Thanks, Murdock, I appreciate that. Let's go out on the porch."

We walked out and sat down on some chairs overlooking a beautiful view of the lake. The lake was calm and smooth as glass. The sun was slowly setting, but it would never become completely dark because we were so far north.

I took another big sip of tea. I felt even better.

"I'll give you some advice about living in and succeeding in the White world, if you really want this. You know that there can be a lot of pressure and stress involved in this world. It's a world apart from the reserve."

He reassured me that it was his goal to live his life away from the reserve and away from subsistence living. He respected his family and his culture, but he was determined to leave. However, he didn't understand what he had to do since it wasn't second nature to him, as it was for me or Zack, who took our way of life for granted.

"I don't want to hunt, fish, and trap for a living or fix boat motors. You can see how unhappy I am doing this. I am open to any suggestions because right now it appears that I have no real direction. You have a great intuitive sense that many people do not possess. The Cree people call it 'seeing beyond the hill,' meaning you can see things that can't be seen visually and are not readily apparent. It's a great gift that you have. Some people are more intuitive than others."

"As a doctor, it's part of my job to see things that aren't readily apparent. Sometimes people can't express things well enough for me to easily help them, so I must find other ways. The way I see it, you have a great opportunity right in front of you. This lodge is a big-time corporation. I'll bet the owner of this lodge probably owns other lodges elsewhere. This place is run with true professionalism. I suspect that this lodge alone brings in close to two million dollars per year."

Murdock looked at me with mild shock.

"I never thought of it that way, but I'll bet you're right."

I said, "Look at all they do. It's much more than a fishing lodge. It's run like a high-end hotel with a restaurant, bar, tackle shop, housecleaning, and airport runway. All of this is coordinated from a front office in Winnipeg. I suspect the manager of this place probably makes close to a six-figure salary, if not more.

"Since you're already involved in this business, I think it would be a good place to start to work your way up to the next level. You already know the business on one end, and you have a good relationship with the rank-and-file workers here—the guides, cooks, and housecleaners. The manager of this place personally likes you a lot."

"He does?"

"Yes, I talked to him. He said you were one of the best guides here, and you are from a well-respected family. He also said you are well respected by the other employees. I think now is the time to make your move for a higher position and hopefully a higher salary. I would get to know the manager of the lodge on a more personal basis and then see if he could show you how the business is run."

I continued, "Now, you need to know how to play the part. You must show upper management that you are ready for a move into their realm. Appearance and demeanor are the first step."

"How do you mean?"

"First, you need to be confident without being physically intimidating. Having a rough-and-tough appearance may be respected in the bush but not in the corporate world. I would suggest shaving the mustache, getting a good haircut, and wearing just a little better clothes than the standard employee here. Not fancy, but just a cut above the others. That is, when you're around the lodge and not out fishing.

"Second, improve your demeanor, especially to upper management. Don't be afraid to talk with them about any improvements that you think need to be made. Look them in the eyes, and don't look around the room or at the floor. This would imply lack of confidence. Also make sure you have a strong grip when shaking hands. Again, this implies confidence, which they respect. You need to smile a lot. You must remember, you need to sell yourself to gain higher employment and thereby a higher salary."

"But that's so phony to smile at someone when you don't know them or don't mean it!"

"I know. I understand what you're saying, but smiling disarms people and makes them more receptive to you. I know this is strange in your culture, but I assure you, a good easy smile is a key to success. Think of it as a hunting tactic or a tool to get what you want. Unless you are alone in the bush, everyone must be a salesman in one form or another. Even the president of the United States must sell Congress or the voting public on his way of thinking. The manager of this lodge must sell fishermen to come to this lodge over other lodges, and you have to sell yourself to advance your career. You must be patient, however. As they say, Rome was not built in a day. It takes time and patience to build an empire. One other thing that is important: don't appear too ambitious, even though you are."

"That sounds so hypocritical, like living a lie."

"I know, but you will just have to trust me on this. I know what I'm talking about. Along with a smile, it would be a good idea to learn how to make what we call small talk. Again, I know this will not be easy for you."

"What do you mean, 'small talk'?"

"It means making a quick conversation with someone, not about anything substantial but just keeping communication open. One easy way to start is to ask the person about their family or how their day is going, even though you couldn't care less. By keeping this small bit of communication open, it makes it easier to establish a more significant relationship with the person later. You might consider it a type of diplomacy."

"Again, this seems so phony. It's not what I'm used to. These are not the ways of my people. However, I believe you."

"Look at it like learning a foreign language."

I continued, "The third thing I would suggest would be to get some type of training or preparation that would be applicable to your job. If you could somehow get a college degree, this would give credibility to your advancement in the business world. However, you'll probably use very little of what you learn in school. Ninety-five percent of learning to run a business is on-the-job training. A diploma from a school is pretty much a rite of passage. It's like learning the language of business as opposed to practical application."

"That seems like a waste of time and money."

"I know; there are a lot of things in this world that don't make sense but are nonetheless important stepping stones to your goals.

"The fourth and last thing I would suggest would be to pick your friends wisely. Don't hang around guys who want to party all the time or who are dummies. Find friends who have high aspirations like you. Friends can have a great effect on you and can have an influence on your destiny. If you hang around chickens, you'll learn to fight and squabble for scraps in the dirt. If you associate with eagles, you'll learn to soar high in the sky."

Murdock liked that analogy and nodded in understanding.

It seemed with all the talking and the Labrador tea, my stomach ailment had resolved. We both stood up and shook hands. His handshake was much different this time than the first time we'd met.

He looked me straight in the eyes, smiled, and gave a firm handshake. I couldn't help but give a big smile and chuckle as I said, "Good job, my friend." Murdock then gave a bigger smile in acknowledgment.

The next day was our last day at the lodge. Murdock escorted me and Zack to the airplane and shook our hands. He looked at me and said, "Thanks for everything. I'm so glad we met."

"I am too, Murdock. I may possibly see you next year, eh?"

"I certainly hope so."

Murdock waved goodbye as we boarded the large charter propeller plane. The plane taxied down the dirt airstrip and roared off into the sky. After we lifted off, the plane circled around the lodge. I could see Murdock on the side of the airstrip, still waving.

The next year I scheduled another fishing trip at Big Rock Lodge.

When I got there, I inquired about Murdock as a fishing guide. One of the unique things about this lodge was that you could request a certain guide again if you had worked with him before. The fishing guide whom I talked to explained that Murdock was no longer a fishing guide; he was an assistant manager of the lodge! I thought that was a big step in a short period. As we walked into the main lodge for a briefing by the manager, I was greeted by a young man whom I barely recognized. Murdock!

He was clean-shaven and had a stylish haircut with a small amount of gel. He wore khaki slacks and a pressed white shirt. He greeted me with a big, confident smile and a firm handshake. He looked great!

As Murdock was shaking my hand, he said, "I saw the guest register and saw your name. I'm thrilled you made it back. I don't do any guiding anymore, but I talked with the manager, and he said I could make an exception for you on this trip. I told him it would mean a lot to me."

I replied, "That's excellent. I'm looking forward to working with you again. We'll have great fun. Hopefully no bears or lightning this time, eh?"

Murdock laughed.

I said, "This time you take your fishing rod, and I'll help with the shore lunch."

He looked at me quizzically.

I said, "Look at it this way: you deserve a vacation with a friend. We'll both have some fun for a job well done."

"I would like that. Believe it or not, I don't get to go fishing very often anymore. Oh, by the way, I received a scholarship to the university in business administration. It'll take a while to earn my degree, but in the meantime, I've got a good job here."

"Wow! That's fantastic! Congratulations; you really move fast."

Murdock was extremely grateful for the advice and support I had given him over a year before at a low point in his life. I'm sure he would have done well despite my meeting him. However, sometimes some good advice and a little confidence builder at a low point in someone's life can speed the process up. The most important essential in Murdock's life was a stable and supportive family. Without this I don't think he would have done so well when life took a bad turn. Although Murdock and I came from dramatically different backgrounds, we nonetheless had many similar characteristics. We made a psychological and emotional connection, which made him more open to my suggestions.

Murdock seemed like a flower coming into bloom, becoming who he really was, a confident and ambitious young man with a future. This was a far cry from the unhappy, sullen man whom I had first met a year before. He was now obviously happy with his situation and going in a good direction. I think he'd just needed a little push toward the positive. I think he was now well planted in both worlds, White and Native.

I said jokingly, "Your future looks so bright you're going to need to wear your wraparound shades all the time!"

"Ha ha ha. You think so?"

"What do you say we go fishing?"

"Sounds good. I'll get ready."

We walked out of the expansive lodge, opening the heavy log doors to the outside. I put my arm around Murdock, looked at him, and said, "You have come far, my friend; you have come far. I'm proud of you!"

THE VEHICLE

When one tugs at a single thing in nature,
he finds it attached to the rest of the world.

UNKNOWN

M y good fishing buddy Dallas and I were waiting patiently on a dock for our fishing guide to show up. We were stand-ing in front of our tackle boxes, holding our fishing rods and staring out over the vast expanse of Great Slave Lake in northern Canada. We had been ready to go an hour before our scheduled date with our fishing guide. It was unusual for a fishing guide to be late. When you arrange to meet a fishing guide at a certain time, it's like one of the ten commandments. For that matter, one of the unwritten rules of any sportsman is that you will never be late for a fishing time. It's the eleventh commandment that wasn't written in stone. Fishermen show up on time no matter the temperature and whatever the weather! It was not only bad manners, but it was also a waste of time and money. The best fishing is usually in the early morning, and you're missing a potential trophy fish you traveled thousands of miles and spent a lot of money to get.

Both Dallas and I were starting to fume, with me being more on the irritated side. We had traveled for days and been on four separate airplanes to get here to the middle of nowhere. The lodge was quite small. There were only four other fishermen staying there, all of whom were already out fishing with their guides. We had been told that our guide was quite experienced and that he was the nephew of the owner of the lodge. If this guide didn't show up soon, the owner and manager of the lodge were going to get a real earful. This fishing lodge had the reputation of catching the largest northern pike in the world, and we were anxious to have at it. We had been anticipating and preparing for this trip for nearly a year. While Dallas and I were standing there waiting, I recalled the process we had gone through to get here.

I first learned about this fishing lodge when I picked up a fishing magazine at the supermarket with an article titled "Ten Best Places in the World for Giant Pike." On the cover of the magazine was a photo of an enormous northern pike being held by a fisherman with a broad grin. I wanted to be that man in the photo. Pike had been my favorite fish to catch since I was a young boy, so the magazine immediately struck my interest. I'd been hunting big pike nearly all my life. I leafed through the magazine to the pike section. Number one on the list was Thompson River Big Pike Lodge. There were a few photos of some of the largest pike I had ever seen. That was it—I was sold! The Thompson River is a small river running into the south side of Great Slave Lake. The lodge was located on the river just at the entrance to the lake.

I later talked with Ben, who managed the lodge. He was a retired Chicago policeman who was a straightforward and no-nonsense type of guy, but friendly. He handled all the business of the lodge, including advertising, booking guests, and setting up booths at sports shows in various cities to promote the lodge. The lodge was on tribal land and was owned by one of the tribal leaders of the Dene tribe, which is a branch of the Cree. The owner had a hands-off approach to the day-to-day management and left running the place up to Ben. It was the only fishing lodge on the south side of the lake, which is an enormous area. The closest human habitation was Fort Resolution, approximately 150 miles away. The main access was by boat or plane since there were only rudimentary roads to this small settlement of two hundred people on the Dene tribal reserve.

I knew little to nothing about Great Slave Lake except that it was a large lake in the Canadian far north. It is the second-largest lake in Canada, the tenth-largest lake in the world, and deepest lake in North America at over two thousand feet deep. It covers over ten thousand square miles and is roughly the size of Belgium. It was named after the "Slavey" Indian tribe, a branch of the Dene, nothing to do with a person in bondage. The lake is in an intermediate area between the arctic tundra and the boreal forest of Canada.

The lake is frozen from November until mid-May. I had booked the trip for the first week in June. I knew that the large pike would be in the shallows warming themselves after a long winter and that they would be especially hungry.

In early May I began checking the weather conditions of the area around the Thompson River and Great Slave Lake on a daily basis. It was still frequently below zero with occasional blizzard conditions. I started to be concerned by mid-May, when I noted that the area was experiencing record cold temperatures and the lake was still frozen solid. I made several phone calls to Ben. He reassured me that the ice would be out by our scheduled trip. By the end of May the temperature was above freezing, but not by much. I couldn't imagine how the many feet of ice on this huge lake could melt within two weeks. Nevertheless, we were going to proceed with our scheduled flights.

Dallas and I began the multiple flights taking us from Kansas City to Detroit to Calgary, Alberta, and then to Yellowknife, Northwest Territories. It was a long day, to say the least. The whole time I was wondering whether the lake was still frozen. Would our long trip end as a scenic weeklong tour of the small town of Yellowknife?

When we finally reached Yellowknife and climbed down the ladder from the small propeller plane to the tarmac, it felt like walking into a freezer. We had just come from eighty-degree weather to low forties with a good wind making it feel much colder. We walked into the small airport terminal and saw a large stuffed polar bear next to the baggage claim. I thought, *How appropriate.* We had now entered another world: the frozen north.

Dallas and I watched as the luggage and fishing equipment slowly moved in front of us. I picked up my equipment and luggage. Dallas got his fishing equipment but was missing the rest of his luggage, which contained his clothing and miscellaneous gear for a week of life in a cabin. We waited patiently at the baggage claim without any sign of Dallas's missing luggage. After spending many frustrating hours with the baggage-claim people, we were told that his luggage was still in Calgary and had not been transferred to our plane. All Dallas had to wear was what he had on. The airline wasn't sure when they could get Dallas's baggage since the bags were with another airline. The only airline that came to Yellowknife was a small, obscure one that serviced remote towns of the Canadian far north.

We were scheduled to fly out early the next morning by pontoon plane to the lodge on the opposite side of the lake. We left the airport exasperated, with more questions than answers. Fortunately, Dallas is an even-tempered fellow. His view of the situation was, it was what it was, and we'd have to deal with it. I would gladly have shared what I had with him, but he was three times my size.

After we checked into the hotel, our next plan was to buy a new wardrobe for Dallas. This included rain gear as well as everything else.

As Dallas and I were waiting for a cab outside the downtown hotel, an Indigenous man and two Indigenous women staggered up to us, put their arms around us, and asked if we wanted to party. They had obviously been partying all day and were barely able to stand. Two of them held on to my shoulders, and the other was holding on to Dallas for support so they wouldn't fall. They kept babbling incoherently. They seemed to be saying that they loved everyone, and "It's all good." They seemed harmless but quite impaired. We peeled their arms off us and pointed them in the direction we wanted them to go away. We said thanks but no thanks, and they stumbled along down the street. We then noticed large numbers of people staggering around, milling about on the street corners and in parking lots and alleys. All told around fifty mostly Indigenous people, appearing disheveled and somehow impaired. This was an afternoon on a weekday. There was no holiday or festival that would explain the drunk people. Dallas and I found it quite odd that so many obviously drunk people were wandering around for no clear reason.

The cab rolled up, and we jumped in. We had been given the locations of several clothing stores by the hotel concierge. As we were driving to the clothing shops, we asked the cab driver about all the drunk people.

He said, "Oh, yes, they are always here. It's a real tragedy. Usually it is alcohol, but they will get messed up any way they can—pills, drugs, or whatever. Sometimes they sniff glue or paint."

I knew the latter two could cause permanent liver and brain damage, even if used only a few times. The cab driver went on to say that these people didn't work and were on government welfare.

I thought, *It's such a tragedy that so many native peoples have fallen into such a downward cultural spiral.*

Our cab driver was a tall, thin Black man. His skin was so dark that it was almost a deep purple. He had a thick foreign accent. I asked him, "Are you from Sudan?"

"Oh, yes! Do you know Sudan?" He turned around and flashed a wide smile.

I asked a further question: "Are you a Dinka?"

"Oh, my, yes, yes! How do you know this? How do you know about my tribe?" His exquisitely bright white teeth beamed through his broad smile.

"I know several Dinkas where I live." I had also studied the Dinka tribe in a college cultural anthropology course.

Our cab driver was overjoyed that someone knew about him and his people. He couldn't contain his white-toothed smile. The Dinka are from southern Sudan in Africa. They are some of the tallest people on earth. Their skin has some of the darkest pigment on earth. They have an unmistakable appearance. They are a proud people whose entire society revolves around cattle. The more cattle you have, the wealthier you are. A coming-of-age ceremony for young men involves leaping up onto the cattle's backs and stepping over the backs of the entire herd without falling. The Dinkas are generally Christian and have been severely persecuted by the Arab Muslim northern part of Sudan. Many have been driven out of their homes, and many have been killed because of their religious faith. The cab driver's name was Abdu. It seemed ironic that he had come from one of the more isolated areas in the world, clear across the globe, to another of the world's most out-of-the-way and isolated areas. One climate was terribly hot and dry, while the other was cold and damp for most of the year.

"Were you able to walk across the backs of your cattle?"

"Oh, my, yes. I didn't fall once. My parents were so proud of me!"

"How did you wind up in Yellowknife?"

"My brother and I were able to get out of a refugee camp since we were driven from our homeland. Many of our friends and family have been killed for being Christians. If you were caught, you might have a chance to live, maybe, if you converted to Islam, but we would never do that. Even then, they would probably kill you anyway or sell you into slavery. My brother and I walked in the bush many days to Kenya, where there was a refugee camp for my people. During our long trek we had to frequently hide from the people who attacked our village. We also had to avoid lions, hyenas, and poisonous snakes, which were present and always a danger. Many times, we slept at night in trees to avoid the dangerous nocturnal animals. We frequently could hear the animals below in the bush stalking us. After many days we reached Kenya and relative safety. The refugee camp there was not a good place to live with no future. At least we had food, water, and shelter. Living there was better than the alternative—death. I have many relatives still in the refugee camp. I pray that someday we will be reunited. Canada was the first country to accept us. We heard there were all sorts of different jobs available in Yellowknife because it's so cold and dark in the winter that no one wants to come here. We planned to eventually go to the United States. Everyone is rich there, and it is so much warmer."

"Warmer, yes, but not everyone is rich."

"Yes, but you have the opportunity to become rich if you try hard."

"That may be."

I told him of Dallas's clothing dilemma. We made a definite connection with Abdu. I got the feeling he wanted to spend as much time as possible with us. He was so excited that someone knew about him and where he had come from. He and his brother were probably the only Black people in town, and certainly the only people from Sudan.

"Oh, yes, I will help you on your quest to find clothing! This can be a difficult thing because there are not many large people here. Most of the native people are quite short, and Yellowknife is a small town." He knew English well. His use of language was quite proper and formal, but with a distinct African accent.

Abdu took us from one place to the next. He made the hunt for Dallas's clothes an adventure that he took personal responsibility for. There weren't any clothes to fit Dallas in any of the stores. Abdu voluntarily went off the meter and waited for us while we shopped. It was a huge benefit to us not to have to call another cab whenever we left a store, especially since cabs in the small town of Yellowknife were at a premium.

While we were being driven from one clothing store to the next, Abdu gave us a grand tour of Yellowknife. Just past downtown by the lake, he pointed out an enormous dark rock, as large as several buildings. He said, "This rock is one of the oldest rocks in the world. It is estimated to be nearly two billion years old, nearly as old as the earth itself." He then pointed toward the lake. I noticed that the lake was still frozen, and my heart dropped, although I didn't say anything. I thought, *We're going to get to know Yellowknife really well over the next week since we'll be unable to fish.* I was planning to call the manager of the lodge as soon as we got back to the hotel to discuss how to proceed with the lake still being frozen.

While pointing toward the lake, Abdu focused our attention on twenty or so houseboats. They were all brightly colored and appeared quite unusual. He told us that the people who lived on the houseboats were not required to pay property taxes. However, they were required to supply their own power and other utilities, which could be a lot of work for most of them. Most of the people living there were free-spirit types. He told us that there was a reality television program about several of the people who lived there, but he had not seen it. The most difficult time for those people was when the lake was just starting to freeze and when it started to thaw out. That's when the ice is too thin to walk on and too thick to drive a boat through. During those times they were pretty much trapped.

Abdu pointed out the provincial capital and a beautiful museum next to it. He said that a lot of people lived in Yellowknife because of government work. There were also many people there because of the nearby diamond and gold mines. He and his brother had planned to work in the mines, but the mines had recently cut back production and were not hiring new people.

Abdu said, "It worked out well because I like driving a cab. I get to meet new people all the time. However, none are as friendly as you two. If not for our church, we would be miserable here. The church has brought us into contact with many wonderful people. It is all in God's hands, so I'm not going to worry."

I replied, "Yes, it is in God's hands."

After striking out at five different clothing stores because they didn't have large enough sizes, Dallas and I were frustrated. Abdu seemed to sense our dejection when we walked out of the last clothing store.

He said, "Do not despair! We will eventually succeed in your quest to find large clothes. I assure you of this. I think I know of one last place that may have something. It is called Canadian Tire Company."

It was like a Western Auto store in America. Who would have thought that they would sell men's apparel in the same place that sold tires and automotive parts? In the far back of this warehouse-type store, beyond the multiple rows and stacks of tires, was a small clothing area. Dallas found a heavy insulated blue plaid flannel shirt in his size after using a ladder to get the shirt from the top shelf. However, there was nothing else in his size.

Dallas said, "Well, this is going to have to do."

As we walked out of the store, Abdu was overjoyed. "Oh, my, what a beautiful blue plaid shirt!" He gently felt the shirt with his hands and said, "It is quite thick. I think this beautiful shirt will serve you well against the cold. Now you need something to break the wind and protect you from the rain."

Abdu took us back into the store, and we purchased a carton of extra-large durable yellow plastic trash bags and some heavy rope. Abdu made a hole in the end of a trash bag for Dallas's head and on the sides for his arms. He then tied a rope around his waist to make it fit closer to his body. This self-made piece of apparel served as an effective windbreaker and raincoat.

Dallas had proven to be always optimistic and upbeat even under less-than-ideal circumstances. We had made a terrible situation into a totally acceptable situation, thanks to our new friend from Africa.

Abdu took us back to the hotel. We thanked him for his help and gave him a big tip. He was quite grateful. He got out of the cab and shook our hands with great exuberance as well as slightly bowing his head, which is the custom of his Dinka tribe.

He said, "I am so happy that our quest for clothing was successful. Please call me anytime if you need transportation. It has been wonderful getting to know both of you! I pray to God that it his will that we meet again."

He then gave me his card to call if needed. I gave him my card and told him to look me up if he or his brother were ever in Kansas City. I told him that I would be happy to be a sponsor for him if he decided to come to the United States.

He looked at my card and said, "Oh, you are a doctor! Thank you, Dr. Graham, for your offer of such generosity and kindness. I do hope I see you again, God willing."

"Yes, God willing," I said.

We thanked him and said goodbye. Abdu left me with such a good impression that I truly wished we would meet again. His story was so compelling, and he seemed to be such a devout Christian that one could only wish to help the young man from Africa.

As we walked into the hotel lobby, we saw two middle-aged men sitting on a couch with their fishing-rod cases and tackle boxes by their feet. They were arranging their many lures. They looked pretty glum. I asked them, "Are you guys planning to go fishing?"

"We were, but we just found out that the lake around our lodge is completely frozen. I guess it's been the latest ice-out in years because of the extra-long winter they had here." They were going to a different lodge than Dallas and me; theirs was on the north side of the lake, the opposite side from where we were going. I asked them, "What are you going to do?"

"We don't know; we're trying to figure that out now."

I couldn't help noticing their fishing lures in their open tackle boxes along with their rods. The fishing rods they had brought were nearly twice as large as mine. Their lures were quite large, some nearly a foot long, with various wild shapes, colors, and flashy feathers. I immediately felt that my equipment was inadequate. I wondered, *Do I know what I'm getting into? Do these guys know something I don't? Are these monster pike here going to break my rods and destroy my lures, or will they look at my lures, laugh, turn up their noses, and swim away?*

The open tackle boxes looked like a circus was going on within them. With so many crazy colors along with small propellers, tiny glass eyes on some lures, and large, bright feathers sticking out, I expected to hear music coming out of the huge tackle boxes, followed by a parade of bizarre, multicolored creatures. I had never seen lures like this sold at my Midwest tackle shop. It seemed they were prepared for large saltwater fish like marlin or barracuda. All their equipment was top-of-the-line.

I said, "I've never seen anything like these lures before."

"That's because they're not in production yet. We test these lures for the manufacturing company. They pay for our trip. Not a bad deal, eh? Some of the lures we made ourselves during the winter months and presented them to the company. We have to go through the process of getting a patent, which is a lot easier if you do it several times. If the lures are accepted for production, we get a cut on the sales. This is our new job since we retired from our corporate business jobs."

"So how do you guys like your new life away from the corporate world?"

They both looked at me, smiled, and said simultaneously, "We love it!"

As fishermen, it seemed that these guys really knew what they were doing. I said, "It looks like you fellows are going after some big fish."

"Have you ever been here before?"

"No."

"Just you wait. You'll see—that is, if the ice is out where you're going. We come up here every year. You will catch more and bigger pike than you ever have before."

Both men were retired and in their late fifties. They were tall and appeared athletic. They were in excellent physical condition despite their age. They reminded me of two older Viking warriors. I think they had both found their true calling outside the corporate boardroom. To put that much creativity into making lures along with marketing them requires a significant amount of ingenuity and follow-through for your business objectives and is not a simple thing to do. These were highly intelligent guys who now knew exactly what they wanted in life and were out to get it while having fun along the way.

Their main objective in life now was to catch big musky and northern pike. Their whole summer was filled with a schedule of various fishing trips. I don't think money was too great of a problem for these two guys. They had probably done well in their previous jobs and were now picking up their retirement checks along with their new business venture. We talked for some time, trading fish stories and showing each other photos of big fish on our cell phones. They gave me some tips on great places to go fishing in the future.

These two friendly guys were from Wisconsin and were primarily musky fishermen. Musky fishermen are a breed apart from other freshwater fishermen, I have noted. This type of fishing requires big, heavy equipment and a lot of patience. You don't frequently catch muskies, but when you do, they are large, and you can be in the fight of your life.

Musky and pike look quite similar and are frequently found in the same waters. Muskies tend to grow a little larger on average and are found only in northern waters flowing south, as in southern Canada and the northern United States. Muskies are much more difficult to catch than pike. They tend to be more hesitant to attack lures than pike, and northern pike are much more common than muskies. Although there were no muskies in Great Slave Lake, the pike here were equal in size to big muskies farther south. In the winter, the two men went to Florida to fish saltwater. They had become professional sport fishermen. I thought, *Wow, what a lifestyle!* However, right now they were none too happy because of the ice.

Across the room on one of the several sofas were a middle-aged man and a woman in her late twenties or early thirties. They had on matching red down coats with several official-looking patches. They were both smiling and seemed bored just sitting in the lobby like the rest of us. I had time to spare, so I walked over and asked if they were scheduled to go fishing as well. They said they were part of a Canadian government scientific team on their way to a research station on the tundra in the high arctic. One was studying the permafrost and changes in animal populations. The other was studying ionizing radiation in the arctic and associated atmospheric changes.

"It sounds interesting. How long are you going to be there?"

"For about three months."

"Doesn't it get a little boring being shut in for so long?"

"It's not too bad. It makes you focus on your work. You can evaluate the data you collect and write the scientific paper in a fairly short period because you don't have the distractions you would have if you were back in civilization. In fact, we expect to generate several papers. We certainly get a lot of reading done. The research station has a gym and a pretty good mess hall and lounge. The food is not bad. It's like summer camp for scientists."

"Do you get to go outdoors?"

"Oh, yes, but up there on the tundra, there's not much to see. It's pretty bleak. It's nearly completely flat from horizon to horizon. The Arctic Ocean is nearby, but it's no Riviera. The mosquitoes are the worst on the planet. Even strong insect repellent is only a minor deterrent."

"It sounds lonely."

"We have satellite phone communication with our families, so it's manageable. The amount of data that we collect keeps us busy evaluating it for the entire year. We both feel we're doing beneficial things for humanity. That's what keeps us going."

"I would certainly agree with that. More power to you."

"If it wasn't so interesting, this line of work would probably drive you crazy."

The two scientists were quite pleasant and had easy smiles. They seemed to enjoy talking about their work and their lives. We went on talking in more detail for some time. I had just enough general knowledge to follow what they were talking about. I had had some experience in cancer research and cell biology as a young man earning a master's degree prior to medical school. During that time, I had published a few scientific papers. I could appreciate the amount of work and effort that is required in scientific research for so little gain. There certainly is not a lot of money in being a scientist. However, where would humankind be without them? We would still be living in caves and working with stone tools. To be a scientific researcher requires an altruistic attitude for the greater good of humanity, as opposed to personal monetary gain. I have great respect for people who can do this.

As we were talking about scientific research in the arctic, we heard a commotion by the front door. Three disheveled, partly drunk Indigenous men were serving themselves coffee from the complimentary coffee machine for guests of the hotel. They were obviously not guests and had come in off the street. Each of the men wanted to have the first cup of coffee, and they were pushing each other around, jockeying for position to get the first cup.

The hotel employees at the front desk noticed the men but decided to just let it go. The commotion and hassle of kicking them out probably weren't worth it unless things became much worse. Each of the men put a handful of sugar cubes into his coffee cup. They reminded me of the Three Stooges fighting for position in the coffee line. After several cups, they wandered toward the door. As they ambled out, one of the men knocked the hat off another from behind for pushing ahead of him for the coffee. He picked his hat up off the floor and then retaliated by pushing the other guy out the door. There were a few curse words as they slowly shuffled out of the hotel and back onto the street. The people at the front desk just ignored them and went about their business. For all I knew, this could have been a daily ritual.

I couldn't help but reflect on all the different people I had come into contact with today in the Canadian subarctic, from research scientists to drunk Indigenous people to an African refugee to professional sport fishermen. Who would have thought there would be so much diversity in the middle of nowhere? It was interesting, to say the least.

I called Ben, the manager of our lodge, and he again reassured me that the ice was out at our destination lodge. I told him, "Great, we will see you tomorrow!" Dallas and I spent the evening at a sports bar having hamburgers and Molson beer and watching the Stanley Cup ice hockey championship on television. The only sport that is even thought about in that part of Canada is ice hockey. There was nothing in this bar to make you think that there was any other sport in the world.

The next day we boarded a pontoon plane in a small bay that was free of ice. We took off and got a good look at Yellowknife from the air. It looked like it had grown out of a large rock. The entire lake as far as we could see was frozen solid. There was complete white all the way to the horizon. Even after an hour's flight over the huge lake, we saw nothing but ice. I thought, *This pontoon plane is going to have a tough time landing on ice if the lake doesn't change quickly.*

Eventually we saw a river entering the main lake that was ice-free. We saw the lodge on the river next to the lake. There was also a small strip of open water along the lakeshore. The pilot banked over the lodge and landed in the river. The landing was smooth, and we taxied up to the dock adjacent to the lodge. We unloaded our gear and brought it up to our plywood cabin. There was a woodburning stove inside. We met Ben and the cooks in the main lounge and dining hall. It was cozy and comfortable but definitely no-frills. There was one large dining table for the fishermen. There was a nice porch looking out over the lake from the combined dining and main lodge area.

It was still early in the morning, so we got our fishing gear together and went down to the dock to meet our guide to go fishing. The sun was out in a clear blue sky. It was fairly cold, with a slight breeze making it feel much colder. I put on a winter coat. I was a little concerned about Dallas with his makeshift apparel. He appeared perfectly comfortable, but I knew Dallas was not one to complain.

All the other fishermen got into their boats with their guides and took off fishing. Dallas and I stood there on the dock, waiting for our guide to show up and fuming. I was thinking about all the things I was going to say to our tardy guide and his employer.

Suddenly we saw an aluminum fishing boat with an outboard motor ripping at top speed around the point where the river went into the lake. I thought, *This must be our guide.* It seemed we had waited much longer than we really had since we were anxious to get out on the lake and go fishing. The guide was about twenty minutes late, still not good but not atrocious.

The boat was still going at top speed as it bore in close to the dock. I asked Dallas, "Is this guy going to ram the dock?" Dallas and I stepped back off the dock, anticipating a crash. Just when I thought there would be a collision, the boat was turned 180 degrees right in front of the dock and came to a stop perfectly placed within inches to the side of the dock. It was crazy but incredibly skillful.

A young Indigenous man stood up and said, "Are you Bruce and Dallas?" We told him that we were.

With a big smile he said, "What do you say we go fishing? Sorry I'm late, I wanted to make sure this motor was in tip-top condition for you guys. I changed the spark plugs and the oil, and now it runs great. I think we've got the fastest boat here! By the way, my name is Johnny Two Knives." We all shook hands.

Johnny could not have been older than eighteen years old. I noticed that he had all sorts of car-racing patches all over his coat, such as Ferrari, Lemans, Ford Mustang, Lamborghini, Daytona, and Pennzoil, among other insignias. For a heavily used seventeen-foot aluminum fishing craft, his boat was nearly spotless. I noticed that it had a wax coating as well. I thought, *Who in the world would wax and tidy up an old aluminum fishing boat?* I had the feeling that we were jumping into this young lad's hot rod.

As we sat down in the boat, Johnny said, "Are you after big pike today!"

"Yes, we are."

"Well, I know where to find them."

With that said, he gunned the engine full throttle, jerking Dallas and me back before we regained our seated position. The boat peeled away from the dock and rounded the corner of the point, entering the main lake. Johnny took the corner into the lake like a race-car driver at the Indianapolis 500 rounding a curve. This made a huge wake away from us. Dallas and I held on to the sides of the boat with both hands to stabilize ourselves. It felt like a ride at an amusement park. We looked at one another and both smiled. I got the impression that Johnny liked speed. The sharp turns and speed of the boat might have upset many people. However, instead of being alarmed, Dallas and I thought it was quite fun. Johnny's sunny disposition, big smile, and out-of-the-ordinary boating skills had made us forget about being angry and frustrated. Within minutes our moods had completely changed, like the boat making a 180-degree turn. My bad attitude had been disarmed within minutes. He obviously knew how to drive the boat well and took pride in his abilities, not only in driving the boat but in its maintenance.

As we were cruising along at maximum speed, I looked back at Johnny. He was in a slouched position with one shoulder much lower than the other opposite the throttle of the engine. He had one leg stretched out. He had the appearance of a pimp in the inner city driving his Cadillac around the "hood."

"You look comfortable."

Johnny gave a big smile and said, "I am." Dallas and I started to laugh.

"Hey, Johnny, how long have you been driving a boat like this?"

"Since I was six years old. I grew up on the lake at Fort Resolution. There aren't that many cars there, or for that matter many roads. There is one gravel road to Yellowknife, but it takes around eight to ten hours to get there since it's on the opposite side of the lake. We used boats a lot when I was growing up. My uncle was able to bring all the materials to build the lodge by barge from Fort Resolution to here. My dad and uncle used to take us fishing here ever since I can remember, even before the lodge was built by my uncle.

"You're a doctor, right?" he asked.

"Yes."

"We could sure use your help on the 'res'. There are a little over two hundred and fifty people there. We have a health clinic and a nurse practitioner sent by the government. She's real nice, but she's no doctor. If something is bad, we have to call Yellowknife for an airplane as an ambulance." Our conversation with Johnny involved yelling over the high-pitched loud roar of the motor at maximum speed and rpm.

I turned around and looked forward over the great expanse of this huge lake. I felt the cold wind blowing in my face. The rocky shoreline was covered with gray-green moss, orange lichen, and large blue-green spruce trees. Because of the vast area of frozen lake, the whole environment smelled like dry ice, as if we had entered a giant freezer. There was no sign of civilization anywhere. We were certainly back in the North Woods. It felt good to be on an adventure in the bush again.

It had been over a year since I had been in the wilderness on a fishing trip. This was something I looked forward to every year in either Canada or Alaska. These yearly expeditions seemed to recharge something in me. It wasn't the fishing itself, although that was the goal and gave a purpose to the adventure into the wild. In recent years fishing had seemed more like a vehicle to propel my spirit where it wanted to be. I could shed the trappings of a more fast-paced, high-pressure "civilized" life, filled with artificial drama, and revert to my more primitive self, devoid of pretense. Something that felt more natural. Basically, a sense of freedom.

I have often wondered if human beings were really made for our urban environment. Civilization has packed people together with millions of others, living in an artificial asphalt, plastic, and concrete world. Humans evolved over countless thousands of years in small hunter-gatherer bands living in a hostile wilderness. I can't help but think that the feeling of freedom when I return to the wilderness is somehow related to a deeper instinct to go back to where we all began, to where humankind evolved, to unearth the ancient feelings we all have buried in our souls. In essence, where humans were really meant to be.

I asked Johnny, "Is the ice going to present a problem with the fishing?" The day was clear and cold. There was a hundred-yard strip of open water between the shoreline and the sheet of ice on the frozen lake.

"Nope, not at all. All the areas where we'll be fishing are free of ice."

"Hey, Johnny, could we motor over to the edge of the ice just to take a closer look?"

"You got it, boss."

He turned the boat ninety degrees on a dime, running at maximum speed without slowing down, again creating a large wake. Dallas and I grabbed the sides of the boat to stabilize ourselves. Johnny obviously liked the sensation of sharp turns at high rates of speed in his hot-rod boat. It didn't bother me if it wasn't dangerous. Johnny abruptly cut the motor down to a slow troll as we approached the edge of the ice.

As we came closer to the edge of the massive sheet of ice that extended thousands of square miles, a strange sound permeated the entire area. Johnny stopped the motor. It was a sound like millions upon millions of tiny crystals hitting each other, making a high-pitched tinkling sound like thousands of miles of tiny wind chimes. The sound echoed off the large granite cliffs of the shoreline close by. The ice was not a solid sheet, nor was it slush, but what appeared to be billions of small crystals slowly undulating with small waves knocking them against one another to make the sound. The sound of the natural wind chimes surrounded the entire region, creating an almost sublime experience. We just sat there for a while, taking in the strange phenomenon. Even Johnny was impressed. Over the past fifteen minutes I had forgotten about being angry at Johnny for being late, and for the moment, I even forgot about fishing.

We all sat in the boat in silence for a while, taking in the sounds and the grand vista of the frozen lake that stretched as far as the eye could see.

Eventually Dallas said, "What do you say we go fishing?"

I replied, "Let's do it!"

With that, Johnny started the engine and rocketed off. Not more than ten minutes had passed when Johnny slowed the motor to a troll. We were close to the shore of the lake, less than fifteen yards away. The shoreline was a fifty-foot granite cliff extending into the depths of the lake below.

"Let's try this spot here for a while. There's often something big hanging around the base of these cliffs. There's usually not a lot of fish here, but the ones that are here can be real monsters."

Dallas and I were relaxed as we talked with Johnny. We cast our fishing lines out, trolling our lures behind the boat.

Johnny said, "One of these days I'd like to go to Los Angeles and get into movies or get into racing cars. That would be so cool!"

Before Dallas or I had a chance to laugh or respond in anyway, my lure was hit by something big. It bent my extra-heavy rod nearly in half. I initially thought my lure was snagged on a rock, but it started moving rapidly, going deeper and deeper. It was giving huge jerks on the line. Whatever it was, it was bending its body nearly in half and then swinging back the other way in a violent, jerking manner. What came to my mind was a gigantic mosquito larva vigorously bending and pumping its primitive body back and forth. I could tell this fish had a lot of weight to it. I kept the rod tip up in the air; however, with each bend the fish made, my rod would respond by jerking rapidly up and down. I had never fought a fish like this before.

Johnny said, "Oooooh, Bruce, you got something big!"

It seemed to have more power and strength than a pike, making longer runs without tiring. Big lake trout are very strong and powerful,

but they don't jerk and bend like what was on the end of my line. The way this fish struggled was unlike any fish I had ever caught. It was big, whatever it was.

My mind was totally focused on playing this fish. The line would scream out of my reel, and then I would slowly retrieve the line after the fish had completed its run. I didn't want to make any mistakes. I could tell that unless I played this fish perfectly, it would either break my line if I brought it in too quickly or throw the lure out of its mouth if my line was too loose. Either could happen in less than a second. I took my time and played it very carefully. I didn't want to lose this fish! I started to slowly bring the fish closer to the boat, but I still couldn't visualize it. The fish ran under the boat to the opposite side. I had to switch places with Dallas and go around the boat, following the fish. I looked down into the depths of the crystal-clear water. Now within eyesight, I could see a large silvery fish thrashing its entire body back and forth. It was amazing that it hadn't thrown the hook by now because of the violent and rapid movement. Because of its silvery color, I thought, *Oh, a lake trout! If it is, it's going to be a record.* This fish was nearly half the size of the boat! Slowly, slowly the fish began to tire, and I brought it up from the depths next to the boat. It was much too large for a net, so we used a fish cradle to land the large beast.

Johnny yelled, "It's a coney!"

"A what?"

"An inconnu, and a big one!"

"What's an inconnu?"

"It's like a big whitefish. They live in the deepest parts of the lake. Every spring just as the ice goes out, they come close to the shore to feed. They only stay for around a couple weeks and then they go back to the deep water, and you don't see them for the rest of the year."

I noticed that it had dorsal fins and a V-type tail fin. The anatomy of this fish showed that it was built for power and speed. The fish looked like something one might catch in the ocean rather than a freshwater lake.

Inconnu are found only in waters of the far north, lakes and rivers flowing into the Arctic Ocean or the Bearing Sea. They are bright silver with long, powerful bodies and look like tarpon except that their mouths are not as large and they are found only in freshwater. Like sharks, they must continually have water flowing through their gills. Thus, they must constantly swim. Because of this constant movement, they are very strong and muscular. This fish was fifty-seven inches long and over thirty-five pounds. This was the largest freshwater fish I had ever caught. After a quick photo we released it, and it swam away. I sat there in the boat, exhausted. Not only had fighting this giant fish for over thirty minutes taken it out of me physically, but I was mentally exhausted from the intense concentration of the fight. This was the first fish caught on the trip, within the first hour of fishing. I didn't know how I was going to top this.

After a brief rest we continued to slowly troll past the cliffs and then across a channel between the mainland and a large island. In the middle of the channel, I could see multiple dorsal fins breaking the water surface and then going down.

I asked Johnny, "Do you have dolphins in this lake?"

"No, a school of coneys are coming in." I had never seen such a sight in freshwater. It was like a school of porpoises.

Dallas and I caught several more inconnu. We were having a real time. Later we went to a large, shallow bay and caught numerous big northern pike and walleye. We caught over 120 fish that day. We released all of them except for some of the walleye that we took for lunch. I had never seen fishing quite like this. We caught several trophy pike as well as numbers of all sizes.

Throughout the week the fishing remained outstanding. Dallas's makeshift coat and rain gear were holding up well despite the cold temperatures and occasional rain. He did look a little odd with a big yellow trash bag over his body tied around his waist with a rope, but who cared? The odd apparel was doing its job.

Johnny knew every spot to catch fish. He knew the topography of this area by heart. He had been fishing this area since he was a child. He even knew where to find all the unseen submerged boulders that fish might be lurking behind. Johnny was doing his job as a fishing guide well.

Johnny was talkative and lively. He asked us if we had seen various movies. His taste was the action-adventure movies that any eighteen-year-old young man would like. He loved all the kung fu movies with Bruce Lee and Jackie Chan. As he talked, he made a few karate moves with his hands.

"Those guys are so fast you can barely see their hands move. Then before you know it, they hit you on the side of the head with their foot! They're so powerful they can put holes in walls and break cinder blocks with their hands. Those guys are intense!"

We all started to laugh. He also loved the Transformers and, of course, James Bond. It seemed that he knew every scene and what was said in each of these movies by heart. He must have seen them hundreds of times.

"How do you know about all this movie stuff?"

"We got satellite TV about five years ago. We don't get many stations, and we get only a few movies, but that's life on the 'res' you know. There's not much there."

The next day we walked down to the dock, where Johnny was waiting for us in his boat. I asked how he was doing this morning as we walked toward the boat to go fishing.

He replied, "Yo, dude, it's all cool today." At the same time, he made a gang sign with his hand.

"Johnny, would you cut that stupid stuff out? You don't even know what that means. You've been watching too much TV."

He broke out laughing and replied, "I thought that would get a rise out of you." We then jumped into the boat for another day of fishing.

As we rapidly cruised away to our next fishing spot, I asked Johnny, "What do you like to do better, hunting or fishing?"

"I like to fish, but hunting is my favorite by far. In the late fall the tribe goes on a communal caribou hunt thirty miles to the north. We all travel by snowmobile, like an army. We shoot as many caribou as we can to sustain the whole village over the winter. It's a blast! My people have been doing this for thousands of years. Instead of dog sleds in the past, we now have snow machines thank goodness. It's kind of like a rite of passage into adulthood for a young man to go on your first caribou hunt. In the spring we all go by boat to the shallows of the lake and hunt ducks and geese on their migration from the south to their nesting grounds farther north on the tundra, close to the Arctic Ocean. We sometimes can bag nearly a thousand birds during the hunt. Between those two hunts, everyone at Fort Resolution has enough meat to last them all year. Individually people go hunt moose as well. Some people still run trap lines, but that's less and less common these days because of government assistance. Plus, the cash return on furs these days is much reduced because of commercial fur farms. It's just not worth it to be a trapper anymore. It's kind of sad to see a way of life dwindle away like it has. For hundreds of years trapping was the mainstay of tribal life for men, but not anymore. The government just pays us a monthly stipend. Basically, paying people not to work. This has led to a lot of problems for the people living on the res."

Dallas and I had witnessed the amount of alcoholism and unemployment in Yellowknife among the Indigenous population. This has been a controversial subject for the Canadian government, paying people living on the reserves a salary whether they work or not, thus creating an incentive not to work, followed by drug and alcohol abuse with all the associated social problems.

There has also been much criticism of Indigenous people hunting as many animals as they wish on First Nations land regardless of whether the animal is in season elsewhere. Conservation and hunting organizations are concerned that the populations of certain species may be depleted. I was told by some sportsmen that the "Native people shoot anything that moves at any time." The Canadian government has given the First Nations people nearly total autonomy over their reserve land. It makes sense since it was their land to begin with. For the present, wildlife management on the reserves is up to the council of each tribe.

As the days went by, the lake ice completely melted. This happened much more rapidly than I would have thought possible. Every day was great fishing. It was refreshing to be around Johnny with his youthful exuberance and good humor. We were all having a great time.

One day we ventured farther away from the lodge than we had previously to fish for lake trout. It took us nearly an hour to get to this spot. After catching a few nice-sized trout, we returned to the lodge. Johnny abruptly stood up in the boat while he held his hand on the throttle. He stopped his usual chatter and stared at the shoreline. He said, "There's something funny over there. I'm not sure what it is. Do you guys want to look?"

"Sure, let's check it out."

We motored toward the rocky shoreline and beached the boat. We secured the boat and jumped out. We followed Johnny up onto a rocky ledge for about twenty yards. Johnny looked down and said, "Oh, man, this is so bad!"

Dallas and I walked up to him and noticed a dead black bear. Its abdomen had been cut open and its genitals removed. Neither the skin nor the meat had been removed. Johnny knelt, took his hat in hand, and inspected the carcass in more detail.

"This is a relatively fresh kill. The bear was killed for its gallbladder and its genitals. They sell them on the black market and send them to Asia. Some Asian people think that the gallbladder of a bear has a medicinal effect on certain ailments. They also think that eating the genitals of a bear will help with their sex life. This is a real shame, and it's illegal. Unfortunately, there's a lot of money in it. Man, this is so messed up!"

"Do you know who may have done this?"

"I have my suspicions. I know one guy who is suspected of these things, but no one has ever caught him red-handed. He always seems to have a lot of money but never has a steady job. In every town there's always one bad apple. I know that he was visited by the RCMP [Royal Canadian Mounted Police] in the past, but they couldn't pin anything on him to prosecute. This is so bad to kill a bear like this for stupidity, no matter how much money they give you. It's just so wrong!"

We looked around the area for a while. There was evidence of an abandoned campsite where the poacher had stayed. We found a tree stand with empty shell casings around where he had laid an ambush for the bear.

Johnny said, "The only place the poacher could have come from would be Fort Resolution, where I live. That's the only human habitation for hundreds of miles. The poacher wanted to go as far away as possible from the 'res' because it's illegal and poorly thought of by the people as well. It's just a shame. It would be different if the poacher needed the meat or fur, but to kill a bear for this purpose is bad. The older people of the tribe revere the bear as a kindred spirit to the tribe.

It's thought that to kill a bear without a good purpose will bring bad luck. Unfortunately, there are probably many areas where the poacher has ambush sites for bears, and what we see here is just the tip of the iceberg, so to speak. The bush is such an immense area without any people. Anyone can easily get away with poaching."

We went back to the boat to return to the lodge. How Johnny knew there was something amiss in the bush as we were passing by remained a mystery to me. The Indigenous people of this area can detect any slight disturbance in nature that White people have no idea of.

I could tell this event with the bear had affected Johnny. He became silent and expressionless, which was a dramatic departure from his usual bubbly, highly charged personality. Although Johnny had immersed himself in White culture via TV, he had clearly retained some of his basic tribal values regarding the bear.

Johnny said, "Asian superstition is big business around here. Thousands of people from Asia come here to Yellowknife to witness the aurora borealis every winter. Most of them are young couples from China, Taiwan, Japan, Korea, Singapore, among many other places. They believe that if conception of a child occurs under the northern lights, that it will result in a gifted child. I guess they never asked themselves why all of us Indian people are not all gifted, genius, wonderful people!"

I wasn't sure if this was just a myth or a rumor. I wouldn't think that people that believe in the medicinal benefits of bear internal organs may believe in special properties given off by the aurora borealis would be too far of a stretch. However I doubted the validity of Johnny's story. Either way, Johnny believed they did as well as some lodge owners.

Johnny continued, "All of the hotels and lodges around here are filled all winter. One lodge just up the river has either cabins or tepees available. The top of the tepee is open to the sky so people can see the northern lights above them. The way the tepee is marketed is that you'll get a higher dosage of the northern lights unencumbered by a ceiling or solid wall. No matter the 30-below temperatures. How they feel like doing it at those temperatures is beyond me. They do have a small campfire in the middle of the tepee. However, living in a tepee, no matter what the fire is like, is going to be really cold. One of my jobs in the winter is to keep a pile of wood stocked outside for them to use. Those people that rent a tepee are required to rent a cabin as well if things don't work out for them outside. Most will stay in the tepee for just a few hours and then retreat to the cabin when they get too cold.

"It's also my job to entertain these people when they're not indoors trying to make superbabies. None of them know any English, making it difficult to teach and show them things. I have all sorts of activities for them if they wish. We take hikes through the bush and along the lakeshore with snowshoes. I take them on rides through the bush and on the frozen lake with the snowmachine and sometimes a dog sled if they want.

"They're such spastics! They're always falling. They just aren't used to deep snow, and for the most part, they're not very strong. I think they don't live very active lifestyles at home and aren't used to a lot of physical activity. They don't follow instructions well because they don't understand English. It seems they're always getting themselves in trouble, and I bail them out. Don't get me wrong, I think these people are overall polite, nice people. They generally don't have big egos and aren't overly demanding. They're generally easy to work with. They take pictures of everything. They will frequently lose their cameras in the snow and then go nuts until we usually find them. It's hard to take photos with mittens on, you know. One guy wanted to take a picture of me with a feather in my hat like a 'real Indian.' Can you believe that? They're like infants in this country. These people know nothing!

"There are so many of these people that the streets of Yellowknife are crowded during the winter. It's big business for Yellowknife during this time. They bring in lots of tourist money for the town. I suspect that some of the poached bear organs are sold to these people during this time. This would cut out a middleman and give more money to the poacher. If not, the bear parts are easily shipped overseas."

What Johnny was telling me made sense. When I had searched the Internet for fishing lodges on Great Slave Lake, much of the lodge's advertising was not for fishing but for the northern lights in the winter. I thought it odd that "cheesy" pictures of hearts and little cupids with arrows were part of the sales ads. I noticed that the rates to stay there were double and sometimes triple those for the fishing lodge in the summer. These people obviously had a lot of money or were willing to pay a lot for the benefit they hoped to gain from their experience.

After our ten-day fishing adventure, we returned to Yellowknife airport, where Dallas picked up his luggage that had been left in Calgary. He had been without it for the entire trip. He picked up his bag and said, "Well, this was a big help!" He then threw his big yellow trash-bag windbreaker into the nearest trash bin.

"What, you don't want to keep your big yellow trash bag for a memory?"

We both had a big laugh and then boarded the plane. I thought of Abdu and our dilemma of trying to replace Dallas's lost gear. I hoped that I might see that polite, devout young man again. I thought the only thing that was holding him and his brother in Yellowknife was the relationship he had with his church.

As the plane took off and flew around Yellowknife, I noted that the ice was completely gone from the lake. I was amazed that it had melted completely within a week. My thoughts shifted to the two professional sport fishermen. I hoped they had been able to salvage something out of their fishing trip. My suspicion was that they had been able to get in at least half of their trip. I was grateful for the tips they had given me for other fishing spots to check out in the future.

When I looked over the large lake, I remembered Johnny and his youthful exuberance and positive attitude. His fun-loving personality couldn't help but rub off on you. Although he talked about going to Hollywood or driving race cars, I didn't think he would ever leave the area for long. He loved what he was doing too much. I suspected he would spend some time in a city, like Calgary or Winnipeg, for a while, like so many young Indigenous men. However, he liked the bush and his family too much to be gone very long. He had never been in a town larger than Yellowknife. A large urban city would be a big shock for him.

As we gained altitude, the vast, uninhabited forest dotted by thousands of lakes stretched as far as the eye could see. We had done so many things and met so many interesting people within just a ten-day period that it seemed like a year. The fishing had been fantastic, but when I thought about the trip in its entirety, the fishing itself was almost a sidelight to the overall adventure and the feeling of profound freedom. The trip was not just about fishing. When driving on a long road trip, it is fun to take a short, fast ride in a high-powered sports car periodically, but the adventure is the road trip itself. I looked on the fast sports car as catching the fish—exciting but fleeting. The greater adventure and meaning came from the trip itself, the feeling of freedom, of removing myself from the superficiality and pretentiousness of urban civilized living, of returning to my true self. This is what the wilderness brings to me. Fishing is the *vehicle* to get me to that place.

SEEING BEYOND
THE HILL

Solitary trees, if they grow at all, grow strong.
WINSTON CHURCHILL

A must-do for any freshwater sport fisherman, especially fly fishermen, is to fish for salmon and trout in Alaska. This had been on my "bucket list" nearly all my life. I had watched many thrilling videos of thousands of multicolored salmon swimming in masse up Alaskan rivers and streams in plain sight from the riverbank or a boat, with a resultant fish-catching extravaganza. Another big perk to fishing in Alaska is that many of the fishing lodges fillet, package, and freeze your catch to be sent back to your home vacuum packed. One could in theory have hundreds of pounds of delicious salmon fillets for months, if not years.

Salmon can grow quite large, depending on the species. Their strength and their fighting ability are renowned. They have all recently come from the ocean, where they are constantly swimming, making them powerful with tremendous stamina. Nature has prepared them for the challenges of swimming upstream against a strong current, jumping over waterfalls, and eluding predators such as bears, otters, and eagles to reach their spawning destination in shallow gravel-bottomed streams far from the mouth of the river from where they came.

The barriers to a trip to Alaska are many, not including the distance and expense just to get there. Fishing for salmon there is entirely different than fishing in the lower forty-eight. It's a big departure from just throwing a lure into the water and retrieving, as one does for bass or pike. It's even different than fly fishing for trout in the lower forty-eight. The fly-fishing equipment required in Alaska is much heavier and involves buying entirely new gear—new rods, reels, line, lures, waders, and other equipment, just to start.

I was finally going to make the trip with Edward, an old fishing friend who had made regular trips to Alaska for years. He invited me to go with a group of twelve other fisherman friends, so I grabbed at the chance of a lifetime. He would know the ropes: where to go and what to do. This would save a lot of time and effort for someone who was going in cold not knowing the area. It would also greatly improve my chances of a successful fishing trip to go with someone who'd had success in the past. After ten months of preparation, we were finally off to the Wajimi River on the Katmai Peninsula in southwest Alaska. The fishing lodge was about fifteen miles outside the tiny village of King Salmon, Alaska. There are no roads to King Salmon. Access to the outside world is limited to plane or boat. The town revolves mainly around tourism and sport fishing. There is a national park close to the area, but it does not get a lot of tourists because of its remote location and difficulty of access.

We landed in King Salmon, and the fishermen disembarked from the plane to the terminal to pick up their baggage and fishing gear. My gear was late coming from the plane. As I patiently waited for my luggage, Edward and the rest of the group hurriedly loaded into a van going to the lodge and unknowingly left me stranded, waiting for my luggage. Because of the remote location, cell phones were nonfunctional.

After my baggage finally arrived from the plane, I looked around the small airport terminal. It was entirely empty except for the airline employees at the desk. The airline personnel were not expecting any more flights that day. They were busy packing up and ready to lock the doors. I asked them how I could get to the lodge or what I could do. They just looked at me with unknowing blank stares and shook their heads. They had never heard of the lodge I was supposed to be at. I doubted that their primary job was with the airlines. The motley crew of young people all wore street clothes: plaid flannel shirts and dirty blue jeans. They looked like they wanted out as quickly as possible to go party. They certainly didn't give a hang about my predicament. I pulled my heavy gear outside the terminal as the airport was locked up and the employees fled the scene. Most of the crew jumped in the back of an old pickup truck and peeled out down the dirt road in front of the airport. The remainder were just milling around, waiting for someone to pick them up.

It was one of the hottest summer months on record in Alaska. It felt more like Arizona in the summer than Alaska. I sat there for around thirty minutes pondering my next move, hoping that my group had realized they were missing someone and return in short order.

Next door to the gravel airport parking lot was an official-looking place with an American and an Alaskan state flag outside. I dragged my heavy gear over to the building with the flagpole since I didn't trust my valuables to be left unattended, even if it was in the middle of nowhere Alaska. I have learned from experience that one can never underestimate human greed given an open opportunity, no matter the location. Plus, the airline employees didn't look like the most responsible crew I'd ever seen. I dragged my heavy gear into the small, official-looking

log building. I was not about to let my baggage out of my sight. I didn't
need one more disaster added to my current problem.

The building was an information and tourist center with a small
museum as well. The two elderly managers were extremely friendly.
However, none of the phones worked, and there was no cell-phone connection to the entire area. They obviously didn't get much business and
wanted to talk as much as possible to alleviate their own boredom. They
told me their entire life story and the entire history of King Salmon, as
well as Alaskan state history in general. Then they wanted to know all
about me and my life. They offered to drive me over to the lodge when
they got off work in five hours, even though they weren't quite sure
where it was. They were willing to drive around through the bush and
make a try. How that was going to work I had no idea.

After talking with them for over an hour, I pulled my gear outside
and sat down on my bags, frustrated. As I was sitting there in the heat,
bored and quite disgusted, I began to realize that my friends were not
coming anytime soon. I saw an older man trying to fix a flat tire on
his pickup truck in the gravel parking lot of the airport. The truck was
jacked up when he realized he didn't have a spare tire. I walked over to
see if I could be of assistance and to alleviate my boredom. He was a
nice guy. He told me he was from Michigan, and he spent his summers
in Alaska at a lodge. As luck would have it, the man was the owner
of the lodge where I was going to spend the week fishing. One of his
employees came, fixed the tire, and then drove us both to the lodge.
When I got to the lodge, nobody had realized I was missing after four
hours—even Edward. I doubted they would have noticed I was gone
after a week!

Everyone was preparing to go fishing. The lodge manager, who was
the owner's son, was assigning fishing guides to each two-man group.
There would be three people, including the guide, on each seven-

teen-foot aluminum boat. Unknown to me until now, Edward's son, who had recently graduated from high school, had been staying at the lodge for the past six weeks. He had hoped to become a fishing guide at the lodge for a permanent full-time job. However, things hadn't worked out for him. He was required to do a lot of work that he didn't relish doing, and he didn't have the social skills or maturity to fit in well with the lodge or the clients. He was planning to go back home with our group when we left. In the meantime, he had quit being a fishing guide and was going to spend the time fishing with his dad. Edward and his son would be in the same boat instead of me. They would have a fishing vacation together over the next week before both would leave for home.

With this change of events, I was left alone in a boat with a guide. That didn't bother me too much, but it's always nice to share your fishing adventures with a friend. Even though I was not in the greatest mood after being left for four hours at the airport, I was willing to roll with the new reality and not get upset. From my past experiences on many fishing trips, rarely does the trip go as planned. There's always some glitch to deal with, big or small. The bottom line was that this was my vacation. I rarely get time off work, and I was going to enjoy myself whatever the circumstance.

The manager of the lodge had to make some quick rearrangements because Edward's son was essentially quitting. He came up to me and said, "Bruce, you're going to be with our newest guide, Lavender."

I looked directly at him and said, "Lavender? What? A GIRL? Your *newest* guide?" I was shocked at the thought of some little girl in the middle of nowhere Alaska as my guide, and a rookie at that.

"Oh, you're going to love her. She is an excellent guide."

"Are you sure she knows what she's doing?"

"I would recommend her without any reservations. I guarantee that you'll be pleased."

"Is she willing to do all the hard work that requires a lot of strength that a standard guide does?"

"Lavender is as strong as most of the guys around here and is more than willing to get her hands dirty if need be."

"She's willing to clean and fillet the fish?"

"Sure, that's part of her job."

I took a deep breath, put my hands in my back pockets, and looked away with obvious irritation. It didn't seem I had a choice. I was highly skeptical. Lodge managers always say reassuring things about their worst guides. I had seen this before. I knew the consequences of a bad or inexperienced fishing guide. It could destroy your whole trip. I was now having a hard time not showing my displeasure.

As I was talking to the manager and looking out the front door of the lodge onto its large, expansive wooden deck, a tall, slim woman walked in, wearing aviator shades and a baseball cap. She came up to me purposefully and removed her shades. She was drop-dead gorgeous! She had a big smile with perfect white teeth. It was the genuine smile of someone who was comfortable with herself.

She said, "Hi, my name is Lavender," as she stuck out her hand to shake. Her handshake was firm and confident. I was completely taken off guard by her beauty. She was about five foot ten and wore no makeup. She had light auburn hair and braided pigtails. Her happy blue-green eyes looked right into mine without pretense or unease. I could tell she was not the type to let her beauty define her.

"Pleased to meet you. I'm looking forward to working with you."

Trying hard to respond to her disarming good manners, I replied, "Pleased to meet you."

After recovering from my initial shock, I reminded myself of my initial concern about a quality guide and her effectiveness to perform her job.

"So, how long have you been guiding in Alaska?"

"This is my second year."

I wasn't overly impressed with that answer. "How have you done so far?"

"We've caught a lot of fish this year. It's been a little slow lately because of the heat, but I think that will change shortly."

"Do you know how to fly fish?"

"That's what I do best. I've been fly fishing since I was five years old."

"I'm relatively new to fly fishing. My son-in-law recently got me into the sport two years ago. I've never caught any big fish like you have here in Alaska on a fly. However, I have spin-cast fished all my life."

"That's no problem. If you have difficulty, I'll teach you."

Our conversation was so positive that I was having a hard time holding on to my displeasure. Her directness and clear intelligence had temporarily disarmed me. I tried hard to regain my tough questioning process, so I relied on the fundamentals of physiology and gender difference.

"So what if I have to pee and we're in the boat?"

"Just stand by the edge of the boat, unzip your pants, and pee off the boat like you usually do. We always bring toilet paper if you need to go to shore into the bushes."

"You don't have any problems with that?"

"We're all human beings, and this is the Alaskan wilderness. No one cares."

"What if you have to go?"

"I just pull the boat over to the shore and find some bushes. There's no shortage of them up here."

"Well, OK, I guess we've got everything straight. By the way, what's your last name?"

"Lilly. Lavender Lilly."

I thought, *Her name fits her well. Unique and pretty. However, we'll see how she does her job.*

I could tell Lavender had noticed my reluctance to trust her as a quality fishing guide. However, it didn't seem to bother her. She took my skepticism in stride and confidently reassured me. I suspected that she was used to this sort of questioning. However, as the saying goes, I'm from Missouri, and you're going to have to "show me." In short order I would see if she really could do the job.

The next morning I walked down to the dock with all my fishing gear, ready to go. As I approached the dock, I saw Lavender already sitting in the boat with her aviator shades, baseball cap, braided pigtails, and big smile. I think the most beautiful and disarming thing about her was her smile.

"Good morning. Are you ready to do some fishing?"

I smiled back politely and said, "Yes, ma'am, let's go!" She gave me an enthusiastic feeling, as if saying, *Let's go out and have some fun!* There was nothing fake about her. Her positive attitude was infectious. As I stepped onto the boat, she gave me the sensation of being on an athletic team ready to go into action, a sensation I was all too familiar with from my younger days but had nearly forgotten.

When the boat took off, I noticed that our engine wasn't as fast and powerful as those of most of the other boats. I figured that the more powerful boats went to the guides on a seniority basis, and since Lavender was the newest guide, she probably got the poorest equipment.

The other boats sped off and left us far behind. They were off to the best fishing locations. As we slowly followed in our boat. I began to think that this girl was nice, but the trip was going to wind up a disaster, and we wouldn't be catching many fish, if any. My previously positive mood slowly began to turn foul. Negative thoughts were slowly creeping in. I thought, *What a waste of my valuable time off of work and wasted money*. I was starting to silently fume. So far the trip was far below my expectations. I was now in a terrible mood, with no confidence in my female guide. However, I didn't let my displeasure show as I stared ahead toward the expansive river in front of us.

We went to an area where there was a bend in the river with a large eddy. The other boats were already lined up in a row along the eddy. The fish were supposedly congregating in this place. When salmon migrate up rivers from the ocean, they frequently travel in large groups, or pods. The pods usually rest temporarily during their migration in areas of decreased current to regain their strength. This location was where most of the action had been on the previous days.

We maneuvered into place along with the other boats. There were a few fish being caught, but nothing spectacular. It was still hot, and the fish were not very active. When one boat would float out of position, others would jockey into the spot, which occasionally caused some displeasure and animosity with the guide of the boat that had lost its spot. I could tell these other guides were highly competitive. The great majority were young White men in their mid- to late twenties. All appeared athletic and in good condition. They were all expecting a big tip if the fishing was good and were determined to out fish the other guys.

After about forty minutes I had two strikes but no fish landed. I didn't say a word, but I wasn't pleased with being in a row of boats, jockeying for position. It just didn't seem like an Alaskan wilderness experience, even if we were catching fish, which we weren't. It reminded me of other rivers I have fished where the fishermen were shoulder to shoulder, fighting each other for the best spot to cast. That is not what I call fishing. To me it's not all about catching fish, although that is a big plus—it's about being isolated in the wilderness and solitude.

I silently cast my fly time and time again, concentrating on the cast placement and then the retrieve, not saying a word but quite unhappy.

Somehow Lavender picked up on my displeasure even though I hadn't said anything. She said, "Why don't we try somewhere else?"

I put down my fishing rod, looked back at her, and said, "Yes, I'd love to. Let's go!"

So off we went, leaving the crowd of boats behind. I didn't care if we caught another fish if we were out of that mess.

As we were leaving the throng of boats, Lavender commented, "It seems to me that you're not the type of guy that likes to fish around crowds. I'm the same way."

I smiled at her and said, "How did you know?"

"Call it woman's intuition."

"What do you say we use that intuition of yours to catch some fish."

"I'm on it, boss."

We motored into a bay, close to the entrance of a clear stream running into it. She stopped the motor and said, "Let's try here."

I stood up in the front of the boat and cast my big pink-and-purple feathered streamer fly out as far as I could manage. I began the retrieve, stripping my line in slowly with a slight jerking movement. I felt a sudden and violent hit. I quickly pulled my line and raised my rod to set the hook. My line began streaming out of my reel. The fight was on! The fish went back and forth and around the boat. It then went on a fifty-yard run into the main river. It took out all my line down to the back of the reel. The fish was so strong I couldn't turn it. I had to just let it run until it tired out. Eventually I managed to get the fish close to the boat. It wasn't that the fish was necessarily tired, but I just maneuvered it closer to the boat. Lavender lunged at the fish with a large net like a cobra striking its prey. She was fast as lightning, with pinpoint accuracy.

"Got him!" She lifted the net up in the air and said, "Yes!!"

It was a beautiful ten-pound silver salmon. She seemed as happy as I was. We were both smiling, and then we began to laugh. My foul mood had vanished as quickly as it had appeared.

"Good catch, Bruce; you played that fish well," she said, beaming her beautiful smile.

Over the next hour I caught one more large silver salmon. I looked ahead at a small, shallow river running into the bay. I thought I saw some movement on the surface of the river just ahead suggestive of fish. It would certainly make sense since salmon swim upstream to shallow creeks to spawn.

Lavender saw me looking at the stream and said, "Let's go upstream a bit and see what we can find. You seem like the adventurous, independent type." I turned around to look at her and smiled my approval. She again seemed to be reading my mind since I had not voiced anything about entering the small river. I doubted the river was large enough to accommodate our boat, but I thought it was at least worth a closer look.

We slowly and carefully motored up to where the stream became shallow with scattered boulders. The boat was starting to scrape the bottom of the stream. I thought, *This will be as far as we go.*

To my utter surprise, Lavender jumped out of the boat, waist high to her waders, and began pushing the boat upstream against the current. I helped by poling with a paddle and deflecting the boat away from small boulders. I knew pushing this heavy aluminum boat against the current, filled with gear and me, was no easy task. There were very few fishing guides who would have done what Lavender was now doing. I was amazed not only by her strength but by her willingness to jump into the water without question when she thought it might enhance my fishing success. She pushed the boat about thirty yards upstream until we got to a point where the stream widened and became deeper. I looked over the side of the boat and was shocked. There were literally hundreds of big silver salmon swirling around in a circle. Lavender pulled the boat to the bank. I hopped out and began casting into the swirling mass of fish.

Again, a sudden hit. However, this time the line went limp. I quickly realized the fish was speeding toward me. I couldn't strip the line in fast enough to keep up with the fish coming directly at me like a speeding bullet. The large silver salmon broke the water's surface and flew vertically into the air, twisting and turning. At the highest point it jerked its head, broke my line, and swam away. The air came out of my lungs. My arms fell to my sides along with the limp, broken line. I felt like yelling and swearing, but I didn't. That was the best fish of the day, likely over twenty pounds. There was really nothing I could have done to avoid what had happened. It was just a smart fish and bad luck.

Lavender gave a loud sigh and reassured me that it was just unlucky. She gave me her rod to keep me fishing while she repaired my line. This is what a premier guide does, but many don't. A good guide keeps you in the game fishing, even if your line breaks. She was aiming to please, and not just because it was part of the job. She had already done far above that. She had done all these things because they were the right thing to do. She did them out of instinct. She did them because they came naturally to her.

I was thinking that this woman was an outstanding fishing guide. She looked at me while she was busy mending my line and smiled. She knew what I was thinking. Without any verbal communication, she and I became mentally connected. We looked at each other and laughed. We each knew what the other was thinking. She knew she had gone above and beyond what a good fishing guide would do, and she knew I knew it. At that point we gained a mutual respect and admiration for each other. She had proven herself to me.

I caught many more fish, and Lavender quickly scooped them up with the net and put them in the boat. She was thrilled and showed her excitement with each caught fish. I asked her, "Why don't you do a little fishing?" She looked at me with a big smile and said, "Really?" She jumped at the chance. It's not often that guides are allowed by their clients to fish, but it seemed more fun when she and I were fishing together, especially since I didn't have Edward with me. I suddenly realized that it had all worked out for the best that Edward was fishing with his son and I was fishing with my new buddy Lavender.

She was a true master with a fly rod. She floated the fly out in the air with ease, elegance, and accuracy. Her casting was beyond great technique. It was art. It was inspiring to watch her. Her movements were an amalgamation of directed, coordinated strength and elegant delicacy. It was truly a thing of grace and beauty; she was a performing artist. It was almost like watching a professional ballet dancer. Every move was closely choreographed from years of practice.

While I watched her perform her art, Greek mythology came to my mind. She reminded me of Diana, goddess of the hunt and nature. I closely watched her technique to gain pointers on improving my own fly-casting skills. She proceeded to catch several more fish than I. I netted the fish she caught, assisting her. They were all large silver salmon. We gave each other high fives after each catch. I could tell she loved this. I got a big charge out of just watching her have so much fun.

When we broke for lunch, she retrieved several sandwiches from the large wooden lunch box and some cold drinks from a thermos. We sat in the beached boat, talking with ease after a good round of successful fishing.

"I haven't had so much fun with a client in a long time, maybe forever."

"I had a memorable time as well. My first Alaskan salmon on a fly."

"Today reminded me of fishing with my dad when I was a little girl in Montana. He taught me how to fly fish. I grew up in the mountains.

We used to go fishing all the time. We used to have so much fun. There's really nothing I like better than to go fly fishing."

She smiled as she talked of her memories, intermittently taking bites of her sandwich. It was my impression that her father was no longer a part of her life, either by death, divorce, or some other situation. There seemed to be a gap or an empty area in that part of her life that needed to be filled. I could tell that at one time she had been quite close to her father. She said that she was the oldest, with two younger half-siblings, and that she was pretty much on her own. It was my impression that she didn't have a strong support system and that she was totally independent.

I replied, "Well, I guess you're in the right business, and it's up to you to chart your own destiny with the skills you possess."

"That's about right," she answered, nodding.

She then began to ask me about my life and family. She showed great interest in my medical stories. She was enthralled with every word I said. She seemed like a little girl being told stories of life-and-death drama and my lifesaving adventures as a surgeon. I told her stories of my own family and that I had a daughter roughly her age.

"Your daughter is a very lucky girl to have a father like you."

"Well, thank you. I feel that family is the most important thing in life."

"I think so too. I wish everyone thought like that," she replied. I picked up a subtle feeling that her family was not as stable as she would have liked.

She came across as a wholesome, good person who wanted a family and was entirely on her own. I couldn't help but think that this woman would be a great catch for some lucky young man.

That afternoon the fishing slowed considerably. We were essentially sight fishing. We could see the salmon and were casting the large streamer flies in front of them. It became obvious that the salmon were not hungry and hunting for food. They were striking at the flies because of the annoyance of something being right in front of them, so accuracy of the cast was key to fishing in this stretch of the river.

The salmon's main objective was to spawn and not to eat, especially when they had reached this far upstream from the river's mouth at the ocean. The more recent the salmon to the river, the more likely they are to attack a lure for food.

After a successful and enjoyable day of fishing, we motored back to the lodge. We had caught far more salmon than any of the other boats. The other guides and fishermen stood in disbelief as we unloaded our catch at the dock.

Later that evening we had a delicious dinner of freshly caught salmon. I noticed that Lavender ate alone at a counter next to the kitchen. She mainly talked with the female cook and was quite reserved with the other guides, who were boisterous young men sitting together at their own table. Aside from the female cook, Lavender talked mainly with Roy, who was the oldest and most experienced of the guides. He was in his mid- to late thirties, short, outgoing, and had a crazy laugh, which he used with regularity. It seemed that he was Lavender's friend and mentor for guiding. Roy seemed to be a respected buddy to everyone. He had been guiding nearly all his life. In the summer he was a fishing guide in Alaska, while the remainder of the year he was a fishing guide in Michigan, mainly for trout, salmon, and steelhead.

I also saw that Lavender was much more reserved and formal toward me when we were at the lodge and around other people. I think she was trying to maintain her professionalism. I thought that was quite appropriate. It showed me that she had a lot of style. In older terminology, she had a lot of "class." The other guides sat at their table, devouring their food like a pack of ravenous animals, while Lavender sat at the counter slowly and delicately taking her meal while talking with the female cook.

Frequently some of the other guides would walk by and flirt, making provocative remarks. She would smile and turn away with no interest whatsoever. These young men lived in a bunkhouse and had minimal contact with women for the entire summer. I couldn't imagine why Lavender would put herself in a position like this just for a job, even though she loved guiding and fishing. She stuck out like a sore thumb, even though she was a consummate professional. I thought there had to be something else here for her to be alone with a bunch of guys in the middle of nowhere Alaska for an entire summer.

She wouldn't allow herself to get too close to any of the guides or male staff of the lodge because it would look inappropriate and cause friction with the other young men. I thought it must be a stressful and lonely existence. She surely had a lot of guts, though. I later found out that she had a long-term boyfriend who was a fishing guide in a lodge downriver. She couldn't get a job at his lodge, so she had gotten one at the lodge closest to his.

The next couple of days the fishing was slow. However, we continuously brought in more fish than the others. We received a lot of envious and even jealous comments from the others. My relationship with Lavender changed from a client-guide relationship to two friends fishing, having fun together. She was always positive, upbeat, and beaming her always present big smile. She was an excellent conversationalist, and we kept up a continuous banter all day. She had excellent general knowledge about most things and a keen interest in the things she didn't know much about. I could tell she was well educated, with an active and clear mind. She was a pure joy to be with in so many ways.

The slowdown of the fishing was not only from the heat. We had gotten word that a flotilla of commercial fishing boats was harvesting the new pods of incoming salmon at the mouth of the river. No new fish were swimming upstream. The commercial fishing boats were allowed to periodically harvest the fish and then stop on other days to allow the sport fishermen a catch. During this slow time, we focused our fishing mainly on large rainbow trout. They were not as affected by the heat and were indigenous to the river; thus, they were not affected by the commercial fishing. The trout are frequently found behind the salmon after they spawn, eating the salmon eggs. Alaskan rainbow trout grow to be some of the largest in the world from eating large amounts of protein readily available from millions of salmon eggs and salmon meat after the salmon die.

Lavender anchored the boat in the middle of the river over a submerged sandbar with deeper areas on each side. We both jumped out of the boat up to our thighs in a fast-moving current. It was a little worrisome since the current was so fast and I was not always sure of my footing. I didn't know the location of any potential drop-off to deeper water, so I didn't stray far from the boat. Lavender sure didn't lack guts to jump out of the boat in this situation. It didn't seem to bother her at all. The current was uncomfortably fast. I could imagine how some terrible mishaps could occur in this situation.

I was having some difficulty casting my lure in the right area, especially since a light wind was affecting my fly-line placement. In this location on the river, accuracy of the cast was the key to success. She demonstrated the proper technique multiple times, but I couldn't quite do it. She could cast nearly thirty yards away with pinpoint accuracy. I was again amazed.

She put her rod down to focus her attention on helping me. Any other guide would have been frustrated and given up or not even attempted to instruct me on better technique. She seemed like a mother kindly and patiently teaching her young, uncoordinated child to tie his shoe. She worked with me on technique for over forty-five minutes, never losing patience. Her voice was reassuring after multiple terrible casts. She was an excellent coach who never gave up on the rookie who had some unseen potential. Eventually I got the hang of it and started making some good casts, to my amazement. Lavender gave me constant positive encouragement. She even gave me a small cheer when I made a good cast.

"Yeah, that's a good one, Bruce!"

After being instructed on where and how to cast a lure that imitated a cluster of salmon eggs, I caught a huge rainbow trout. It was a tremendous fight, taking some time to land, especially since the trout was swimming rapidly downstream with the current. I had to move the trout slowly and skillfully to the side of the river, where Lavender was waiting with her large net. The fish was thirty inches long, a trophy by any standard. It was the largest rainbow I had ever caught. After gently raising it out of the water and obtaining a photo, I released it back into the river. I was overjoyed. Lavender seemed to take as much pleasure in the catch as I did. We gave each other a high five. Later I caught a few other good-sized trout, but not nearly the length of the first one.

We decided to break and have some lunch. With considerable difficulty, I climbed back into the boat with my fishing rod and heavy waders. I crawled over the side of the boat and rolled into the bottom slowly coming to my knees. I was relatively old but still in decent condition. As I sat down and looked over at Lavender in the water, she leaped into the boat with the nimbleness of a predatory cat, despite her heavy waders. This feat of strength, agility, and balance took real ability. I know of very few strong young men who could have vaulted into the boat from being partially submerged in water, as she was, in addition to having a fishing rod in one hand. I could barely believe what I had just witnessed. This was no ordinary woman. She must have had some kind of extraordinary training in her past. I became intrigued by my new guide. I thought, *There's a history to this girl that she has not disclosed.*

She began to prepare our sandwiches from the lunch box. There's nothing like a good morning of fishing to make the lunch taste so much better. It felt like a reward for a hard-won victory. While we were having lunch, I took a drink of hot, strong coffee from the thermos that she had brought.

I said, "Thanks, coach, I appreciate your patience."

"You're welcome. It's part of the job," she said, beaming her big smile.

I chuckled. "No, ma'am, you went far above and beyond the job. I don't think anyone else here at this lodge would have had the patience to work with me with such diligence. Plus, I wouldn't have caught that trophy rainbow trout."

"It's fun for me. It brings back many fond memories of when I used to play sports and coach as well."

I was right about there being a history behind her physical prowess as well as her coaching ability. Lavender went on to tell me she had played basketball all through high school and college. She was the captain of both teams. Her small college team won the Division III national championship. After two years she was recruited and subsequently transferred to Oregon State University on an athletic scholarship for the opportunity to play Division I basketball. Early in her stay at OSU she received a terrible foot injury that required several complicated surgeries. She never fully recovered and still had chronic discomfort from a steel plate in the arch of her foot. The injury ended her athletic career. Her hopes and dreams were to take OSU to national prominence and to someday play professional women's basketball.

"Basketball was everything to me. I was crushed. It's still painful to think about, to put everything you have into something and see it washed away forever."

I knew to be successful or even competitive at that level in collegiate sports takes everything you have. I told her that I could identify with her since I'd been knocked out of collegiate wrestling due to two separate knee injuries after working my way on to varsity and obtaining an athletic scholarship. At the time I'd been devastated as well. She looked into my eyes and nodded understandingly. I told her that in the long run, it's the things you learn playing sports that improve your life, not the winning of awards or championships. Although in the moment that's all that matters, in the big picture, learning determination, courage, leadership, resilience, and the ability to work with and inspire others is the important thing. I told her that given time, the wound of perceived failure would heal, and she would look back at those memories with great fondness.

She said, "I know you're right, and I understand everything you're saying. But it still hasn't been that long. I appreciate your insight. It's good to hear from someone who understands my feelings. It seems that you have intuition as well. Maybe we are kindred spirits?"

"Maybe, ha! You mean I have male intuition?"

With that, we smiled and shook hands. She said, "Something of that sort."

"Better days are ahead for you. This I'm sure of," I said with a reassuring smile. "What position did you play?"

"In high school I was a forward, and in college I was a point guard. The girls in college were taller and more athletic than the ones in high school. I was quick and could usually give a head fake or quick pivot around most anybody to beat them one on one. I was good at long distance shots, getting more than my share of three-pointers."

"I'll bet there are some photos of you and your championship teams at the schools you played for."

"Oh, yeah, there is a team photo at both schools. There's also an individual photo of me posing in an action picture, holding a basketball, at both my college and high school as the captain of a championship team and being an all-American."

"Wow, that's quite an honor! Your parents must be quite proud of your basketball accomplishments."

She looked away and replied, "I'm not sure my parents even knew I played basketball."

"Ah, come on, an all-star like yourself?"

"In all the years I played basketball, winning state championships in high school, national championships in college, nobody from my family ever came to a game I played in. I've never received a lot of support for anything in my life from my family. They never even asked me about basketball. At the time I thought that they just didn't understand sports. But later I realized it may have been something more. I had to have a job all my life to pay for anything I wanted or, for that matter, anything I needed. Fortunately, I had an athletic scholarship through college."

I could see that athletics had given her a direction, discipline, and even meaning to her life that was missing at home. I think she instinctively knew that basketball had served as a stabilizing force in her life.

"You might say I was self-sufficient since I was able to walk. My family was poor. One year we were homeless, and I lived in a tepee with my mother and two younger half-brothers. I was partly responsible for raising and caring for both, along with my mom. I wasn't very social in school because I didn't have the time. Between school, basketball, having a full-time job, and helping raise my brothers, there wasn't much spare time outside of sleep. I guess it kept me on the straight and narrow, so to speak. Not much partying for me."

"Wow, that must have been a unique experience. When was the last time you talked to your mom or any of your brothers?" I got the distinct impression that her father hadn't been in her life since she'd been a child, so I didn't press that issue.

"We're not very close. I talk to my mom about once a year. She has a lot on her plate to take care of. We get along OK, but she's just distant. It's not like there is anger or bad blood between us. It just always seemed that I've been kind of an outsider in my own family, but not in a mean way. I've always been on my own."

Lavender exuded the confidence and maturity that come from having been given a lot of responsibility at an early age. However, with maturity came a certain loneliness. Someone who'd missed out on childhood. I thought maybe there was some division in her family because she had a different father than her siblings. However, I wasn't going to delve into that issue unless she brought it up.

"You know there is an old saying from a very wise man: 'Solitary trees, if they grow at all, grow strong.' It seems to me that you're a strong, beautiful solitary tree."

"You might be right. I never really thought of it that way, being alone and all. I guess the tears I should have shed are still in me. However, I never let my family issues get me down. I'd like to be closer to my family, but as the saying goes, it is what it is, and I can't do much about it."

"I think it gives you total freedom to choose what you wish in life, unencumbered by expectations or what other people may think. On the other hand, when times are tough, it's always nice to have family around for support. Does your mom know that you're a fishing guide in Alaska?"

"I doubt it."

"You really should try to reconnect with your entire family despite their unfriendliness. The Bible says that you should honor your mother and father. In fact, it's one of the ten commandments. You don't have to like them, but at least respect them, which means continued contact, even if you get the cold shoulder."

"Yeah, I guess you're right."

"If I were you, I would take a leadership role in this situation. Disregard their poor behavior. Stay confident in yourself, and lead them in the right direction toward love, no matter their response. They seem like misguided children. Given time, I'm sure they will see the light, even if they don't admit it. They will at least see the good in you, and who knows, this may rub off on their own lives. I think it will be good for you and your future. To do this, you'll need to grow a thick hide and not get too upset with being initially rebuffed."

"Yeah, it's always been something I wanted to do but I never was persistent at, like basketball or coaching."

"Yes, to grow love takes persistence. Your family will see what a wonderful young lady you've become. You can be an example for them to follow. A light in the dark. And yes, you are a stunningly beautiful bright light! If you were my daughter, I would be tremendously proud of you."

An instant after my last comment, she immediately looked into my eyes as if taking a quick glimpse of my soul to confirm the truth of what I had just uttered. She smiled as if she could see my honesty. She then looked out at the river and said, "Thanks, Bruce. I appreciate that.

"Bruce, it seems that you are extremely dedicated to your profession."

"Well, yes, I think I am. I take it very seriously because people's lives are in my hands. I feel that it is a sacred honor to care for people in need. When I was a young man, I transferred the hard work and dedication I had in athletics to medicine."

Lavender replied, "To really excel in anything takes complete dedication."

"I would agree," I said.

The next day Lavender, Roy, two other fishermen, and I were scheduled to fly in a pontoon plane to a smaller river that ran into the Wajimi River and was teaming with trout and arctic char. It was known, however, for its sizable grizzly bear population. I asked Lavender about what precautions we were going to take with the bears. She assured me about the usual things that I already knew: make plenty of noise on a trail so you don't startle them, stay at least fifty yards away from a bear, and don't bring any food.

She continued, "Plus I have plenty of bear spray."

I smiled and said, "Bear spray, huh? I'm sorry, but if a charging, angry grizzly bear is that close to you, I wouldn't bet my life on some spray to turn that eight-hundred-pound grizzly around. I have seen bears put their heads into beehives to get honey despite being stung repeatedly on their sensitive noses."

"I do have a .50-caliber Magnum pistol I could bring if that would make you feel more comfortable?"

"Uh, yes! It would definitely make me feel more comfortable."

The next day we flew into a small lake and hiked about four miles to the river. The river was beautiful, with a waterfall at one end. Many large bears were congregating around the falls, fishing for mainly red sockeye salmon. It was an amazing sight to see numerous large bears catching salmon in their mouths in midair. We steered far and wide away from this area, even though it was the best fishing spot, and went fishing far below downstream.

I asked Lavender, "Did you bring your gun?"

"Oh, yeah," she said, opening the front of her jacket to reveal the largest handgun I had ever seen. It was encased in a shoulder holster with the gun lying in front of her chest. She looked like something out of *The Untouchables* or the Secret Service. A .50-caliber gun is used not only to kill large animals, such as elephants, hippos, and lions, but also to take out and disable large machinery, such as trucks and troop transports. I immediately felt more secure.

It was an incredibly successful fishing day. Every third cast we caught a trout, grayling, arctic char, or sockeye salmon. It was one of the most memorable fishing experiences of my life. Lavender and Roy were having a great time as well. We released all the fish that were caught after taking photos. We hadn't seen any signs of bears while we were fishing this area.

When the afternoon came, we began to head back to the lake to meet the pontoon plane. We were all walking single file along a heavily wooded trail. Thick brush up to our chests on each side of the path could easily hide a potential bear in ambush. For that matter, we might awaken and startle a sleeping bear. We were talking and making noise as per our protocol to alert any bears in the vicinity so they could move away without being surprised.

Lavender and Roy were leading, and I was behind them with the other fishermen behind me. As we turned around a bend in the trail, we suddenly saw two bears charging down the trail directly ahead of us. They were running full speed around the bend in the trail. Roy and Lavender directed us all off the trail. Even though we were making noise, the bears kept coming fast. They had no intention of stopping. Within an instant, they ran right past us as if totally oblivious to our presence. We were only ten feet away from them as they came barreling through. I quickly glanced at Lavender and noticed that her hand was gripping her gun and not the bear spray. To our great relief, the bears quickly passed.

The two small bears were adolescent yearlings, chasing each other down the trail just having fun like two teenage boys. They never even noticed we were there.

Smiling, Lavender looked at me and said, "Well, so much for the bear spray." She put her gun back into the leather holster in front of her chest.

I was nearing the end of my trip to Alaska. One day Lavender was much more talkative while I was fishing, her mood was almost bubbly. She said, "I'd like you to meet my fiancé and tell me what you think." Lavender had a big smile and exuberant eyes as she revealed her future plans with this young man.

"So, who is this lucky guy?"

"His name is Steven. He's a fishing guide at another lodge down the river. He's coming over this evening to see me!"

"How long have you known Steven?"

"I met him last summer while we were both guiding. I've never had a real boyfriend before. When we met, you might say I was swept off my feet. It seemed he was everything I've ever wanted. We moved in with each other at his home in Florida after the summer. He's a fishing guide there for saltwater fish. Sailfish, tarpon, sea bass, marlin, and lots of other fish. I help with his guide service. It's much different than here. We have to catch live bait before the clients arrive every day. The boats are much larger since they go in the ocean and carry groups of fishermen. It takes a lot of preparation for each group we take out. There's a lot of boat maintenance as well. It's a lot more labor intensive than it is here, but the pay is far better. I take action photos of the fish and the clients. It's wildly popular and serves as a real memento of their big catch."

I looked at some of the photos she had somehow transferred from her camera to her cell phone. They were amazing in their color and clarity. There was so much precision that I could see the droplets of water and the spray creating a subtle rainbow effect off a sailfish being landed by a client in a boat. The photo not only showed masterful technical ability but was a true work of art with its color and composition.

"I also help him on the accounting and business end of things to make things more profitable."

"Wow, you're a real asset to this young man. What do you like most about Steven?"

"I love that he is so close to his family, who are all wonderful people. We eat dinner at his parents' house every Sunday. His mother and I get along great. I even help her cook meals."

"There has to be something wrong with a person who couldn't get along with you."

"He's also a hard worker and fun to be with. He isn't very good with the business accounting, but that's where I come in and help."

"He sounds like a good fit for you."

"Oh, yes, I think so!"

"So when is the big day?"

"Well, we haven't decided on a specific date yet. That's something we're going to talk about. I'd like you to come to the wedding if you could find the time."

"If you're getting married, I'll be there! I'd like you to meet my wife, Barbara, as well."

"I would love to meet her; she sounds so wonderful!"

"She is. That's why I call her Saint Barbara."

I suddenly got a hit on my fishing line. After a prolonged fight, I landed a pink salmon and then a red-and-green sockeye in its spawning colors. After we released the fish, our conversation changed.

I put down my fishing rod and said, "I think this would be a good time for lunch." We pulled off to the side of the riverbank and tied the boat to a tree. It was a beautiful day. The temperature had dropped to the upper 60s, and the fishing was much improved.

As we were eating our sandwiches, I asked, "What do you want most in life?"

She responded quickly and strongly, "A good husband and a family." She clearly knew what she needed in life and was trying hard to fulfill that need. She desperately wanted to remedy that deep loneliness she'd had since she was a little girl, that hole in her life that needed to be filled or repaired. She wanted to be as dedicated to love and a family as she had been to basketball.

"I can't think of anyone who would make a better wife than you. Steven is a very fortunate young man. Besides being beautiful, of course, you have so many incredible qualities. You possess a rare quality. You have the ability to read people, to sense someone's feelings that aren't overtly showing. You may call it intuition; some people call it a sixth sense."

I continued, "An old Cree man once told me that certain people can see things 'beyond the hill.' Meaning that they can see or sense things that are not obvious or in plain sight. You have this ability. People who possess this unique gift are usually highly intelligent, which you obviously are."

She replied, "It's funny you should bring this up. I think you have that same ability. It seems to me that we think very much alike. It's rare that two people can immediately hit it off so well in such a short time as we have."

"It does seem that we have similar thought patterns. I've tried to develop this ability of 'seeing beyond the hill' because it's part of my job as a physician to try to see things in people that they don't readily share with me. It helps me in their care. I learned long ago to listen to my clinical instincts before a patient becomes obviously worse. Many times, by the time a person's vital signs and laboratory values deteriorate, it can be too late to fix the situation."

As we motored back to the lodge, I could tell she was excited to see her fiancé. She was gunning the boat motor as fast as it could go.

When we got back to the lodge, she tied the boat to the dock. I carried my fishing gear up to the lodge, took off my waders, and got into my regular clothes. When I walked out onto the deck of the lodge, I saw Lavender with a young man by the dock. She saw me and waved for me to come down.

I walked down toward the couple. Steven was a large, nice-looking young man with a full brown beard and a big smile. Lavender was beaming as she introduced us.

The first thing I noticed was that he wanted as little physical contact as possible with Lavender. It seemed as if he didn't want to touch her despite her wanting to hold and hug him. He moved away when she got close. It had been over a month since they had last seen each other. He was trying to avoid close contact with his future wife. We made small talk for a while. We talked mainly of fishing and about his home in Florida.

After talking with Steven for a while, Lavender said as she looked up at him, "Have you decided about a wedding date yet? I'd like to invite Dr. Graham."

He was evasive with his answer. He clearly didn't want to talk about it. I could tell, since I had been a young man at one time, that there was no love or any kind of excitement in him for her. I felt sure he was going to give her some bad news about their relationship.

I had a sick feeling as if someone had hit me in the gut. Lavender had given him so much of her love and time for nothing. For over a year she had built her whole life around him, and he was going to discard her like a piece of trash. I could tell she was heading for a crushing blow. I hated to see her hopes for the future dashed on the rocks. It was going to be another hit to her like her injury knocking her out of basketball, only possibly worse. She was totally devoted to this guy. He was obviously not mature enough to see the beauty and quality he had in his hand. I thought one day he would regret losing this girl. I could tell he knew that I knew his true feelings for Lavender.

I looked at him and said, "Son, I hope you realize what an amazingly good woman you have."

"Oh, I do!" But he tried to avoid eye contact, looking down at the ground.

I thought, *No, you don't, you fool! All this time you've been using this young lady, leading her on, and lying to her. You've been telling her things she wanted to hear without meaning any of it! You are nothing but a big, immature adolescent, a child in a man's body!*

I was so mad I could have hit him. However, I was polite and didn't let my feelings show. I could read him like a book, and he knew it! I could tell he felt guilty about the impending breakup that Lavender knew nothing about. She was about to be hit broadside by a truck that she didn't know was coming.

I thought, *One day when you eventually grow up, you're going to regret breaking up with this wonderful girl. That is, if you ever do grow up, which is doubtful. I think you want a mother and not a wife!* Being a man-child is unfortunately becoming more prevalent in this society these days.

Lavender was still beaming her big smile, oblivious to his real feelings for her that lay just "beyond the hill" out of plain sight.

I was told long ago by an old Cree shaman named Dark Eye that when you fall deeply in love with someone, you give them a part of your spirit that can never be retrieved no matter what happens with the relationship. If the relationship ends, which often happens, your own spirit can be diminished to the point where there is little left to give another. Nothing is left but a scar. I was hoping that Lavender had more than enough spirit left in her heart to recover. I was sure she did because she was a strong person, but nonetheless, she was going to be badly hurt.

Later in the evening at dinner, I ran into Lavender.

"Well, what did you think of Steven?"

"He's a nice guy and a handsome fellow." I was expressionless and left it at that. It was not my place to tell her what I thought was the truth about Steven. I was able to see "beyond the hill" about Steven, but love and hope for the future had blinded Lavender to what was on the other side of that hill with him, just as my initial preconceived notions of Lavender's gender and guiding abilities had blinded me to what was "beyond the hill" about her.

I could tell immediately that Lavender knew exactly what I was thinking. I think it was what I didn't say that tipped her off. She was then immediately able to see "beyond the hill" with me. She didn't say anything or show any emotion, but she and I both knew what the score was. That moment of realization must have been devastating to her, but she didn't let on. I think deep inside, she must have known about Steven's true feelings all along but had put reality out of her mind for wishful thinking.

I asked her, "So what did you and Steven decide about the wedding?"

"He said he didn't want to talk about it right then. Unfortunately, he had to leave right after you two met."

I just shook my head in acknowledgment, not saying anything further. I thought, *He chickened out on giving her the bad news. What a coward!*

The next day as I was leaving the lodge, I ran into Lavender; we shook hands as she stared into my eyes. Within that instant of eye contact there was an entire story that both of us knew. I had spent ten days with her, but it had seemed like a year. I guess you can get to know someone pretty well spending ten hours a day alone in a boat with them for ten days, working for a common goal of catching big fish.

I told her, "You'll do well; I have full confidence in you. Trust your inner senses and keep trying to see beyond the hill."

She gave me a big, tight hug. I told her, "You can call me anytime, and you're always welcome at my home in Kansas City for as long as you wish."

I could see her eyes begin to well up with tears. It was the first time I had seen her so vulnerable. She had obviously received the bad news from Steven.

I said, "You will always have a friend in me." I knew Lavender would eventually be fine because she was like a strong, solitary oak tree. She was used to adversity and weathering storms. I knew she would be resilient. However, she was going to have some real pain in the short run, which I hated to see. It reminded me of an old blues song that went, "When things go wrong with you, it hurts me too."

I heard later from Edward that Lavender and Steven had broken up, and she had a new boyfriend with a good reputation. I knew the young man and liked him a lot.

I suspect that she has honed her sixth sense to where hopefully there will be no blind spots in the future, improving her ability to *see beyond the hill*. Hopefully I have improved as well.